# About the Author

**Michael J. Arata Jr.** has been in the security profession for 20 years. He has held positions as Vice President of Corporate Security and is currently a security consultant. He possesses the following security-related certifications:

Certified Protection Professional (CPP)
Certified Information System Security Professional (CISSP)
Certified Fraud Examiner (CFE)

He holds the following degrees: a Master of Public Administration, a Bachelor of Arts in Public Administration, and a Bachelor of Science in Fire Protection and Safety.

# Dedication

To my wife, Karla, without whose understanding and encouragement this book would not have been written. This includes all the late nights writing and re-writing it. Also to my son and daughter for understanding that dad needed to spend time completing this book.

# Author's Acknowledgments

To the editors, Nicole and Jen, at Wiley Publishing. They did a great job in making sure the book's information was easy to understand.

## Publisher's Acknowledgments

We're proud of this book; please send us your comments at http://dummies.custhelp.com. For other comments, please contact our Customer Care Department within the U.S. at 877-762-2974, outside the U.S. at 317-572-3993, or fax 317-572-4002.

Some of the people who helped bring this book to market include the following:

*Acquisitions, Editorial*

**Project Editor:** Nicole Sholly

**Executive Editor:** Bob Woerner

**Copy Editor:** Jennifer Riggs

**Technical Editors:** SaberGuard Identify Theft Solutions and IDEXPERTS

**Editorial Manager:** Kevin Kirschner

**Editorial Assistant:** Amanda Graham

**Sr. Editorial Assistant:** Cherie Case

**Cartoons:** Rich Tennant (www.the5thwave.com)

*Composition Services*

**Project Coordinator:** Katherine Crocker

**Layout and Graphics:** Samantha K. Cherolis, Christine Williams

**Proofreader:** Bonnie Mikkelson

**Indexer:** Estalita Slivoskey

---

**Publishing and Editorial for Technology Dummies**

    **Richard Swadley,** Vice President and Executive Group Publisher

    **Andy Cummings,** Vice President and Publisher

    **Mary Bednarek,** Executive Acquisitions Director

    **Mary C. Corder,** Editorial Director

**Publishing for Consumer Dummies**

    **Diane Graves Steele,** Vice President and Publisher

**Composition Services**

    **Debbie Stailey,** Director of Composition Services

# *Identity Theft*

...rata Jr.

WILEY

Wiley Publishing, Inc.

**Identity Theft For Dummies®**

Published by
**Wiley Publishing, Inc.**
111 River Street
Hoboken, NJ 07030-5774

www.wiley.com

WILEY

# Contents at a Glance

# Table of Contents

# Introduction

*I*n this book, I tell you how to prevent identity theft and what to do if you're a victim. If you're wondering what sort of information is vulnerable and should be shredded, or how to reclaim your credit if you've been a victim, this is the one-stop reference for you. Today, the name of the game is making yourself a hard target, and armed with this book, you'll do exactly that.

## About Identity Theft For Dummies

Here are some of the things you can do with this book:

- ✔ Know the signs of whether you've been a victim of identity theft.
- ✔ Read and understand your credit report.
- ✔ Know what to do and how to clear your name if you're a victim.
- ✔ Find ways that help prevent you from becoming a victim.

## Foolish Assumptions

Please don't take offense, but I have made the following few assumptions about you (which help you use this book to its maximum potential):

- ✔ You can use a computer to surf the Internet.
- ✔ You're up to adjusting Security settings for your computer by using the Control Panel, even if you're not quite sure how to do this yet. (I tell you how to do this in Chapter 12.)
- ✔ You don't give up your personal information readily.
- ✔ You're careful about the e-mails you open.
- ✔ You're willing to take an active part in protecting your identity.
- ✔ You're careful about what sites you go to on the Internet.

# Conventions Used in This Book

To help you navigate this book easily, I use a few style conventions:

- ✔ Terms or words that you might be unfamiliar with in the context of identity theft, I *italicize* and define.

- ✔ Web site addresses, or URLs, are shown in a special monofont typeface, `like this`.

- ✔ Numbered steps that you need to follow and characters you need to type are set in **bold**.

# What You Don't Have to Read

You don't have to read anything that doesn't pertain to what you're interested in. In fact, you can even skip one or more chapters entirely. Don't skip too many, though, because all the chapters are chock-full of useful information and interesting content. As for the few sidebars you see in this book, feel free to ignore them because they contain, for the most part, tangential information that, while interesting, isn't necessary for you to know in order to protect yourself from identity theft.

# How This Book Is Organized

*Identity Theft For Dummies* is split into seven parts. You don't have to read it sequentially, and you don't even have to read all the sections in any particular chapter. You can use the Table of Contents and the index to find the information you need and quickly get your answer. In this section, I briefly describe what you'll find in each part.

## Part 1: Getting the Scoop on Identity Theft

This part defines identity theft — who it affects, how it happens, what information is vulnerable, and how to protect that information from being stolen. I also cover what personal information is being stolen and what to do about preventing that from happening.

## Part II: Determining Whether You're a Victim

The chapters in this part describe the signs to look for to determine whether you're a victim. You see how you can use your bank statements as an identity theft prevention tool. You also see how to order and read your credit report. I also tell you what to look for when reviewing your bank statements, both checking and savings.

## Part III: Being Smart with Your Sensitive Information

Here I give you a look at some good identity theft prevention techniques. I provide some tips on securing your personal information. Watching what you throw away and being careful what you say and do in public places and online are good identity theft prevention techniques. I caution you about using your wireless laptop computer to check that bank account in an Internet café or on a public computer in a library.

## Part IV: Arming Yourself against Potential Identity Theft

In this part, you find out who you can join forces with in the identity theft battle: government agencies and online companies, which help keep you from becoming a victim or help you if you already are a victim. I outline several common scams identity thieves use to steal your identity. I also give you a rundown of identity thieves' methods so that you won't fall prey to their scams.

## Part V: Safeguarding Electronic Information

Today, you use computers more than ever in your daily life, and this includes online banking and bill paying. So this part provides information on how you can protect your personal information while online. Also included in this part of the book, I review the security features of Windows, XP, Vista, and 7 to help you secure your computer from unwanted intrusions and viruses.

## *Part VI: Taking Back Your Good Name*

If you need information on what to do if you're a victim of identity theft, this part is for you. You also find information in this part about placing a fraud alert on your credit report, obtaining a police report, and completing an identity theft affidavit. Finally, this part tells you when and how to close compromised accounts and open new ones.

## *Part VII: The Part of Tens*

Every *For Dummies* book has this special part, which features lists with helpful tips and tricks. Here you find ten tips for helping you more easily reclaim your identity and good name, a list of resources you can use to help prevent identity theft, ten security tools, and ten scams to avoid.

# *Icons Used in This Book*

What's a *For Dummies* book without icons pointing you in the direction of really great information that's sure to help you along your way? In this section, I briefly describe each icon I use in this book.

When you see the Tip icon, pay attention — you'll find an extra valuable tidbit that may save you from becoming a victim of identity theft.

Heads up when you see this icon — here's where I tell you mistakes you can make that will almost guarantee that you will become a victim of identity theft, and what to do to avoid making those mistakes.

This icon indicates a gentle reminder about an important point.

This icon marks real-world scenarios that help illustrate the concept at hand.

# *Where to Go from Here*

From here, most folks like to browse the Table of Contents and find something about identity theft that they want to know more about. The great thing is that you don't have to read the book in order, chapter by chapter. You can skip around and go right to the sections of the book that interest you.

If you haven't been the victim of identity theft, you may want to focus on the sections that address preventing identity theft. On the other hand, if you have been the victim of identity theft, you may want to focus on the sections that address how to reclaim your good name and credit. Chapter 17 lists resources where you can find additional information and help.

# Part I
# Getting the Scoop on Identity Theft

## The 5th Wave
By Rich Tennant

"So, someone's using your credit card info to buy stylish clothes, opera tickets, and exercise equipment. In what way would this qualify as 'identity theft?'"

# In this part . . .

Identity theft is the fastest growing crime in recent years. To fight this crime, you need to know what it is and who it affects. You need to know what information is vulnerable and how to exercise prevention so that you don't become a victim. I cover all this in Part I.

# Chapter 1

# Who's Stealing What ... and What You Can Do about It

*I*n this chapter, I explain who identity theft affects, how it happens, and what personal information it involves. Although identity theft is pretty unnerving, a greater understanding of it can be empowering. After you find out what identity theft is all about and how it occurs, you can protect your personal information from falling into the wrong hands — and you'll know the best way to take action if it does.

## Taking a Look at the Fastest Growing Crime

*Identity theft* happens when someone (the identity thief) uses another person's personal information (such as name, Social Security Number, and date of birth) to fraudulently obtain credit cards or loans, open a checking account, or otherwise gain access to money or goods in the other person's name.

Identity theft takes three primary forms: financial, criminal, and medical. *Financial* identity theft includes activities like credit card fraud, tax and mail fraud, passing bad checks, and so on. Of course, the identity thief's objective is to not pay back any of the *borrowed* money but, instead, to enjoy spending it. *Criminal* identity theft is used to commit crimes in another person's name and to finance criminal activities with the use of credit cards in someone else's name, selling people's identities, and even terrorism. *Medical* identity theft is when someone assumes your identity for medical reasons and/or for someone else to foot the bill.

In 2007, the U.S. Congress recognized the growth of identity theft and amended the Identity Theft and Assumption Deterrence Act (which was originally introduced in 1998), making identity theft a crime. In September 2003, the Federal Trade Commission (FTC) released the results of an impact survey that outlined the scope of the crime. The survey statistics show the following:

- 8.4 million Americans have been the victims of identity theft in 2007.

- The total cost of this crime to financial institutions is $49.3 billion, and the direct cost to consumers is $5 billion.

- The FTC noted identity theft as the fastest growing crime. The FTC will conduct an "Experiences of Identity Theft Victims" study with data from 2008. The FTC is also seeking comments on "Credit Freezes: Impact and Effectiveness in 2008." The results will be available in 2010.

- In 2007, identity theft led the list of top ten consumer complaints to the FTC.

Identity theft continues to be a concern for Americans, and it's still the number one complaint filed with the FTC. If the economy continues on a downward trend, identity theft will continue to be an issue for those with good to excellent credit. The number of people with stellar credit is dwindling because of the recession the U.S. is currently experiencing. So if you have good to excellent credit, you need to be even more vigilant to prevent your identity from being stolen.

Identity theft isn't just using someone's stolen credit card to make purchases, it is actually opening accounts in someone else's name and using them. Stealing the credit card is fraud but does not entail assuming the cardholder's identity. This distinction is important because when you report a stolen credit card, it isn't classified as identity theft. Stolen credit cards are still an issue though, and you must protect your credit card(s). I discuss how to accomplish this task in Chapter 6.

Some other interesting stats from the FTC study that you may find surprising are

- ✔ In more than 25 percent of all cases, the victim knows the thief.
- ✔ In 35 percent of those cases, the thief is a family member or a relative.
- ✔ Almost 50 percent of victims don't know how their information was stolen.
- ✔ The average out-of-pocket expense to individuals is $500.

So who exactly are the people who fall victim to identity thieves? Read the upcoming sections to find out the *who* and the *how* of identity theft.

## Who identity theft affects

In addition to the statistics I note earlier, the FTC survey findings show that identity theft can happen to anyone with credit, bank accounts, a Social Security Number (SSN), a date of birth (DOB), or other personal identification information. That is, almost every man, woman, or child is a potential target. Yes, even children are susceptible to identity theft because all children have a SSN and all children have a DOB. Identity thieves don't care about age; they just want personal information that they can use to obtain credit. The credit bureaus will not have a file for a minor until the first application for credit is made. If someone is using the child's SSN to obtain credit, there will be a file. There have been cases where minor children have a number of open accounts that they did not open, and it is a headache to clear up the mess.

The sad part is that you can be a victim and not know right away. For example, you may find out you're a victim only when you go to buy a car and get turned down for credit because your credit report already shows you own three cars, but you aren't driving any of them. If you catch identity theft early, however, you can minimize the amount of time and money necessary to clear your name.

A current trend shows that people steal their children's or other family member's SSN to obtain credit. In these cases, the children are under the age of 18 and aren't aware that their credit is being ruined by a family member. In some cases, an *infant's* credit has been ruined — and the child can't even talk or walk yet. When these children get older, they face a tough world at a disadvantage of having bad credit and may not even be able to get a job based on their ruined credit history.

Anyone, even a celebrity, can become a victim of identity theft. For instance, Tiger Woods, Robert De Niro, and Oprah Winfrey have all been victims. No one is immune, and straightening out the resulting mess can take years. But you can protect yourself by practicing identity theft prevention (see my crash course in Chapter 2 and find more details in Part III) and looking for the telltale signs in your financial information (see Part II).

## *How identity theft happens*

Unfortunately, identity thieves can easily obtain other people's personal information and ply their trade. For example, suppose that you lose (or someone steals) your wallet. In your wallet are your driver's license (with your name, address, and birth date), multiple credit cards (gas cards, department store cards, and at least one major credit card), ATM cards (if you're forgetful, with associated personal identification numbers [PIN] numbers written down), and medical benefits cards (with your SSN as the identifier). Some people even carry personal checkbooks and their actual Social Security cards in their wallets. Get the picture? All the information an identity thief needs is right in one place.

Identity thieves can also obtain your personal information through *dumpster diving* — a midnight garbage safari activity. Yes, these thieves literally go through the garbage cans in front of your house and scrounge information, such as cancelled checks, bank statements, utility bill statements, credit card receipts, and those preapproved credit card offers you've been discarding. I discuss what thieves may be looking for in your garbage and what you can do to thwart them in the section "Knowing What Information Is Vulnerable" later in this chapter. You can also find more details in Chapter 6. Those who work for a company and handle personal information are also a threat, and they can steal personal information and sell it to those who want to use it.

Remember this advice: *If you don't shred, it isn't dead.* The non-shredded personal information you've tossed in the trash becomes fair game, and the identity thief thanks you for being so thoughtful.

Although identity thieves have many ways — some rather high tech and sophisticated — to obtain your personal information, wallets and garbage are the most common targets. The point is that after the thief has your personal information, he can assume your identity (at least financially) and start making purchases, getting cash or loans, and otherwise using your good credit.

# *Knowing What Information Is Vulnerable*

We live in a numbers society: phone numbers, personal identification numbers (PINs), driver's license numbers, credit card numbers, date of birth (DOB), Social Security Numbers, bank account and 401K numbers . . . you get the idea. As the lyrics of the song "Secret Agent Man" tell us, "They have given you a number and taken away your name." Also, employee and medical record numbers and other tidbits of information are used to identify people as persons today, and that fact gives meaning to *personal identification information* because all these numbers are keys to your identity on the phone, online, or in writing.

The vulnerable personal information that identity thieves use is as follows:

- ✔ **Social Security Number (SSN):** This is, of course, the nine-digit personal identification number (compliments of the federal government) that everyone needs to get a job, pay taxes, and apply for credit. The SSN is the key to the *kingdom* — your financial kingdom, that is. The identity thief uses your SSN to apply for credit, file false tax returns, get a job, open bank accounts, and so on.

- ✔ **Date of birth (DOB):** A DOB is a piece of the personal information puzzle, but if an identity thief has this piece by itself, it's not a problem. When the thief uses your DOB in conjunction with your SSN, she can become you.

- ✔ **Mother's maiden name:** This name is used to verify your identity when accessing financial information. Identity thieves use your mother's maiden name to verify their identity as yours to access your financial records and open new accounts in your name.

- ✔ **Personal identification numbers (PINs):** Usually a four- (or more) digit number used to access your bank accounts when using your ATM card.

- ✔ **Passwords:** Your passwords are the keys to any information stored electronically. When the identity thief has your password, he has access to the information you're trying to protect, such as bank accounts, online bill paying services, and so on.

- ✔ **Security questions:** You see these questions — such as what was your first pet's name and where did you go to high school — sometimes when you're setting up an online account. These are not real security questions, so don't use real information when answering the questions. The real answers can be easily guessed by potential thieves or, in the case of your alma mater, are a matter of public information. You can make up the answers so they are not easily guessed; you need to remember the answers you choose, though, so if you forget your password, you can still verify your identity by answering the security questions correctly (with your made-up answers).

- ✔ **Driver's license number:** The number used to identify you is printed on your license. When the identity thief has your driver's license number, she can have a phony license made that shows your name and driver's license number with the thief's picture.

By using your personal information, identity thieves can party hard on your nickel and good credit reputation. They spend like there's no tomorrow because they know that someone else (you) is picking up the tab. Identity thieves can use your personal information to open accounts, such as a cellular phone account, in your name. Of course, they don't pay the bills and continue to use the phone until you discover the theft and the heat is on; then they drop that account and move on to another unsuspecting victim.

## Your identity thief doesn't have to be your twin

Many episodes of the old *Mission Impossible* TV show featured one of the IMF (Impossible Mission Force) personnel assuming the identity of an intended target or someone close to the target. In the show, the person assuming the target's identity would wear a mask that resembled the target's face and would learn to speak and act like the target. In real life, an impersonator (the identity thief) doesn't need to look or act like you to steal your identity. All that's needed is your personal identification information and *bingo:* He or she becomes you.

TV commercials for a major bank's credit card offer the best depiction of this real-life situation. In the commercials, you see the victims talking to you about how much fun they've had buying expensive vehicles, taking lavish vacations, or whatever. What you notice, though, is that the

voices you hear don't match the people you see on the screen: a male voice emanates from a female, or vice versa. The voice — gloating over how wonderful it is to get the goods and stick someone else with the tab — is obviously coming from the identity thief while you're looking at the victim.

A world of companies — you've probably seen the TV commercials — today pitch that they can help protect your identity from thieves. For a monthly fee, these companies will help keep your identity safe. In Chapter 9, I show you some of these companies that provide services to prevent identity theft from occurring in the first place. Preventing identity theft should be your goal. However, identity theft may occur even if you guard your identity like Fort Knox guards the gold reserves of the U.S.

## Vulnerable info comes in the mail

To steal your identity, the identity thief uses some of the information you receive in the mail. In Table 1-1, I outline the most vulnerable information that comes in the mail.

| Table 1-1 | Vulnerable Info That Comes in the Mail |
|---|---|
| *Type of Mail* | *Vulnerable Information* |
| Telephone bills and other utility bills | Your telephone number, address, and account number |
| Driver's license renewal | Your name, address, DOB, and driver's license number |
| Monthly credit card statement | Your name, address, card number and type (Visa, MasterCard, and so on), credit limit, and expiration date |
| Bank statements | Your name, address, bank name and contact information, account number, and type. For checking accounts: your cancelled checks, account number, and so on |

| Type of Mail | Vulnerable Information |
|---|---|
| Preapproved credit card offers | Your name and address |
| Paycheck stubs from direct deposit | Your name and address; your employer's name, address, and pay rate; and sometimes your SSN |
| 401K and other securities statements | Your name, account number, balance, name of company holding account, contact information, and sometimes your SSN |
| Personal check reorders (blank) | Your name, account number, address, and bank name and address |
| Blank checks from credit card companies | Your name, address, and account number |
| Annual Social Security account statement | Your name, address, SSN, DOB, and account balance |
| W-2s, 1099, tax returns, and other tax information | Your address, your SSN, and your spouse's and dependents' SSNs. |

The best way to minimize the amount of information you receive in the mail — especially those preapproved credit offers and the blank checks from the credit companies — is to opt out. You can do so by going to www. optoutpresceen.com or calling 888-5OPTOUT. When you opt out, you remove yourself from mail marketing lists. You can request that your bank not send preapproved checks, as well.

With the current economy, fewer credit card offers seem to be coming in the mail than in previous years when the economy was booming. This doesn't, however, make it less of a problem for other bills and information you may get in the mail that can be used to steal your identity. For example, the federal government still sends annual Social Security statements in the mail. On the statement, you'll find your full Social Security Number. Your DOB as well as your address is also on the statement. So protecting yourself from identity theft still means that you need to guard your incoming mail from the United States Postal Service deliveries. This means *not* leaving your mail in the box for a long period after delivery even in locked mailboxes. Several years ago I was the victim of stolen mail because I left the mail in a locked cluster mailbox overnight. Read about this scenario in the nearby sidebar, "Never leave your mail in the mailbox overnight."

CASE STUDY

---

# Never leave your mail in the mailbox overnight

Several years ago during the Christmas season, I discovered missing mail when I went to retrieve the mail the morning after it was delivered. As I approached the cluster box, I noticed that several mailbox doors were open, including mine. Of course, nothing was inside. A thief had used some kind of tool to pry open the box and then cut the locks. On the way to the post office to report the incident, I noticed that several other cluster boxes in the neighborhood were also broken into.

Now this is when the "fun" began. At the post office, I spoke to a supervisor and told him to hold my mail at the post office until they repaired the lock on the box. The supervisor then said I needed to report the crime to the police department in my city. So off I went to the police department to report the crime. I waited with all the others in the lobby. When it was my turn, the clerk asked me why I was there. I said my mail was stolen along with several others in my neighborhood. The clerk then said that I needed to report it to the post office. I said I did and he replied that "it's their jurisdiction." I knew this wasn't right, so I went to the main post office to report the crime to the law enforcement arm of the United States Postal Service, the postal inspectors.

Much to my chagrin, the postal inspectors were no longer located at the main office in my city, and I had to call San Francisco to file a complaint. I left a message. (To this day, I have never heard anything from the postal inspectors, and I assume that the perpetrators were never caught.) I returned to my branch's post office to pick up my mail for the day. The supervisor said that I should file a report with the local police to investigate the crime. So I was off to see the police department *again* to file a complaint and report the theft.

The police report is necessary to file a fraud alert on my credit report for a 7-year, but not for a 90-day, alert. At the police department, I told the clerk I wanted to file a report for stolen mail. She asked what monetary loss I suffered. Without that information, she couldn't file a report. I said, "I don't know; if I knew I would have my mail or wait a minute, let me contact the thieves and ask them. At least maybe I can get them to pay any bills that may have been in the mailbox."

Ultimately, I did get the report without knowing the monetary loss and immediately filed fraud alerts on my credit report. When you file a fraud alert, you need a police report number. Luckily, nothing ever happened from the stolen mail incident with my credit or identity. I was lucky, and none of my bills were late, so either the thieves paid my bills (ha) or only "junk" mail was in the box. So the moral to the story is never, ever, ever, leave your mail overnight in the mailbox even it is locked.

---

## *What you throw away can hurt you*

*Dumpster diving* occurs when identity thieves go through the garbage of potential targets. The only tools they need are a pair of gloves and a flashlight. (The favorite time to go on a garbage hunt is after dark, and the thief must be able to stand the smell — especially on a hot summer night.) The purpose of dumpster diving is to find personal information that you discard without tearing or shredding. What type of information, you may be asking? The following list gives you the answer:

✔ **Preapproved credit card applications:** Throwing away those preapproved credit card applications without tearing, shredding, or destroying them in some way is inviting trouble. An identity thief can retrieve the application from your trash, send it in with the address changed, and receive the new cards in *your name* based on *your credit.* After receiving your card, the thief charges items (or cash advances) to the card up to its maximum in short order. Then she tosses the card and leaves you with the bill.

*Note:* Not as many credit card applications are sent in the mail as in previous years. With so many people delinquent in paying their credit cards, it's no surprise that the days of the preapproved credit card applications may be done for — at least until the economy gets better and more people are working. The credit card issuers are hurting because they're seeing a loss in revenue with more credit card defaults occurring than ever before.

✔ **Credit card receipts:** Although many businesses no longer print your entire credit card number on your receipts, some still do. Check your receipt — if it lists your credit card number, don't leave it behind to fall into the wrong hands.

✔ **Financial statements:** Bank and other financial statements containing your account numbers and (often) your SSN are treasures that may lurk in the garbage unharmed and waiting to be "liberated" by the identity thief.

✔ **Other paperwork:** Old job applications, insurance forms, and benefits summaries are just a few other forms where your information can be found.

The bottom line is to remember to destroy all personal information before throwing it away. Tear, shred, or otherwise destroy those preapproved credit card applications, financial statements, credit card receipts, and so on. Don't make your house a dumpster diving gold mine; what you throw away can come back to haunt you.

# The Role of Technology in Identity Theft

Technology can play a role in helping you prevent identity theft when you browse the Web, shop online, and log in and out of secure Web sites. Technology can also play a role in helping you lose your identity. Online banking, online shopping, e-mail, and blogs are places where people post information about themselves for friends to see. Would-be thieves can see the same information and have a vast arena from which to steal your identity, and they don't have to get smelly going through the garbage. They don't even have to leave the comfort of their home to steal your identity.

## The Internet makes it possible

The Internet isn't owned or governed by any country. Laws do exist against the distribution of certain materials — such as child pornography — in some countries, which is important. But when it comes to e-mails, blogs, and shopping, it is *user beware.* The Internet is a minefield and is potentially dangerous to the user. The best advice I can give you is to be careful regarding what you do, what you post, or where you go on the Internet. I explore ways to protect yourself and your identity on the Internet in Part V of this book.

The two most common technological tools at your disposal are encryption and authentication. If you know the tricks to these tools, they can help you make sure that your information is safe when you're online.

## *Encryption*

*Encryption* uses digital keys to lock and unlock data while it's being transmitted over the Internet, which makes it incredibly difficult for anyone but the intended recipient to see or tamper with that data. With encryption, a key on the sending end scrambles data, and a key on the receiving end unscrambles it. While the data is in *en route,* good encryption makes it virtually impossible for outsiders to peek at or tamper with the data — in your case, your personal and financial data. *Secure Sockets Layer (SSL)* is the standard form of data security on the Internet. SSL uses digital certificates to verify that the two computers in a transaction are who they claim to be before exchanging the keys that encrypt the data.

Before you use your credit card to purchase merchandise online — in fact, before you enter any of your data online — you want to make sure that the site uses 128-bit SSL to keep your data secure. Checking this is easy — in the bottom-right corner of your Web browser, just look for the lock shown in Figure 1-1. If you hover your mouse pointer over the lock, you may even see a tooltip that says SSL 128. When you double-click the lock, you see information similar to that shown in Figure 1-2, which indicates that the site's identity is authentic and the data is encrypted.

Encryption can also be used to protect e-mail messages and attachments as well as files of personal information that you store on your PC or CD. The encryption software Pretty Good Privacy (PGP) enables you to encrypt this data. PGP offers a *freeware* version (software that you don't have to pay for) for home use. (You can download the freeware version at www.pgp.com/products/freeware.html.) For about $50, PGP offers the software with more features, such as the ability to encrypt content on your hard drive when you're not using it (you may want to do this if, for example, you travel often with a laptop that might be stolen or lost).

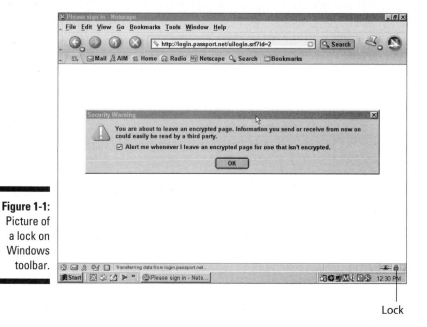

**Figure 1-1:**
Picture of
a lock on
Windows
toolbar.

Lock

**Figure 1-2:**
Web site
verification.

VeriSign offers a method to help you know that the Web site you're on is *authentic* (that is, the site is who it says it is and is encrypting data). A site that uses VeriSign may display the VeriSign logo. (You're most likely to find the logo on the site's privacy and security page.) When you click the VeriSign logo, you're taken to a page that tells you what security measures that site is using through VeriSign.

Because well-known names and logos like VeriSign offer people assurance, of course, online scammers try to use them in unscrupulous ways. Savvy identity thieves can forge a site, copy a logo, or make their own digital certificates. Use SSL and the VeriSign digital certificates and logo as one of many tools to make sure that the site you're visiting really represents the company or organization it claims to be, and see Chapter 10 for more on spotting and avoiding online scams.

## Authentication

*Authentication* is the method used to identify you when, for example, you access your personal information on your PC, Web sites for bank accounts, online bill paying services, and so on. When you authenticate yourself to a PC or a secure Web site, you enter a username and a password or PIN to log in.

The best way to protect your identity through authentication is by using a good password. Choose a password that's hard to guess but you don't need to write down. The password should include a minimum of eight characters with a combination of letters, numbers, and special characters. An example is TGIF!*49. If you have the opportunity to choose secret questions to help prompt you in the event that you forget your password, choose good questions that no one but you can answer, such as a favorite teacher. (People could have access to your mother's maiden name or spouse's middle name.)

# Safeguarding Your Information in Everyday Ways

With identity theft on the rise, you need to be your own watchdog. Table 1-2 lists some everyday do's and don'ts that will help keep your information out of the hands of thieves. I go into more details about preventing identity theft in Part III.

**Table 1-2     Do's and Don'ts to Safeguard Personal Information**

| Do or Don't | Why |
| --- | --- |
| DO buy a shredder. | Use it to shred those credit card applications you receive in the mail and any other personal information you're going to discard. |

| *Do or Don't* | *Why* |
|---|---|
| DO opt out. | So you don't receive credit card applications in the first place. |
| DON'T leave credit card receipts behind. | Take them with you so that they don't fall into unscrupulous hands. |
| DO check monthly credit card statements regularly. | You have 60 days to dispute a charge. |
| DO check your monthly bank statement religiously.* | So you can find out whether any suspicious activity is on your account. |
| DO close unused credit card accounts. | To prevent their use without your knowledge. |
| DON'T give out your SSN. | You only need to give it to the government, your employer, and when you apply for credit. |
| DON'T leave your mail in the box overnight. | You don't want your mail falling into the wrong hands. |
| DON'T give personal information in response to e-mails or text messages.** | You don't want to be the victim of a scam. |
| DO check for the VeriSign logo or the lock at the bottom-right corner of your Web browser window. | So you know that when you type your personal data, the information gets encrypted when transmitted. |
| DO sign your credit card. | Your signature will match the receipt when you sign it. |
| DO ask for EOBs (explanation of benefits) and yearly records from medical providers and insurance carriers. | To make sure that no one is using your medical insurance. |
| DO limit the personal information you put on social networking sites. | The less you post, the better — to keep your personal information personal. |
| DON'T leave purses and wallets in the car, even if the car is locked. | Thieves will break into cars to steal purses/wallets that are visible. If the car is stolen, the thieves have access to your personal information from your wallet or purse. |
| DO make sure that your bills are current. | You know whether your address is current and your bills aren't being forwarded to another address. |

*Find out what protections your financial institution offers. Many offer a password in place of PII (personally identifiable information), so that people with knowledge of that information cannot access your accounts. Some even offer one-time use credit card numbers for online purchases.*

*\*\* Text messaging-phishing by SMS is known as Phexting.*

# Finding Your Allies

You aren't alone in the fight against identity theft. From the federal government and credit card companies to your local police, your allies abound and can help you with many aspects of identity theft. Here are some of your key sources of help:

- **The Federal Trade Commission (FTC):** The FTC provides information useful for preventing identity theft and knowing what to do if you're a victim. Its Web site (www.consumer.gov/idtheft) is chock-full of statistics, information, forms, and more to help you understand and prevent identity theft as well as what to do if you're a victim. When you file a complaint online, the report will be forwarded to law enforcement as well.

- **The Social Security Administration (SSA):** The SSA has guidelines for reporting fraud on its Web site (www.ssa.gov). Also, you need to submit a fraud reporting form to the SSA Office of Inspector General (OIG), which is an investigative branch. The SSA recommends downloading the form, completing it, and then sending it via fax or regular mail to ensure confidentiality. When you report the use of your SSN for identity theft, the SSA will not investigate the identity theft but will look into benefit fraud. The SSA will not issue a new SSN if you have been the victim of identity theft.

- **Most local law enforcement agencies:** These agencies provide information on how to prevent identity theft and what to do if you become a victim.

  For example, the City of Stockton, CA Police Department gives seminars for employees at businesses in the city and for civic groups. They also provide tips on their Web site: Visit www.stocktongov.com, click the City Departments link, and then click the Police Department link. When you report the crime of identity theft to the Stockton, CA Police Department, you call the Telecommunications Center to file a report. The report is taken over the phone, and you're given a report number. Most active federal law enforcement agencies investigating ID theft are the U.S. Postal Inspection Service and the U.S. Secret Service.

- **Internet Crime Complaint Center (IC3):** The IC3 (www.ic3.gov) is a partnership between the FBI, the National White Collar Crime Center (NW3C), and the Bureau of Justice Assistance (BJA). At the Web site, you can file a complaint and read about recent scams and other news. The IC3 reports the complaints to the proper local authorities.

- **Federal Bureau of Investigation (FBI):** Go to www.fbi.gov and look for the Be Crime Smart and Use Our Resources links (on the left side of the page) to find more information.

✔ **Financial institutions and credit card companies:** Most financial institutions provide tips about preventing fraud and knowing what to do if you're a victim. Some institutions provide discounts and links to sites that charge an annual membership fee for providing identity theft protection. For example, I subscribe to a CreditExpert.com service, and the site is part of the credit bureau Experian. See Chapter 5 for more details.

To help stem the upward trend of credit card fraud, the card-issuing companies monitor and look for irregular patterns of use. What you charge on a monthly basis is monitored, and when something varies from the normal pattern, the card company calls and asks whether you made the purchase. For example, when people go on vacation and don't notify the card company, they'll probably receive a call asking whether they made a purchase in X country or Y state. The card companies have used this method for the last ten years, and it's helped reduce some credit card fraud.

✔ **Experienced attorneys:** Although the resources I've just listed are usually quite helpful, you may want to contact an attorney to help you restore your credit and name if creditors aren't cooperative in removing fraudulent accounts from your credit report or charges from accounts. Contact the American Bar Association or Legal Aid office in your area and ask for the names of attorneys that specialize in the Fair Credit Reporting Act (FCRA), consumer law, and the Fair Credit Billing Act.

✔ **Your state's Attorney General office:** Check the Web site for your state's Attorney General office, which has resources about identity theft prevention.

# Getting Back Your Identity and Your Good Reputation

If you have been a victim of identity theft, don't panic. You can do things to restore your identity and good reputation; however, it isn't easy. Estimates of the time spent on getting back your credit and good name are around 600 hours of work, according to a study done by the Identity Theft Resource Center, a nonprofit organization (www.idtheftcenter.org). The study found the 600-hour figure is a 300 percent increase from 2001, when people spent an average of 175–200 hours regaining their names and credit.

After you suspect that your identity has been stolen, you need to take four steps as soon as possible and begin documenting your case. The FTC outlines these first four steps on its identity theft site (www.ftc.gov/idtheft), as shown in Figure 1-3.

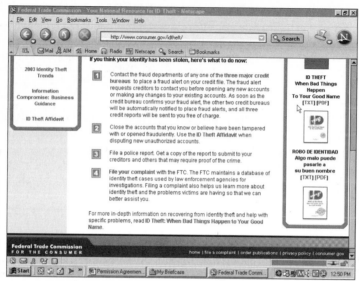

**Figure 1-3:**
Take these
steps right
away if you
think your
identity has
been stolen.

Following is a simplified version of the steps that the FTC outlines:

1. **Place a fraud alert on your credit reports and review the credit reports that you receive as a result.**

   You can contact any one of the three major credit bureaus to place the fraud alert. By contacting one, that bureau is required — by law — to contact the other two bureaus to place a fraud alert on them as well. I discuss the three major credit bureaus in detail in Chapter 5. A new tool that you can add to your toolbox is the credit freeze, which I discuss at length in Chapter 2. If, however, you have filed a fraud alert, you are entitled to a free credit report from each bureau.

2. **Close any accounts that have been tampered with or opened fraudulently.**

   Make sure that you receive a letter stating that the account has been closed and that you receive a clearance letter.

3. **File a report with your local police.**

4. **File a complaint with the FTC.**

   Chapter 2 gives more details about this process for reporting and thwarting identity theft. In Chapter 13, I explain further the process of filling out the required reports. Chapter 14 has helpful information for speeding up the process of closing accounts.

As you begin the process of reclaiming your identity, the paperwork will start to roll in and out of your life. Keeping a good paper trail will help you assemble and support your case. The Identity Theft Resource Center (www.idtheftcenter.org) offers some helpful guidelines for organizing the data. The FTC also gives you tips for organizing your case. The tips shown on the FTC Web site are as follows:

- Follow up in writing with all contacts you've made on the phone or in person. Use certified mail, return receipt requested.

- Keep copies of all correspondence or forms you send.

- Write down the name of anyone you talk to, what he or she told you, and the date the conversation occurred.

- Keep the originals of supporting documentation, such as police reports and letters to and from creditors; send copies only.

- Set up a filing system for easy access to your paperwork.

- Keep old files even if you believe your case is closed. One of the most difficult and annoying aspects of identity theft is that errors can reappear on your credit reports or your information can be recirculated. Should this happen, you'll be glad you kept your files.

# Chapter 2

# Mike's Anti–Identity Theft Crash Course

. . . . . . . . . . . . . . . . . . . . . . . . . . . . . . . . . . . . . . . . . . . . .

*In This Chapter*

▶ Making yourself a hard target

▶ Understanding the laws to protect you

▶ What to do if you're a victim

. . . . . . . . . . . . . . . . . . . . . . . . . . . . . . . . . . . . . . . . . . . . .

*I*n this chapter, I tell you ways to make yourself a hard target. I describe the laws that help protect you from identity theft, including the new changes to the Fair Credit Reporting Act (FCRA). I tell you what to do if you're a victim and how to opt out of receiving preapproved credit card offers.

## Tips for Preventing Identity Theft

You can take preventive measures to help protect yourself from becoming a victim of identity theft. Table 2-1 outlines some things you can do to make yourself a harder target. Making yourself a *harder target* means that you've taken steps to protect yourself so that it's more difficult for an identity thief to steal your identity.

| Table 2-1 | Identity Theft Prevention Tips |
|---|---|
| *Identity Theft Prevention Tip* | *Result* |
| Use a shredder. (See the following section on shredders.) | Keeps your personal information from falling into the wrong hands. |
| Guard those credit card receipts. | Minimizes the risk that someone will get your credit card number from a receipt. |
| Carry only minimal personal information. | Minimizes damage when your wallet or purse is stolen or lost. |

*(continued)*

**Table 2-1** *(continued)*

| Identity Theft Prevention Tip | Result |
|---|---|
| Carry only one credit card. | Reduces the risk — only one card will be lost when your wallet is stolen or lost. |
| Don't leave mail in any mailbox overnight or for extended periods of time. | Reduces exposure to having your mail stolen. |
| Don't mail your bills from unprotected curbside mailboxes or personal mailboxes. | Minimizes the risk that your checks will be stolen, washed, and used by the thief. |
| Pay attention to billing cycles. | If you don't receive your bills on time, follow up with your creditors, because this could signal that an identity thief has taken over your account and changed the billing address to cover his tracks. |
| When ordering checks, have them sent to the bank and pick them up there. | Reduces the risk that an identity thief will steal the new checks from your mailbox. |
| Ask about information security procedures in your workplace, businesses, doctor's office, or other institutions that collect personal information. Ask who has access, what the disposal procedures are, and if the information is shared with anyone else and then verify that the information is secure. | Reduces your exposure. |
| Be stingy with your personal information. The less information you give out about yourself, the more secure the information will be. For example, be careful about giving out your personal information for promotional purposes because this is a common method used by identity thieves to collect information about you. | Reduces the risk that your information will fall into the wrong hands. |
| Don't give out your Social Security Number (SSN). | Keeps your SSN personal. The only time you need to give out your SSN is when you start a new job or apply for a new credit card or loan. |
| Check your monthly credit card statement regularly. | You'll be alerted when new credit cards and loans are opened using your SSN. |

| Identity Theft Prevention Tip | Result |
|---|---|
| Opt out of preapproved credit card applications by calling the toll-free number, 888-567-8688. (See the section "Opt out of preapproved credit card offers" later in this chapter.) | Less risk because you'll receive less marketing mail and calls about credit offers. |
| Purchase a credit monitoring service from one of the three credit bureaus: TransUnion, Experian, and Equifax. | You can detect whether your identity has been stolen. |
| Memorize and randomize your passwords and personal identification number (PIN). Your PIN should not be your date of birth (DOB), phone number, or SSN. | Prevents the ID thief from getting your ATM card and a slip of paper with your PIN when she steals your wallet. |
| When using your ATM card, stand directly in front of the screen and cover the keypad with one hand while you type your PIN. Watch for people lurking around the ATM or pin pad who might be shoulder surfing; if you don't feel comfortable, don't use that machine. | Prevents an identity thief from capturing your ATM PIN. |
| Check your savings, checking, and investment account statements regularly. | You can detect any changes in your accounts that you are unaware of. |

# Buy and use a shredder

Investing in a shredder is worth the money. You can purchase one at a local discount store for around $40. Make sure that the one you purchase shreds the papers so that they can't be easily taped back together. Use a criss-cross or criss-cut shredder that shreds the document into confetti-like material. This way, you don't have strips of paper that can be put back together. The identity thief looks for an easy way to obtain information, and if you shred your documents, they'll look for an easier target. So by purchasing and using a shredder religiously to shred any documents that contain personal information, you'll be that harder target. I have a shredder and use it all the time to shred any documents that I (or my family) don't need or want that contain personal information.

Make a habit of shredding the following documents:

- ✔ The monthly credit card statement after you pay the bill.
- ✔ Bank statements and 401K statements. You don't need to keep every statement you've ever received from your 401K plan, just the first and the most recent three years.
- ✔ Pay stubs from work (after you check your monthly checking statements to make sure that the deposit amount on the statement is correct).
- ✔ Unwanted credit card applications.

## Order and review your credit report

As an identity theft prevention method, order and review your credit reports at least annually. As I outline in Table 2-2 later in this chapter, you're entitled to one free annual credit report from each of the three credit bureaus. Chapter 5 provides details about how to order and read a credit report. (This doesn't stop identity theft, but does help you catch it if it's happened already.)

The revisions to the Fair Credit Reporting Act (FCRA), entitling consumers to one free credit report per year, were signed into law in December 2003 and now are in effect in all states.

Reviewing a credit report is a good way to detect whether someone's using your name to obtain credit. Simply examine the section of the report that summarizes inquiries made by others. Do you recognize the inquiries? Did you make or initiate them? If not, you could be the victim of identity theft.

Look for accounts that you have open but haven't used for a long period of time, and then close the accounts. This keeps the accounts from being used by someone without your knowledge.

The FCRA changes mean that now you get one report a year from each of the three bureaus; do so by going to www.annualcreditreport.com or calling 877-322-8228 (877-FACTACT). In some states (such as Georgia), you are entitled to two reports a year for free. You can space it out and order a different report every four months and monitor your credit. Because many creditors report to credit bureaus only monthly or quarterly, this is the best approach. If you are particularly concerned about your information, you are also entitled to a free copy of all three reports (*above* and *beyond* those you get from annualcreditreport.com). As a result of you placing a fraud alert on your report, it is renewed. You are also entitled to free reports if you are

✔ Turned down for jobs

✔ Turned down for insurance, housing, or credit

✔ Unemployed and looking for work

✔ Receiving public welfare assistance

# Guard your personal information

Don't carry more personal information than necessary. The more information you carry, the greater chance that it'll be stolen. Here are some brief guidelines for what to carry and what to leave behind. Chapter 8 provides more detail, as well.

✔ **Don't carry your Social Security card with you all the time.** If you need the card for identity purposes for a new job, take it with you but guard it. When you return home at the end of the day, take the card from your wallet or purse and put it back in its secure storage place.

✔ **Don't carry personal checks with you unless you're going shopping.** When you carry personal checks, make sure that you guard them. You don't want blank checks falling into the wrong hands.

✔ **Carry only one credit card with you.** You can easily keep track of one card. If you carry several and don't use some of them, you may forget that you have them and not realize that they're missing if they're lost or stolen.

✔ **Be stingy with your personal information.** Be especially stingy with it online and through social networking sites. Don't give out personal information to anyone who asks; always verify the identity of the person asking for the information by initiating the contact to them. Never assume that your caller ID or e-mail is accurate, or that the caller is who she says she is. An identity thief can obtain the information through *social engineering,* which is the art of obtaining more information by using a minimal amount of information to fool the person. For example, knowing your pet's or children's names may help the person find out their birth dates, which you may be using as a PIN.

# Opt out of preapproved credit card offers

By receiving preapproved credit applications in the mail, you increase your chances of becoming a victim of identity theft. All the identity thief needs to do is to steal the application from your mailbox, complete it, and send it in. The thief will use her address, so you won't even get the bills.

You can opt out of preapproved credit card applications by calling the toll-free number, 888-567-8688. The call takes 30 seconds. You can opt out for two years or permanently, and you can opt in at any time. If you place a fraud alert, you're opted out automatically.

When you call, an automated system prompts you for information. One call removes you from the lists at all three major credit bureaus — Equifax, Experian, and Trans Union. I did it, and it's quick, easy, and worth doing. The recording says that the request goes into effect in five business days.

About five business days after the call, you receive a letter asking whether the name and address is correct on the form. If the name and address is correct, sign and date the form and send it to the opt-out department. If your name and address are incorrect, simply make corrections on the form where indicated, sign and date it, and return it. The letter doesn't come with a stamped, self-addressed envelope for returning the confirmation. You need to supply the envelope and the stamp.

To opt out from your own financial institutions and your own credit card company, you need to contact them separately; contacting the three major credit bureaus won't do the trick.

## Opt out of other mailing lists

You may also want to opt out of the Direct Marketing Association (DMA) mailing list. Here's the address:

> Mail Preference Service
> Direct Marketing Association
> P.O. Box 9008
> Farmingdale, NY 11735

 You can also opt out by using four companies that sell mailing lists to other companies. To have your name removed, you need to write to them and send the request by regular mail. I know it sounds like a real pain to have to write and request that your name be removed, but it's time well spent. The four companies' names and addresses are as follows:

> Database America
> Compilation Department
> 470 Chestnut Ridge Road
> Woodcliff, NJ 07677

Dunn & Bradstreet
Customer Service
899 Eaton Ave.
Bethlehem, PA 18025

Metromail Corporation
List Maintenance
901 West Bond
Lincoln, NE 68521

R.L. Polk & Co. - Name Deletion File
List Compilation Development
26955 Northwestern Hwy
Southfield, MI 48034-4716

# Use your debit card carefully

Most ATM cards are a combination debit and ATM card with the same PIN. Debit cards are being used more and more by consumers to make purchases. When you use a debit card, you swipe the card and then the machine asks for your PIN.

Using debit cards to purchase gas can cause you to have an *overdraft* (or non-sufficient funds, NSF) on your account because gas stations block a certain portion of your balance until the transaction clears. For example, if you purchase $20 of gas, the station may block $100 of your balance until the transaction clears. So if you don't keep an eye on your balance, you could go into overdraft and have NSF charges placed on your account.

Another issue to consider is that the card number and PIN can be stolen. Unlike with credit cards, however, you're liable for as much $500 if you don't notify the bank about the stolen debit card within two days. If you don't report the loss of the card within the time limits specified by your agreement with the bank when you signed up for the ATM card, you could be liable for *all* the withdrawals.

Most cardholder agreements specifically exclude fraud by individuals who were at one time given permission to use the account and exceeded that permission. That is, if you "loan" your card once to someone, you may be held liable if they charge it up or steal it later and charge it *without* your permission. However, I strongly recommend that you do not "loan" your debit card to any one, especially if you need to give them your PIN.

# Government Laws to Protect You

The changes to the Fair and Accurate Credit Transactions Act (FACTA) became law on December 2003 (changes took effect December 2004). Table 2-2 outlines the changes.

FACTA provides better protection to you, the consumer, against the fallout from being a victim of identity theft. Following are some of the key provisions of FACTA. Table 2-2 provides additional information.

- ✔ You're entitled to one free credit report from each credit bureau annually. Some states, such as Georgia, are eligible for additional copies under state law. Additional states have reduced-fee laws for additional copies of your report.

- ✔ If you are the victim of identity theft, you're entitled to additional free credit reports.

- ✔ If you are a victim of identity theft, you need to make only one call to receive advice and set a national fraud alert to protect your credit rating.

    The fraud alert requests creditors to contact you before opening any new accounts or making any changes to your existing accounts. As soon as the credit bureau confirms your fraud alert, the other two credit bureaus are notified automatically to place fraud alerts. The three bureaus then send confirmation letters notifying you that the alerts have been placed and will mail you credit reports free of charge, if you request them by using the phone numbers provided in the letters.

- ✔ As a victim, if you file a police report, the police report will help you to extend your fraud alert or to place a credit freeze on your report for no charge because you were a victim of identity theft.

    Neither the fraud alert or the credit freeze will block fraudulent information from appearing on your credit report. This is why I urge you to take full advantage of the free credit reports to keep tabs on what is happening with your credit.

- ✔ The company that is going to issue credit is supposed to ensure that all requests for credit are legitimate after you flag your report and make notice that you suspect you are a victim of identity theft.

    Some companies ignore the fraud alert altogether while others will call and verify that you placed the request for credit. Others will request proof of your identification before moving forward or denying the credit.

- ✔ The fraud alert places a statement on your report, for anyone who might be reviewing your credit report, that you are a victim of identity theft.

The alert does not bar the potential creditor from issuing credit. The credit bureaus have no obligation to ensure the legitimacy of a request for your credit beyond the controls they normally have in place. It is the company that is reviewing your credit that has the responsibility to take action to ensure that the application is not fraudulent.

✔ Any person on active military duty overseas can place special alerts on their reports while deployed overseas away from their usual duty station.

✔ Lenders and creditors are required to take action even before the victim realizes that she is a victim of identity theft.

✔ Debt collectors are now required to report fraudulent information to creditors.

✔ Under FACTA, you have access to specialty consumer reports, such as those provided by ChoicePoint and Lexis Nexis. You also have access to check reports (from Chex Systems, Scan, and TeleCheck), in addition to medical records, payment history, insurance claims, tenant history, criminal background, and employment history. Literally hundreds of companies fall under the requirements of FACTA, and so they are too numerous to mention here. To find out more, go to

```
www.privacyrights.org/fs/fs6b-SpecReports.htm
```

### Table 2-2     The Fair and Accurate Credit Transaction Act

| New FACTA | How It Helps Prevent Identity Theft |
| --- | --- |
| You're entitled to one free credit report per year per credit bureau. | Check your credit report for free. |
| Lenders are required to honor seven-year extended fraud alerts. They often don't honor 90-day alerts. Instant creditors can and will ignore alerts. | Lenders must verify applicant's identity. |
| Fraud alerts can be extended with a police report. | You can request an extension of up to seven years. |
| Fraudulent activities to be reported. | You will now be notified if you have a fraud alert on your credit report in a letter by the three bureaus. You can now order free credit reports from all three bureaus to monitor your report. |
| By 2007, printing entire card numbers on receipts was eliminated. Only the last five digits appear on the receipt. | Helps you keep your credit card numbers more secure. |

*(continued)*

**Table 2-2 (continued)**

| New FACTA | How It Helps Prevent Identity Theft |
|---|---|
| One call opt-out of pre-screened credit offers. | If you call one phone number, you can opt out from receiving promotional prescreened credit offers. |
| You can choose to have only the last four digits of your SSN print on your credit report, if you receive the report in the mail. (You can also still get a report with your full SSN on it.) | Protects your SSN from being overexposed. |
| All creditors have to provide to you in writing why you were denied an application for credit as a result of information found on your credit report. You will receive notification and your rights to the copy of the report with information so you can dispute it. | You know the reason for rejection and are aware if you're a victim of identity theft. |

# Steps to Take If You're a Victim

Sometimes, identity theft can't be prevented. Here's how it can happen. An insider — someone who works for a retailer, credit card company, bank, Department of Motor Vehicles, or Social Security Administration — sells your information to the identity thief. This scenario occurs with low frequency, but it does occur. You can't do much to prevent a situation like this one. That's why you need to remain vigilant and check your accounts and your credit report regularly.

If you discover that you are a victim, do not panic. If you're diligent about checking your accounts and monthly bills, and reading your credit report at least once per year, you'll discover early on whether you've been a victim. Early discovery makes it easier to address the issue and get your good name back.

Table 2-3 outlines the steps you must take if you discover that you're a victim of identity theft. The sections following Table 2-3 provide more detail for each of the steps.

For help with contacting local law enforcement, use these two links:

  ✔ The FTC link:

     www.ftc.gov/bcp/edu/microsites/idtheft/consumers/defend.html

✔ The FTC letter to law enforcement link:

`www.ftc.gov/bcp/edu/microsites/idtheft/downloads/memorandum.pdf`

| Table 2-3 | Identity Theft Victim's Checklist | |
|---|---|---|
| *Notification* | *Action* | *Result* |
| Local police | Call police where you live to report the crime. | You get a report number. |
| Credit bureaus | Complete identity theft affidavit to place a fraud alert on a credit report.<br><br>Review credit report and dispute any information that isn't accurate. | Lender verifies applicant's identity. A fraud alert gives you free copies of your report; an extended fraud alert or credit freeze entitles you to two free copies of your credit reports annually rather than just one. |
| Bank | Close compromised accounts, and then complete fraud or forgery statement/affidavit in a timely fashion. | Reduces exposure and allows for proper dispute, investigation, credit, and resolution. |
| Credit card company | Dispute charges you didn't make on your account. | Minimizes impact. |
| Check verification companies | Notify someone at your bank. | Alerts merchants of fraudulent checks. |
| Department of Motor Vehicles | Request that a notation be made (if possible) that the license has been lost or stolen and try to replace the ID ASAP. | You gain a new driver's license. |

Two check verification companies include Chex Systems (800-428-9623) and Certegy (800-437-5120). I discuss these and others further in Chapter 14.

## *Reporting the crime to law enforcement*

Reporting the crime to law enforcement used to be a chore. Not all states have passed legislation to mandate that local law enforcement agencies take reports of identity theft, but most law enforcement agencies will take reports because of all the recent publicity regarding identity theft.

To report identity theft in most jurisdictions, call the local law enforcement agencies nonviolent nonemergency phone line. Do *not* call 911; the crime isn't a life-threatening situation. The phone book or local law enforcement agency Web site has phone numbers to specifically report these types of crimes. Some states and local agencies provide online methods for reporting nonviolent crimes. You should check with your local law enforcement agency's Web site for more details, as well as your state's Attorney General office Web site.

After you make the call, the agency may send someone to take the report. In California, most jurisdictions don't even send a sworn officer when your car has been stolen — they send a community services officer. This probably follows for an identity theft case. Regardless, you'll have a report number to file with your theft affidavit.

After the report is taken, it's assigned to the detective bureau or squad responsible for the type of crime reported. A detective will open a case file and may do a follow-up contact with you. You need to send the report number and a copy of the report to the credit bureaus as well as all those businesses that have opened credit or sold merchandise that was unauthorized.

## Employing the credit freeze

The *credit freeze* is another tool in the fight against identity theft. The freeze works the way it sounds: A frozen river doesn't move until it thaws, and in a similar way, your frozen credit report is locked until you give permission for the data release. Thirty-nine states and the District of Columbia allow credit freezes by law. California was the first state to pass a law allowing credit freezes. The most recent data (as of November 2008) shows that Michigan, Alabama, South Carolina, Alaska, Ohio, Arizona, Georgia, Idaho, Iowa, Missouri, and Virginia don't have credit freeze laws.

The credit freeze helps you by not allowing an identity thief to open new accounts using your name, SSN, and so on without you knowing about it. This is another tool to prevent you from becoming a victim of identity theft because it stops any access to the credit report by blocking the process of issuing credit. No tool is 100 percent effective. (I hate to say it, but it's true.) Companies that you already have accounts with can access your credit report around the credit freeze. There are accounts that can be opened even with a credit freeze, such as medical identity theft, criminal identity theft, payday loans, utility accounts, and others. So it is important for you to check your credit report even if you have a freeze on your report.

When you initiate a fraud *alert,* you need to contact only one credit bureau and then that bureau contacts the other two bureaus and informs them of the fraud alert. To initiate a credit *freeze,* you must contact all three bureaus. The fraud alert is free, but it lasts for 90 days and can be extended to 7 years.

The credit freeze is in effect until you remove it. The credit freeze can cost $15 per bureau ($15 × 3 = $45) to put it on your report and $18 per bureau ($18 × 3= $54) for you to remove it (or *thaw* it).

In all the states that have freeze laws, you don't have to pay a fee if you've been the victim of identity theft and have a valid police report. The fees vary from state to state if you have not been a victim of identity theft and do not have a police report. There are five states that only permit those who have been victims to use the credit freeze: Washington, South Dakota, Kansas, Arkansas, and Mississippi. You don't have a time limit for keeping the credit freeze on your report, and it remains on your credit report until you remove it by paying any applicable fee.

Generally the freeze can be removed by using three methods: a temporary lift for a single creditor, a temporary lift for a period of time, and a complete removal of the freeze. You need to check with your state for specific details of how the credit freeze works where you live.

To find out about your state's credit freeze law and to place a freeze on your credit report, follow these steps:

1. **Go to `www.creditcards.com`.**

   You're taken to the CreditCards.com home page.

2. **Just below the credit card logos in the upper-right corner of the screen, type** credit freeze **in the search box.**

   You're taken to a screen with a list of links.

3. **Near the top of the list, click the Details of Credit Freeze Laws in All 50 States link.**

   All the states are listed in alphabetic order.

4. **Click your state.**

   You're taken to a page showing a table that provides details about your state's credit freeze law.

   The information is easy to read, and the table provides the cost for placing the credit freeze on each bureau's credit report and the cost for you to remove it. Also, the table provides information on how long the freeze lasts when you place it on your report. In most states, the freeze is permanent until you remove it. In several states, the freeze is for seven years and then it expires.

5. **Look at the How to Place Freeze column and follow the guidelines for your state.**

   The process to place a freeze on your credit report varies from state to state, so I can't provide all the details here.

You can also find information about credit freezes here:

```
www.consumersunion.org/campaigns/learn_more/003484indiv.html
```

Most state Attorney General Web sites contain information on credit freezes as well as form letters to help you exercise your rights to free reports, fraud alerts, and credit freezes.

A credit freeze is not a panacea for protecting you against becoming a victim of identity theft. The freeze process is a long and complex process, and it is recommended mostly for those people who are repeated victims of identity theft. The best defense is prevention and being vigilant about checking your credit report at least annually.

In the states that don't have credit freeze laws, the credit bureaus set the fees and the rules. To find out the cost of freezing your credit report and the cost for thawing your credit report, contact each of the three credit bureaus (TransUnion, Experian, Equifax).

In 2007, the AARP conducted a survey and found that most Americans were unaware that they could place a freeze on their credit report. Maybe public service announcements about the credit freeze law within each state would help get the word out.

## *Other essential actions you must take*

Here are some other things you must do immediately if you discover that your identity has been stolen:

- ✔ **Place a fraud alert on your credit report.** This is an important step in regaining your good name and credit. Chapter 13 provides more details about this topic.

- ✔ **Close compromised accounts.** If you discover that you've been a victim and some of your accounts have been compromised, close them immediately. See Chapter 14 for more details.

- ✔ **Call your credit card company.** If you review your monthly statement and find an item you want to dispute, call the credit card company. Chapter 4 provides more information about compromised accounts.

- ✔ **Contact your bank.** Call your bank if a discrepancy exists on your monthly checking account or savings account statement.

- ✔ **Contact the Post Office Inspector General.** Do this only if the situation involved mail theft.

- ✔ **File a complaint with the Federal Trade Commission (FTC).** The FTC has a complaint form on its Web site (www.ftc.gov).

CASE STUDY

# How I caught up with a thief

Several years ago, I discovered — by reviewing my monthly statement — that someone was using my credit card without my authorization or knowledge. On that statement were several charges on the card I didn't make. To remedy the situation, I called the card company, and it immediately removed the charges and sent me a letter stating that it was investigating the disputed charges. If those charges were found to be legitimate, the amount would be added back into my balance on the next statement. Typically, credit card companies also request a written statement (sometimes called a statement, or affidavit, of fraud). The charges were fraudulent and recurred for several months, so the card company recommended that I cancel the card, which I did. They issued a new one immediately with a new account number and transferred any legitimate charges pending to the new account. My credit report reflected the credit card account was closed due to fraud, and the new account was listed above the closed one.

***Note:*** Your credit card issuer may not address the situation presented above in the same way as mine did, but you need to report any charges you did make to them immediately. This was a unique situation where the credit company fraud investigators were working on a case where the companies and charges in questions were happening to other cardholders as well. This is why it is extremely important to check *every* charge on your statement *every* month.

# Part II
# Determining Whether You're a Victim

"That reminds me — I have to figure out how to straighten out my credit report after having my charge cards stolen and used in four different states."

## In this part . . .

How do you know if you're a victim? You look for certain signs, such as a sudden change in your credit score for no apparent reason. You need to know how to order and interpret your credit report and what to look for on that report that may signal that someone else is using your credit. I cover all this and more in Part II.

# Chapter 3

# Smelling a Rat: Recognizing Common Signs of Identity Theft

## In This Chapter

▶ Knowing what to do if you're a victim of mail theft

▶ Defending yourself against identity theft and credit card fraud

*I*n this chapter, I tell you how to recognize the signs that you're an identity theft victim. The signs of identity theft I outline are the first signs people typically notice, but you can also find clues in your bank statements, investment statements, and credit report. What you don't know can hurt you! For details on what to look for in bank and investment statements, see Chapter 4. For details on credit reports, see Chapter 5.

## Suspecting a Thief at Your Mailbox

You know your normal billing cycle, and when your bills don't arrive on time, you need to find out why. You could be the victim of mail theft.

I'd like to improvise on the old saying that *nothing is definite except taxes and death* and say *there's nothing definite except taxes and bills*. When your bills don't arrive on schedule, you need to be concerned. Don't panic; simply follow these steps:

1. **Contact your creditors.**

   Call your credit card company, gas card company, and all the others that are late, and find out whether the bill is late for some reason (keep in mind that bills are almost never sent out late). Also ask when the bill was sent.

2. **Contact someone at the post office and let her know that you suspect you're the victim of mail theft.**

   Offer to the post office the missed billing cycle and the information from the company you contacted about when the bill was sent. You may want to ask to speak directly to the local Postal Inspector's Office.

Besides your bills, you also receive bank statements regularly. Check your files to see when you last received your bank statements. If you haven't received the statements monthly, you might be the victim of mail theft. Contact your bank and ask when your statements were sent.

To help track bills on different cycles, you can use the Calendar feature in Microsoft Outlook. You can enter the date the bill arrives and then determine when the next is due. Most bills are on a 30-day cycle. After you get the receipt for the bill, make an entry on the next month's calendar and check the recurring event feature. You can also check the notification box so you receive an audible notification on that day. If you don't have access to the Microsoft Outlook Calendar feature, you can use any calendar to enter the information.

Another indicator of mail theft is when you receive notification from a financial institution confirming your requested change of address. If you suspect mail theft, check your credit report, which may reflect the incorrect address that was filed in the change of address form. You can dispute the incorrect address and have it corrected.

# Recognizing When Something Is Wrong, and What You Can Do about It

No question about it: It pays to monitor your bills every month, using the credit card receipts for the month. This is your first line of defense against credit card fraud and identity theft.

Here are the general steps you need to take if you notice charges you haven't authorized on your bill:

1. **Call your credit card company and dispute the charge.**

   Ask for the credit card fraud department. Let the department know that you've been a victim of identity theft; then point out what charges you're disputing and why. Make sure that you get the name of the person you're speaking to, correct spelling, and so on.

Document the conversation by writing down the date and time of the call, as well as the name of the person you spoke to. Follow up your phone conversation with a dispute letter and send it to the company by Certified Mail. You'll receive a letter in the mail from the credit card company outlining your conversation and listing the disputed charges. (See the section "Large unknown purchases on your credit card bills" later in this chapter for more details.)

To help you track your progress, check out this link, which provides a sample record keeping log:

```
www.ftc.gov/bcp/edu/resources/forms/chart-course-
        action.pdf
```

For large dollar charge disputes, follow up your phone conversation with a letter disputing the charge.

2. **File a dispute letter.**

   The FTC provides a good sample dispute letter here

```
www.ftc.gov/bcp/edu/microsites/idtheft/downloads/
        dispute-letter-for-exisiting-accounts.doc
```

3. **Order a credit report and review it carefully.**

   Dispute any unknown charges and information. Place a fraud alert on your credit report if you suspect that you're the victim of identity theft. Turn to Chapter 5 for a rundown on how to interpret your credit report.

4. **Review all your bank statements and balances to make sure that they're correct and show no signs of tampering.**

   If you see signs of tampering, have your bank freeze the accounts. For example, look for withdrawals from your account that you didn't make.

5. **If you suspect that you are an identity theft victim, complete an identity theft affidavit.**

6. **Contact the fraud departments of your credit accounts and explain that you have been a victim of identity theft and are interested in further precautions they may have to offer you.**

   Some will add a password to your account and others will "flag" your account or take other security precautions for free.

7. **File a police report.**

   This can extend your fraud alert to seven years, and the police report will also make reluctant financial institutions take your fraud claim seriously.

The following sections describe the most common ways that people realize their credit card or identity is being used without their authorization, and what you can do in each instance to reclaim your good credit.

## Denied credit for a large purchase

The setting is a car dealership. You have the type, model, and color car you've longed for. You test-drive it, and you make an offer to the salesperson. You haggle for a time and finally come to an agreement. You complete the loan application. The salesperson says it will take a few minutes to run your credit report. After what seems to be an eternity, the salesperson comes back and says, "I have bad news: You were not approved for the loan." You say, "But that can't be — I have good credit."

You're permitted by the Fair Credit Reporting Act (FCRA) to know the reason why you were turned down for the loan. After you review your credit report, you find credit card accounts you didn't know you had, and you own two other cars you've never driven, or seen, for that matter.

What's happened here is that you may be the victim of identity theft and didn't know it. Now your work is just beginning. You must get back your good name and credit. You should dispute the information on your credit report that is incorrect with the credit bureaus; if this does not clear up the issue, you need to contact the original creditor.

You can get the contact information from the credit report. When you contact the creditor, ask to verify the last four digits of the Social Security Number on the account. Now you will have to give them the last four digits of your SSN to verify if this is the SSN on the account in question. For a good explanation on disputing credit report information, go to

```
www.creditinfocenter.com/repair/
          DisputingWithOriginalCreditor.shtml
```

This scenario actually happened to someone and was told to me by that person. The scenario can happen to you, especially if you have good credit. I can't stress it enough: You need to know if someone is using your credit and name without your knowledge, and one of the best ways to detect the theft early is to review your credit report regularly. Chapter 5 explains how to order and read your credit report.

Review your credit report *at least* annually, as well as review your credit card and bank statements regularly. By *regularly,* I mean every three or four months. You can use your annual free report from each bureau and space them out at three-to-four months intervals. When you perform the checks consistently, you will know immediately if something is wrong. The sooner you find out, the easier it is to minimize the fallout. When you find an issue on your report, you should report it immediately. Early detection will help protect you from being held liable for the charges you did not make.

## *Receiving credit card bills from cards you didn't apply for*

In your mail today, you receive a surprise bill from a credit card you didn't apply for or didn't even know you had. The charges on the card are for things you haven't purchased and for a trip to a place you have never been. Something is wrong. You're thinking it's probably a mistake. You double-check the name and address on the bill, and sure enough, it has your name and address.

Here's what you do right away:

1. **Verify that the credit card company is legitimate.**

   Phishing could be the issue here. Verify the company by using the online yellow pages, your state Attorney General's office, or the BBB. You can also do a company search on Google to verify the address and company's phone number.

   When you contact the company, DO NOT ask them to look you up by name; instead, they may ask for the last four digits of your SSN. If they say they found an account, ask to speak to their fraud department immediately. Then provide notification in writing that you are disputing the charge. If it is fraud, then continue with these steps.

2. **Order your credit report and review it carefully.**

3. **Place a fraud alert on your credit report.**

4. **Complete a fraud affidavit and send it to the credit card company that sent the bill.**

You should not pay any balances that are fraudulent. If you pay, you own it. Do not fall victim to predatory collection practices. Check with your state Attorney General's office about the laws that collection companies must follow in your state. Know your rights!

If people at the company attempt to pressure you into paying, just tell them that you're filing a complaint with the Federal Trade Commission (FTC) and your state's Attorney General and remind them of the FACTA (Fair and Accurate Credit Transactions Act) provision that they can't demand payment if you've been the victim of identity theft and have identified the charge as fraudulent.

# Receiving calls from bill collectors for stuff you didn't buy

You are watching your favorite TV show, when suddenly the telephone rings: It's a bill collector calling about a delinquent bill. You have no idea what the caller is talking about. You start checking, but you know you didn't purchase the item the bill collector is talking about. Here's what you do right away.

1. **Take a deep breath.**

2. **Ask the bill collector to send something in writing.**

   This could be a phishing call, so be stingy with supplying information; instead, make the caller give you information. The Fair Debt Collection Act and state laws prevent collection agencies from calling you if you ask them to stop calling you.

   Representatives of collection companies cannot threaten you, harass you, use obscene language, publicize the debt, or misrepresent the debt. You can sue for damages under the act if they do.

   Keep a notebook by the phone, and make notes of all the conversations, including the times and dates of the calls, and the names of the callers; also keep any letters you receive related to the communication.

3. **Order a credit report and then:**

   a. *Review it carefully.*

   b. *Dispute any unknown charges and information.*

   c. *Place a fraud alert on your credit report if you suspect you're an identity theft victim.*

4. **Call your credit card company and then:**

   a. *Get the new charges since the last billing cycle.*

   b. *Dispute any charges that aren't yours.*

   c. *Change your card or account number if compromised.*

   d. *Contact the fraud department of your credit card company.*

5. **Review all your bank statements and balances to make sure that they're correct and show no signs of tampering.**

   If you see signs of tampering, have your bank freeze the accounts. If there are confirmed signs of tampering, change the card or account number and complete the necessary fraud paperwork.

6. **If you suspect that you're the victim of identity theft, complete an identity theft affidavit, and then send it to all your credit accounts and your bank.**

Receiving a call from a bill collector about a delinquent bill for something you never purchased is a definite sign that something is wrong. If this happens, you most likely are the victim of identity theft, and you need to address the situation immediately. Know your rights when it comes to bill collectors.

## Receiving bills for unknown purchases

The mail arrives; you open it and see a bill for a plasma screen TV for $4,500. You look at the bill and say, "What is this? I didn't buy a plasma screen TV at the XYZ store on an XYZ store credit card." So what do you do? You follow these steps:

1. **Verify the legitimacy of the store with a quick call or online visit to the Better Business Bureau or your state's Attorney General's office.**

2. **Call the store's credit department to inquire about the purchase.**

   Suppose they say that you made the purchase in their Seattle, Washington, store on xx/xx/xx date. You live in Spokane, Washington, and you weren't in Seattle on the day of the purchase. Besides, you never received any plasma screen TV. When you inquire further, you find out that the plasma TV was shipped to an address in the Seattle area that you've never heard of.

3. **Tell the store retail credit representative that you're going to dispute the charge and then order your credit report.**

   The XYZ store credit card account is in the credit history of your report. The report also contains the date the account was opened, which was the date of the purchase.

4. **File a fraud affidavit that shows you were at work on the date of the purchase — you weren't in Seattle — and send it to the XYZ store credit department.**

5. **Call the store credit department and ask them to close the account.**

6. **Follow up with a written identity theft affidavit to the store credit department to close the loop.**

7. **Place a fraud alert on your report immediately.**

8. **Order a credit report from the other two credit bureaus to see whether any other accounts have been opened in your name.**

9. **Immediately send an identity affidavit to any account opened without your knowledge.**

   The fraud alert stops creditors from opening accounts without your knowledge. You have to verify your identity and approve all new accounts while the alert is in place.

10. **Check with the Social Security Administration to see whether your Social Security Number (SSN) was used to obtain a job.**

11. **Inquire at the United States Postal Service to find whether a change of address form was filed on your behalf and report the information to the** *Postal Inspectors* **(the Law Enforcement Division of the post office).**

12. **Keep a written record of all the correspondence, phone conversations, affidavits sent, and so on.**

Receiving bills in the mail with your name and address for purchases you didn't make is an indication that you might be the victim of identity theft. It depends on the name. The more common the name, the more likely it is a mistake. For example, Mary Brown and John Smith are likely to be mistakes. The more uncommon the name — such as Raquel FeDelquizecx — the more likely it is identity theft.

## Large unknown purchases on your credit card bills

When you review your monthly credit card bill, check it against your credit card receipts for the month. If you notice a large charge for something you didn't authorize, contact your credit card company immediately.

1. **Look at the date of the purchase, the location, and the amount. Tell the representative you didn't make or authorize the purchase.**

   The disputed charge is removed from the current month's bill and is investigated to determine whether the charge is legitimate.

   Soon after the phone call, you receive a letter in the mail summarizing the details about the charge and letting you know that the card company is looking into the charge and will let you know of the disposition.

   When the card company completes its investigation and you receive notification that the charge was fraudulent, pay close attention to your credit card bills because someone may have your card number.

2. **Follow up your initial phone call with a dispute letter or the completed statement/affidavit or forgery/fraud (see Figure 3-1).**

Date
Your Name
Your Address, City, State, Zip Code
Your Account Number
Name of Credit Card Issuer
Billing Inquiries
Address, City, State, Zip Code

Dear Sir or Madam:
I am writing to dispute a billing error in the amount of $_____on my account. The amount is inaccurate because the merchandise I ordered was not delivered. I ordered the merchandise on (date) . The merchant promised to deliver the merchandise to me on (date) , and the merchandise was not delivered. (In addition, when I ordered the merchandise, the merchant did not tell me that it would charge before shipping.)

I am requesting that the error be corrected, that any finance and other charges related to the disputed amount be credited to my account, and that I receive an accurate statement.

Enclosed are copies of (use this sentence to describe any enclosed information, such as sales slips, payment records, documentation of shipment or delivery dates) supporting my position and experience. Please correct the billing error promptly.

Sincerely,

Your name

Enclosures: (List what you are enclosing.)

**Figure 3-1:**
Sample
dispute
letter from
the FTC.

Keep in mind the following points:

- The dispute letter is to be sent within 60 days of when the disputed charge appeared on your bill.

- Send the letter by Certified Mail return receipt requested to make sure that the credit card company received the letter.

- Don't send the letter to the address where you send your monthly payment; send it the address for *billing inquiries.* You can find the address for billing inquiries on the back of your monthly bill.

- Enclose a copy of your monthly bill and circle the charge(s) you're disputing. Don't send the original monthly bill — keep it in your files, along with a copy of the dispute letter and the return receipt from the post office after the letter is delivered.

3. **Mark your calendar.**

   The credit card company must *acknowledge* your dispute within 30 days after receiving it. The credit card company must then *resolve* the dispute within two months of receiving your letter but not more than 90 days after receiving your dispute letter.

4. **Call the credit card company to obtain your current balance every week until your next bill arrives in the mail.**

   If you don't recognize any charges, speak to a representative and let him know. You may want to cancel the card, as well, and ask for a new account number.

5. **Check your credit report to make sure that you don't have any other surprises.**

   Closely monitor your bank statements and your investment accounts. Stay on top of the situation so it doesn't escalate into a bigger mess.

# Suddenly . . . several unknown charges on each month's bill

You can handle several unknown charges that appear on your bill each month the same way you address a large unknown purchase, although you may not need to cancel your card.

I've experienced this issue. I called people at the card company and told them which charge I was disputing because I didn't make or authorize it. They removed the charges, and when the charges appeared on the next month's bill, as well, the matter was turned over to the credit card's fraud department. I spoke to the investigator, and he said that they knew about the company making the charges and that they would take care of it. The next month's bill didn't have the charges on the bill. In my case, it wasn't an identity theft; it was credit card fraud. The charges, which were small ($50 to $65 per month), would have continued if I paid them and didn't dispute them. It pays to review your credit card bill closely every month and not just blindly pay it.

This was the second time I had issues with a credit card. Several years ago, I noticed charges appearing on my monthly bill that I didn't recognize. I called the card company and spoke to a representative to question the charges. The charges were removed from the current month's bill. The next month, several new charges appeared on my bill. The charges from the previous month were found to be fraudulent. When I called the card company, a representative suggested that I cancel the card. The company issued a new one and moved my current legitimate charges to the new account. (This is where keeping your receipts for a month comes in handy.)

I received a new card several days after the phone conversation with the credit card company representative. I also put an alert on the card so that I would be contacted by the card company if any charges occurred that seemed to be out of my ordinary pattern of spending. The situation was resolved, and I didn't receive any unauthorized or fraudulent charges on that particular credit card after the card was cancelled and a new account was opened.

The charges on my monthly credit card bill were not large, so they could've gone unnoticed had I not made a habit of checking my monthly bill closely. The fraudulent charges each month totaled no more than $60, and they were usually in $30 amounts for each charge. The thieves limit the charge amounts in hopes that they won't draw attention to themselves, and they bank on the chance that I pay my monthly bills without closely reviewing them.

# Chapter 4

# Homing In on Financial Statements

*I*n this chapter, I *home* in on the bank account twins: checking and savings accounts. I also cover investment accounts, including the most popular, the 401K. I present some reasons why you need to look at your bank account statements regularly and some signs that may suggest you're the victim of identity theft.

## Checking Your Monthly Financial Statements for Surprises

Looking at your financial statements on an ongoing and regular basis helps you keep abreast of any changes in your accounts — especially those changes that may indicate that someone has your account information. If you check statements online or over the phone, you must also be careful about *where* you check your statements.

Check the following financial records every month:

✔ **Bank/savings account statement:** You either get a paper or online statement, at least once per month. The online statements can be reviewed any time. Your bank statement is easy to read. For checking, the statement has the checks you wrote and the account balance, plus all the deposits, ATM/debit card withdrawals, and any other automatic withdrawals you have set up. An online statement shows the amount deducted for each bill you paid, as well as the date.

For savings account statements you will see the deposits, withdrawals, and the account balance for the month.

✔ **Credit card statements:** If you find surprises, dispute them immediately by contacting your credit card company at the number printed on your bill. Tell someone at the company that you're disputing XYZ charges because you didn't make them. Follow up your phone call with a dispute letter (see Chapter 3 for a sample letter from the Federal Trade Commission [FTC]).

In the case of existing or new credit card account fraud, don't pay any amount toward a fraudulent balance. In most cases, this is viewed as accepting responsibility for that debt, regardless of whether you acquired it. In many cases, you know the person who stole your identity. To companies that may doubt that you didn't benefit in some way from the misuse of your information, a payment might as well be a written confession.

✔ **Checking account statement:** Reading and interpreting your checking account statement is easy; you've probably been doing it for years to balance your checkbook every month. When you look at your statement, you see what your balance is at the time of the statement. You also see all the deposits made during the monthly statement period and all the withdrawals including ATM, POS transactions, and the checks that you wrote. By looking at the statement, you can see where you stand financially and you know whether someone's tapped into your bank account.

✔ **401K, stock, and mutual fund statements:** These statements usually come on a quarterly basis. Make sure that you review them to keep tabs on your investments. When reviewing your 401K statements, look at the difference from last quarter gains and losses. This helps keep you updated on your 401K plan. The same goes for stocks and mutual funds.

✔ **Social Security Number (SSN) statement:** This statement is sent by the Social Security Administration; it has your address, SSN, how much you have in your account, and the projected amount of monthly benefit you'll receive upon retirement. The statements are mailed, so remember to get your mail every day. Don't leave your mail in the mailbox overnight.

The following tips highlight a couple points to keep in mind if you decide to check your statements online or over the phone:

✔ **When you check your online statements, be careful if you do so in a public place, such as a library; you never know who's watching.** You don't want to make it easy for someone to get your financial information by using a Wi-Fi connection without using encryption. This goes for laptop computers, an iPhone, a BlackBerry, and so on.

The person sitting next to you or elsewhere in a public place can steal your password when he logs on to your bank accounts if the packets aren't encrypted. The perpetrator doesn't even have to be in the same place as you; he only needs to be in close proximity with a laptop computer, a homemade antenna, and some software to hijack Wi-Fi connections. You probably won't even know that your passwords have been captured until you notice money missing from your bank account.

✔ **If you check your bank account by phone, don't do it in a public place and don't use your cellphone.** I recommend that you use only a hard-wired phone (that is, a landline) to check your bank account information. Cellphone conversations can be captured, even though it's considered *wire tapping* (which civilians can't do and the police need a search warrant to perform). Hard-wired phones must be tapped physically for anyone to listen to your conversation, and that is more difficult than you think. I don't explain how this is done because it's beyond the scope of this book and, oh yeah, it's *illegal*.

See Chapter 8 for more about keeping your private information private.

Replacing financial documents can take a lot of time and effort. You can protect your important documents by storing them in a safe-deposit box at your bank or in a fireproof safe in your house. The documents to keep in a safe and secure place include (but are not limited to) birth certificates, Social Security cards, car/home titles, bank records, insurance papers, and wills.

# Checking Your Bank Statement Religiously

When you review your bank statements regularly (monthly), you'll know around the time your statements will be delivered. If your bank statements don't show up regularly, you may be a victim of mail theft. If your statements don't show up, follow these steps immediately:

1. **Call the bank to see whether it sent the statement or whether there's a delay.**

2. **If the statement was sent, see whether you're missing other mail, such as credit card statements.**

3. **Contact the good people at the post office and have them check whether a change of address form is on file for your address.**

If a change of address form is on file that you didn't make, inform the post office of the fraud.

4. **Contact the Postal Inspection Service and report a mail theft problem.**

5. **Contact your local police or sheriff's department as well to report the mail theft.**

6. **Contact the good people at the bank and tell them about your mail problem, and then close and open new bank accounts. Transfer your money to the new accounts. Ask for new ATM cards and change your PIN.**

You must review your bank statements *every month* to detect theft issues quickly — before they escalate.

Credit card statements are also an issue if not received regularly. Your credit card statement has all the information an identity thief needs to use the card herself. With your credit card information in hand, an identity thief can take an expensive trip on your nickel. She probably won't send a postcard telling you what a wonderful time she's having. In fact, the thief is probably pretty darned glad you aren't there with her. Although it is rare that your credit card statement will have your full account number, expiration date, or CVV code, you still need to watch for signs of theft, which means reviewing every charge every month. Flag the ones you don't recognize and research them; if you didn't make the charge, report it immediately to your financial institution.

If you don't receive your monthly statement from your credit card company, it isn't because it's so grateful that you pay your bill every month on time so it decided to give you a break; more likely, you're the victim of mail theft. Follow the preceding steps in this section if you don't receive your credit card statement for even one month.

# Identifying an Unwelcome Doppelganger

Any unknown activity on your bank statements is a *red flag*. If you identify a red flag, a strong possibility exists that you have a joint account with a thief. When you review your accounts, look for the following:

- ✓ For checking account statements, make sure that all the checks listed in your statement are also listed in your check register.
- ✓ Look for any checks that are made out to Cash and ask yourself whether you wrote the checks.
- ✓ Look for ATM withdrawals you didn't make from savings and checking accounts.

✔ Review instances when you're overdrawn in your checking account.

✔ Note all the withdrawals, especially those that are ATM or online payments from the account. Question any you don't recognize.

✔ Balance your checkbook every month so that you know how much is in the account. This also helps you get into the routine of checking the bank statements so that you know when they should appear in your mailbox.

✔ For savings account statements, make sure that any withdrawals that are listed were made by you.

Reviewing your bank statements regularly is a good way to reconcile your accounts and make sure that your balances are accurate, but you have to do it every month. This way, you can fix issues quickly — before they escalate.

## Withdrawals you didn't make

The Activity Summary and the Withdrawals and Other Withdrawals sections of your bank statements are important; you need to pay attention to them. If you see withdrawals that you didn't make, you must note the discrepancy as a red flag. Definitely call people at the bank and talk to them about the charge.

## Checks you didn't write

As you are reviewing your checking account statement, look for checks written for things that you don't recognize. If the numbers of any of the checks on the statement are out of sequence, make note of it. This is a red flag that something could be wrong.

The other scenario is that you see check numbers for checks you don't recognize. You look at the cancelled checks that come with your statement and then look at your register, and you confirm your suspicions: You didn't write the checks for Cash in the amount shown on your statement.

Don't panic; call your bank and tell somewhere there that you didn't write the checks in question. The dollar amount written on the checks and the check Pay to the Order Of in your register shows the checks you made out were to three entirely different entities, such as your electric utility bill, your phone bill, and your credit card payment.

Here is what you should do if you suspect your checks have been lost or stolen.

- ✔ **In most states, the bank is liable for forged checks, but you must notify your bank in a timely manner.** *Timely manner* is rather ambiguous, so my recommendation is that you check your statement every month and contact your bank as soon as you notice something.

- ✔ **You may want to close the account and open a new one.** The bank will want to know of any outstanding checks you've written so they can be paid when they arrive.

- ✔ **Contact your local police department and report the lost or stolen checks.**

- ✔ **Contact check verification companies to let them know that your checks have been lost or stolen.**

Figure 4-1 shows the First Data Web site, which has links to where you can find First Data consumer support (First Data owns TeleCheck):

```
www.telecheck.com
```

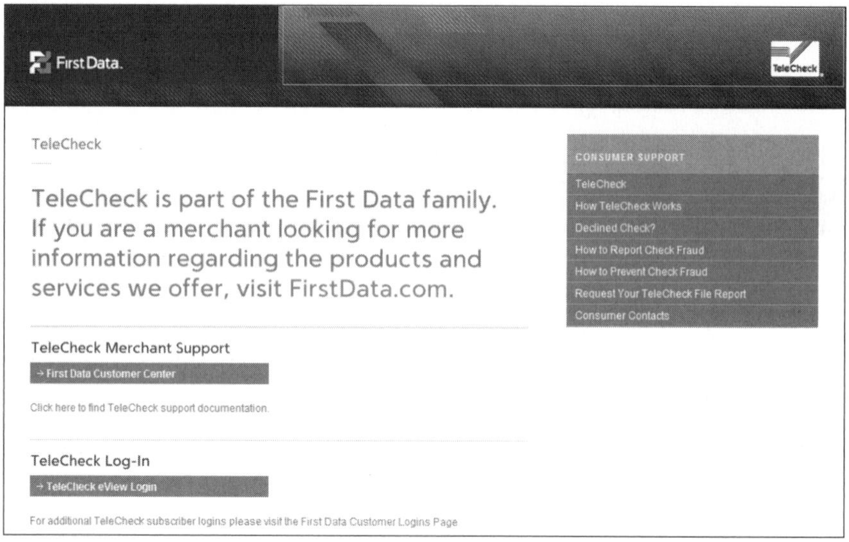

**Figure 4-1:**
First Data Consumer Support.

The site explains what to do if your check was declined, how to report check fraud, and so on, if you lose checks or have them stolen. This Web site gives the phone number for merchants and consumers to report lost or stolen checks. Here are some important phone numbers from First Data:

- ✔ Declined Check Information for Check Writers: 800-366-2425

> ✔ Returned Check Collection: 800-366-1048
>
> ✔ Free annual file disclosure pursuant to the Fair Credit Reporting Act: 800-366-2425
>
> ✔ Fraud, Identity Theft, Forgery: 800-710-9898

## Finding bizarre bank account balances

Suppose that when you review your bank account statements, you notice that the balances aren't what they should be according to your records. You review your statements by checking all your deposits with all the deposit slips you've kept for the month against those recorded on your statement. If they don't match, call your bank immediately and tell someone there about the discrepancy.

The Activity Detail Deposits and Interest section of your bank statement shows the date of each deposit. A description and the amount for each deposit are listed. If your paycheck is a direct deposit, each pay period is listed here, along with any other deposits you made during the month.

Keeping all your deposit slips and your paycheck stubs for the month pays off when you find a discrepancy in your account balance.

After you check the deposits, look at the withdrawals, especially those made with your ATM and debit card. Are they correct? The account statements make it easy to find the information. If you didn't make any one or more of the withdrawals, call your bank and tell somewhere there about the discrepancy.

# Reviewing Investment Account Statements

Check your investment account statements, such as your 401K and IRA statements. These accounts aren't immune from being compromised. The statements are usually quarterly, so you don't get to review them as often as other accounts unless you view them online. Most of the 401K accounts have this option, as do the other investment accounts.

Check the account statements closely to make sure that no one is helping themselves to your money. Look at the balances in the accounts and compare them from the previous statements' balances. You'll see fluctuations due to the stock market conditions, but watch for withdrawals you didn't make or changes that don't seem right.

My advice is to review all your accounts regularly. By regularly, I mean at least monthly, and if the statement is only sent quarterly, you can still access it via the Internet to review it.

# Online Banking

Online banking has grown in popularity. More and more people use online banking because of convenience. You can bank from home and not worry about dressing to go the bank. With online banking, you can check your account statement 24/7, even on holidays, and not have to worry about a paper monthly statement getting "lost" in the mail. You can also use the convenient bill pay to pay your bills online.

Today with the use of a computer you can read your bank statements online and you will be able to see each transaction — even the checks you may have written during the current statement period — deposits, and ATM withdrawals. All that information is available for instant viewing. Reading the statements online will keep you up-to-date on any activity in your account and the chance of the statement being lost in the mail is null. Online banking is a good tool to help you track your accounts and quickly see if something is wrong. The check image is scanned into your statement, and you can view these things:

- Both sides of the check
- Who the check was written to
- The check number
- The amount the check was written for
- The signature of the person who cashed the check

When reviewing the statement, look for deposits as well as withdrawals. Bill pay checks show withdrawals but not a check number because you didn't actually write a check.

Online banking has a cool feature that enables you to look at older statements and track your spending habits — beats sitting at the kitchen table with your paper statements.

For all its advantages, online banking still is not 100 percent free from being compromised. You must still be vigilant to make sure that if you're the victim of someone hijacking your bank account, you can report the criminal activity in a timely manner to recoup your losses.

# Chapter 5

# Interpreting Your Credit Report

. . . . . . . . . . . . . . . . . . . . . . . . . . . . . . . . . . . . . . . . . . . . . . .

## In This Chapter

▶ Demystifying the credit report

▶ Ordering a credit report

▶ Identifying red flags on the report

▶ Disputing the information in your report

. . . . . . . . . . . . . . . . . . . . . . . . . . . . . . . . . . . . . . . . . . . . . . .

*T*his chapter contains information about credit reports. You see how to order them, read them, and dispute any inaccurate information you find in them. Armed with the information in this chapter, you can use your credit report as an important tool in preventing identity theft.

## What Is a Credit Report?

A *credit report* is a factual record of your credit payment history. Based on your credit history, a credit rating (or credit score) can assess your credit risk from high to low. Figure 5-1 shows a credit report from one of the major credit bureaus.

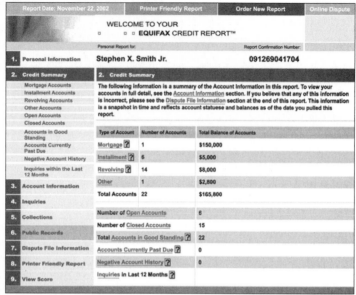

Figure 5-1:
Equifax
credit
report.

The report is broken into the following sections:

- The **Personal Profile** section includes your legal name, Also Known As (AKA), addresses (current and previous), year of birth, and employers (current and previous).

- **Credit summary** is the total number of accounts that you've opened and closed in each category. *Installment* accounts are car loans, furniture on payments, stereo equipment, and mortgage loans; *revolving* accounts are credit cards, lines of credit, and so on.

- **Public records** are court records relating to bankruptcies, tax liens, monetary judgments, and overdue child support payments. These records stay on the report for seven–ten years.

- **Credit inquiries** are either hard or soft. You initiate hard inquiries when "you" apply for credit. Soft inquiries are made by "prospective employers" when they do a background check and by credit card companies for preapproved credit cards. You can stop most soft inquiries by opting out of such as soft inquiries for preapproved credit card offers.

- The **account history** contains the details of each account you've opened or closed.

- Your **credit score** is based on the information in your report relating to your payment history and the number of credit accounts you have open, as well as the balances on the accounts, which is debt to income ratio. *Debt to income ratio* is simply the amount of money you make and the amount you owe. If the ratio of debt is too high as it relates to your income, you'll be denied the loan in most cases because your ability to pay diminishes with each account you open. In other words, you run out of money before all the accounts can be paid each month.

Your free credit report from `www.annualcreditreport.com` will not have a credit score on it. Neither will the one that you receive from placing a fraud alert on your report. Scores are general indicators of how you appear to banks and other creditors. The particular method of calculating the score is a tightly kept secret by the credit bureaus; they admit that telling customers too much about how they are rated would undermine their ability to market those scores of accurate indicators of your behavior in a way that reflects your ability to pay.

You can order your credit report from other online companies (which might charge a fee) besides the three credit bureaus (TransUnion, Experian, and Equifax). Just search for *credit report* with your favorite search engine. Here are two sites where you can obtain your credit report:

- ✔ **FreeCreditReport.com:** You can get a free credit report, and you can also try credit monitoring for seven days. To do this, you need a credit card. Read the fine print on the page; if you don't cancel your membership within the seven-day trial period, you're billed $14.95 each month that you don't cancel the monitoring service.

- ✔ **AnnualCreditReport.com:** Go to this site to receive your free credit report under the law. This site helps you obtain your annual credit report (a report from all three bureaus) free. The cost is $0 — no fee to obtain the report — and no monthly membership is required.

The site also has a Fraud Alert tab (in the upper-right corner). Click this tab to find out how to place a fraud alert on your credit report.

# Obtaining Your Credit Report

To obtain your credit report, simply visit one of the credit bureau Web sites and complete the order form. After your identity is verified, you can view the report online via these secure Web sites and print it. In addition, you can order a printed report over the telephone or by regular mail, which takes about ten days to reach you.

Here's the contact information for the *big three* credit reporting agencies:

- ✔ **Experian:** `www.experian.com`; Find a phone number (888-397-3742) and other ways to reach Experian by clicking the Contact Us link at the bottom of the home page. You can reach a live person at Experian only with a report number. When you access your report online, write down the report numbers immediately.

✔ **Equifax:** `www.equifax.com`; Find a phone number (800-685-1111) and other ways to reach Equifax by clicking the Contact Us link in the bottom-right corner of the home page.

✔ **TransUnion:** `www.tuc.com`; Find a phone number (800-916-8800) by clicking the Contact Us link in the upper-right corner of the home page; on the Contact Us page, click the Personal link.

With any of these three agencies, you can dispute something on your credit report online or by phone. You just need a current copy of your credit report (no more than 90 days old) from the agency you're contacting to dispute an item on the report. All three offer free fraud prevention services, including fraud alert statements that you can place on your credit file if you've been the victim of fraud. Credit monitoring services are also available for a fee.

According to the new Fair Credit Reporting Act (FCRA), you're entitled to one free report per year from each credit bureau, but it is recommended that you get a report every four months. So take advantage of something free and order your credit report quarterly.

The FCRA was signed into law in December 2003 and has been implemented.

All three credit bureaus offer an annual subscription service. Table 5-1 summarizes the services offered and the cost. A sample report (from Experian) is shown in Figure 5-2.

| Table 5-1 | Credit Subscription Services Summary | | | |
|---|---|---|---|---|
| *Company* | *Unlimited Reports* | *Monitor Reports* | *Send Alerts* | *Cost* |
| Experian: Credit Manager | Yes | Yes | Yes | $14.95 per month |
| Equifax: ID patrol | No. First report is included; each additional report is $7.50. | Yes | Yes | $14.95 per month |
| TransUnion | Monitoring service | Yes | Yes | $14.95 monthly for three-in-one report; $11.95 TransUnion Report only |

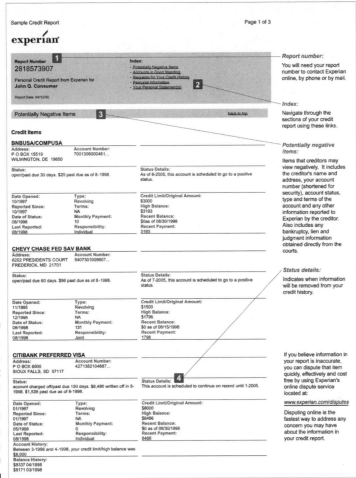

**Figure 5-2:**
Sample
credit
report from
Experian.
(Continued
on the
following
pages.)

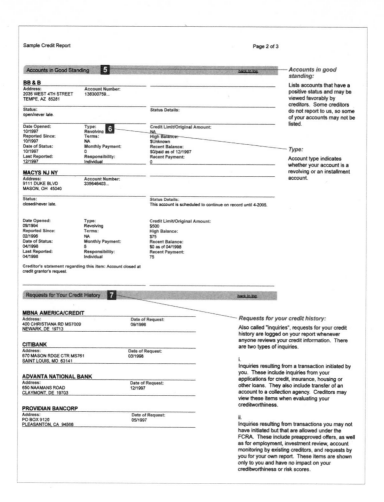

Sample Credit Report                                    Page 2 of 3

**Accounts in Good Standing** 5                                    back to top

*Accounts in good standing:*

Lists accounts that have a positive status and may be viewed favorably by creditors. Some creditors do not report to us, so some of your accounts may not be listed.

**BB & B**

| Address: | Account Number: |
| 2035 WEST 4TH STREET | 138300759... |
| TEMPE, AZ 85281 | |

Status:
open/never late.

Status Details:

| Date Opened: | Type: | 6 | Credit Limit/Original Amount: |
| 10/1997 | Revolving | | NA |
| Reported Since: | Terms: | | High Balance: |
| 10/1997 | NA | | $Unknown |
| Date of Status: | Monthly Payment: | | Recent Balance: |
| 10/1997 | 0 | | $0/paid as of 12/1997 |
| Last Reported: | Responsibility: | | Recent Payment: |
| 12/1997 | Individual | | 0 |

*Type:*

Account type indicates whether your account is a revolving or an installment account.

**MACYS NJ NY**

| Address: | Account Number: |
| 9111 DUKE BLVD | 335646403... |
| MASON, OH 45040 | |

Status:
closed/never late.

Status Details:
This account is scheduled to continue on record until 4-2005.

| Date Opened: | Type: | Credit Limit/Original Amount: |
| 09/1994 | Revolving | $500 |
| Reported Since: | Terms: | High Balance: |
| 02/1996 | NA | $75 |
| Date of Status: | Monthly Payment: | Recent Balance: |
| 04/1998 | 5 | $0 as of 04/1998 |
| Last Reported: | Responsibility: | Recent Payment: |
| 04/1998 | Individual | 75 |

Creditor's statement regarding this item: Account closed at credit grantor's request.

**Requests for Your Credit History** 7                                    back to top

*Requests for your credit history:*

Also called "inquiries", requests for your credit history are logged on your report whenever anyone reviews your credit information. There are two types of inquiries.

**MBNA AMERICA/CREDIT**

| Address: | Date of Request: |
| 400 CHRISTIANA RD MS7009 | 09/1996 |
| NEWARK, DE 19713 | |

i.
Inquiries resulting from a transaction initiated by you. These include inquiries from your applications for credit, insurance, housing or other loans. They also include transfer of an account to a collection agency. Creditors may view these items when evaluating your creditworthiness.

**CITIBANK**

| Address: | Date of Request: |
| 670 MASON RDGE CTR MS761 | 03/1998 |
| SAINT LOUIS, MO 63141 | |

**ADVANTA NATIONAL BANK**

| Address: | Date of Request: |
| 650 NAAMANS ROAD | 12/1997 |
| CLAYMONT, DE 19703 | |

ii.
Inquiries resulting from transactions you may not have initiated but that are allowed under the FCRA. These include preapproved offers, as well as for employment, investment review, account monitoring by existing creditors, and requests by you for your own report. These items are shown only to you and have no impact on your creditworthiness or risk scores.

**PROVIDIAN BANCORP**

| Address: | Date of Request: |
| PO BOX 9120 | 05/1997 |
| PLEASANTON, CA 94566 | |

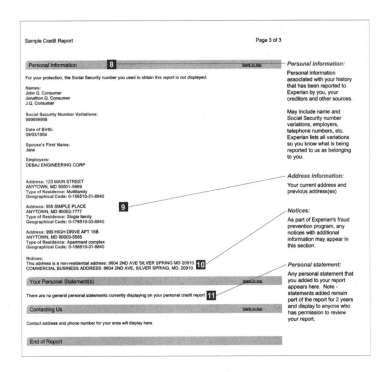

# Reviewing the Telltale Information on Your Credit Report

In this section, I explain the red flags you may find when you review your credit report and how to address them. Your three-in-one report is a good place to start looking.

The *three-in-one credit reports* are not really all three reports in one. Some folks who have ordered the report have found errors on their reports and noticed that the report did not actually contain the numbers from the credit bureaus to dispute the discrepancies. So be aware that the three-in-one report may not be accurate.

## The Personal Profile section

Figure 5-3 shows the Personal Profile section of a three-in-one report. The report lists all the information each of the three credit bureaus has about you in your personal profile. The report even provides a side-by-side listing of the information for easy comparison.

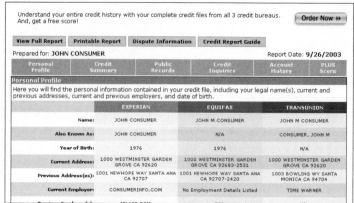

**Figure 5-3:**
The
Personal
Profile
section of
a three-in-
one credit
report.

I recommend that you order and read your free credit report from each of the three bureaus at least annually to ensure that all the credit bureaus are in sync in reporting your information. (You can obtain free annual reports from AnnualCreditReport.com.) You'll be glad you did!

The Personal Profile section of your single credit bureau report in Figure 5-3 includes the following information:

- Your legal name
- Also Known As (AKA); other names associated with your credit files
- Year of birth
- Current and previous addresses
- Current and previous employers

To correct any errors relating to your personal profile, you must prove your identity by supplying the following information:

- Full legal name including SR, JR, III, and so on
- Current and previous addresses for the last five years
- Date of birth
- Two methods to prove your address, such as
  - A copy of your driver's license
  - A passport
  - Proof of a Social Security Number
  - A utility bill
  - A bank statement
  - W-2

Any changes to your addresses that you didn't make are an issue and could be an indicator of fraud. Send a letter to the credit bureau to have the information corrected immediately via Certified Mail return receipt. The *mail receipt* is your record of sending the letter, and the *return receipt* tells you that your letter was received by the credit bureau.

*Note:* The credit report has an identifier number next to each address. This corresponds to the address identifier number in the accounts section of your report. If you have an address that is incorrect but does not have an account attached to it, it is likely an error and not fraud. If the personal section of your report contains a name variation, Social Security Number variation, an incorrect address, and the accounts attached to it are in good standing, this is also likely due to just an error and not identity theft. Both of these errors can be corrected with a simple dispute form with the credit bureau; no affidavit or police report is necessary.

Reviewing your credit report to see whether all the information is correct in each of your three reports helps you clear any inaccuracies before they become an issue. When you see discrepancies, note them and then bring them to the attention of the credit bureau by filing a *dispute* with the bureau that's posted the information you're challenging.

## The Account Information section

The Account Information section lists all open and closed accounts. Make sure that all the information is accurate. Lenders aren't required to report to all three bureaus, so loans are sometimes reported only to one bureau. This is why it is important to get your three-in-one report. This way, you can see whether any accounts have been opened without your knowledge.

## The Credit Summary section

Figure 5-4 shows the Credit Summary section of a credit report. This section of the report is important: It lists all the loans that are currently open, the amount and type of loan, the balance, the name of the company, and whether there any are delinquencies.

Any accounts you didn't open are an issue and may be an indicator of fraud. Also, any loans in collection that you don't recognize as yours are an issue. File a dispute report immediately in either of these instances.

**Credit Summary**

This section gives you a broad look at your current and past credit status. Here you'll find the total number of open and closed accounts in your name, the total balance on those accounts, and delinquencies.

| | EXPERIAN | EQUIFAX | TRANSUNION |
|---|---|---|---|
| **REAL ESTATE:** | | | |
| Count: | 0 | 0 | 0 |
| Balance: | $0.00 | $0.00 | $0.00 |
| Current: | 0 | 0 | 0 |
| Delinquent | 0 | 0 | 0 |
| Other | 0 | 0 | 0 |
| **REVOLVING:** | | | |
| Count: | 8 | 9 | 10 |
| Balance: | $64 | $316 | $316 |
| Current: | 8 | 9 | 9 |
| Delinquent | 0 | 0 | 0 |
| Other | 0 | 0 | 1 |
| **INSTALLMENT:** | | | |
| Count: | 0 | 0 | 0 |
| Balance: | $0.00 | $0.00 | $0.00 |
| Current: | 0 | 0 | 0 |
| Delinquent | 0 | 0 | 0 |
| Other | 0 | 0 | 0 |
| **OTHER:** | | | |
| Count: | 0 | 0 | 2 |
| Balance: | $0.00 | $0.00 | $0.00 |
| Current: | 0 | 0 | 0 |
| Delinquent | 0 | 0 | 0 |
| Other | 0 | 0 | 0 |
| **COLLECTION:** | | | |
| Count: | 0 | 0 | 0 |
| Balance: | $0.00 | $0.00 | $0.00 |
| Current: | 0 | 0 | 0 |
| Delinquent | 0 | 0 | 0 |

**Figure 5-4:**
The Credit
Summary
section.

## The Public Records section

The Public Records section sample in Figure 5-5 is a list of court actions for bankruptcy, tax liens, monetary judgments, and overdue child support payments in some states. The list comes from federal, state, and county court records.

If you find any monetary judgment in a state you haven't lived in, file a dispute immediately. Also, find out more from the court record. The court name and case number are listed on the report, and you can use them to obtain a copy of the record for your review.

**Public Records**

The information in this section comes from federal district bankruptcy records, state and county court records, tax liens and monetary judgments, and in some states, overdue child support records. Public records remain on your credit report for 7-10 years.

| | EXPERIAN | EQUIFAX | TRANSUNION |
|---|---|---|---|
| TYPE: | Suit | | |
| Date Filed: | Jan 12, 1998 | | |
| Reference #: | AB23456 | | |
| Court: | US DIST CT | | |
| Plaintiff: | MARY HARDT | | |
| Liability: | N/A | | |
| Asset Amount: | N/A | | |
| TYPE: | Bankruptcy: CH-13 Filed | Bankruptcy Chapter13-petition filed | Chapter 13 bankruptcy filing |
| Date Filed: | Jun 19, 1997 | Jun 19, 1997 | Jun 19, 1997 |
| Reference #: | CN94847 | CN94847 | CN94847 |
| Court: | US DIST CT | U.S. HIGHEST COURT | NY City Court |
| Plaintiff: | N/A | Marry Jones | KRISTINA CONSUMER |
| Liability: | $4,526 | $25,652 | $50,000 |
| Asset Amount: | $7,580 | $25,600 | $30,000 |

**Credit Inquiries**

This section contains the names of those who obtained a copy of your credit report. Inquiries remain on your report up to two years.

| | EXPERIAN | EQUIFAX | TRANSUNION |
|---|---|---|---|
| WELLS FARGO BANK | | | |
| Banks and S&Ls | | | |
| 1/1/2002 | | | ✓ |
| BANANA REPUBLIC/MCCBG | | | |
| Sales Financing Company | | ✓ | |

**Figure 5-5:**
The Public
Records
section.

## The Credit Inquiries section

The Credit Inquiries section of a credit report features two types of inquiries:

- ✔ **Hard inquiries** affect your credit score, and potential creditors see them when reviewing your report. You initiate these inquiries when you complete a credit application. Mortgage loan applications are hard inquiries.

  If you didn't initiate an inquiry that appears on your report by applying for a loan or credit card, it's an issue! File a dispute immediately.

- ✔ **Soft inquiries** are those inquiries that only you see, and they don't affect your credit score. These inquiries include pre-employment screenings and preapproved credit card offers.

  You can minimize the preapproved card offer inquiries by opting out. See Chapter 2 for details.

## The Account History section

Figure 5-6 shows the Account History section of a credit report. The information includes the account type, balance, account status, the date the account was opened, and the payment status. The payment status is where you find whether the account payments are on schedule as agreed when the account was opened. Look at the account numbers — for security reasons, only the last four digits are printed. Your report will look the same as the sample.

**Figure 5-6:** The Account History section of a three-in-one credit report.

| Account History | | | |
| --- | --- | --- | --- |
| This section contains specific information on each account you've opened in the past. Positive information about your accounts remains on your report indefinitely. | | | |
| BANANA REPUBLIC | | | |
| | **EXPERIAN** | **EQUIFAX** | **TRANSUNION** |
| Account Name: | BANANA REPUBLIC | BANANA REPUBLIC | BANANA REPUBLIC |
| Account Number: | 1212 1212 1212 XXXX | We did not find information for this account. | 1212XXXX |
| Acct Type: | Revolving or Option | | Revolving account |
| Acct Status: | Open | | Open |
| Monthly Payment: | $0.00 | | $0.00 |
| Date Open: | 6/1/2001 | | 6/1/2001 |
| Balance: | $0.00 | | $0.00 |
| Terms: | N/A | | N/A |
| High Balance: | $1,400.00 | | $1,400.00 |
| Limit: | $5,900.00 | | |
| Past Due: | $0.00 | | $0.00 |
| Payment Status: | Pays account as agreed | | Paid or paying as agreed |
| Comments: | CHARGE | | N/A |

| Account Two Year History | | | | | | | | | | | | | | | | | | | | | | | | ? Legend |
| --- | --- | --- | --- | --- | --- | --- | --- | --- | --- | --- | --- | --- | --- | --- | --- | --- | --- | --- | --- | --- | --- | --- | --- | --- |
| Year: | | | | | Year 1 | | | | | | | | | | | | Year 2 | | | | | | |
| | | | | | 2000 > | | | | | | | | | | | | 2001 > | | | | | | |
| Month: | 2 | 3 | 4 | 5 | 6 | 7 | 8 | 9 | 10 | 11 | 12 | 1 | 2 | 3 | 4 | 5 | 6 | 7 | 8 | 9 | 10 | 11 | 12 |
| Experian: | | | | | | | | | | | | | | | | | OK | OK | OK | OK | OK | OK | OK |
| Equifax: | | | | | | | | | | | | | | | | | OK | OK | OK | OK | OK | OK | OK |
| TransUnion: | | | | | | | | | | | | | | | | | OK | OK | OK | OK | OK | OK | OK |

^Top of Page^

MCCBG/OLD NAVY

## *Your credit score*

Your credit score is important to your credit rating and is an indication of what kind of credit risk you are and what interest rate you'll be charged for a loan. Your credit score can also be an indicator that someone has stolen your identity (for example, when your score has a sudden unknown change).

The score is calculated based on the information in your report for that particular bureau. One popular score is the FICO score because it's calculated on software developed by the Fair Isaac Company. However, all three credit reporting agencies have developed their own consumer credit scores. Literally, thousands of credit scores are used; some developed for industry-specific types of credit, such as auto loans or mortgage loans. The score is on a scale in which the higher the score, the better credit risk you are. If your score is 768, shown in Figure 5-7, for example, you're in the Excellent range. Your score is 81 percent higher than most U.S. consumers.

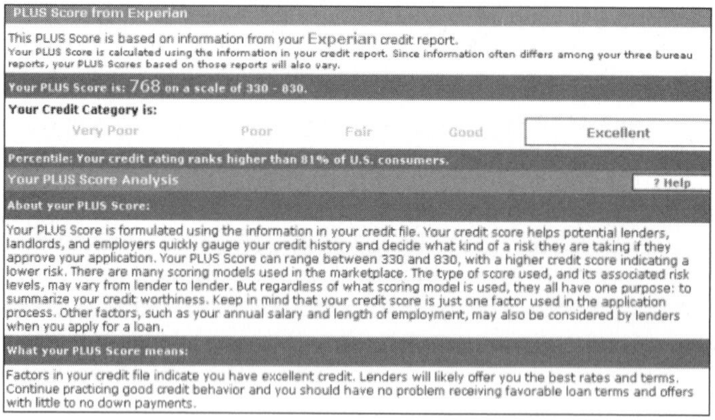

**Figure 5-7:** Sample credit score from Experian.

Table 5-2 lists the score names by credit bureau. I give you the information about credit scores so you know what each bureau calls their credit scores, but these are only the scores derived from the FICO. The higher your score, the better the credit risk you are. Your credit score is affected by the factors listed in Table 5-3.

| Table 5-2 | Sample Credit Score |
|---|---|
| *Score Name Used* | *Credit Bureau* |
| BEACON | Equifax |
| Fair Isaac Risk Model | Experian |
| EMPIRICA | TransUnion |

| Table 5-3 | Credit Score Factors in Order of Importance |
|---|---|
| *+ Factors* | *– Factors* |
| You have a relationship with three or more creditors. | You have too many inquiries in last two years. |
| You don't have any derogatory information on your report. | You have derogatory information, such as charge-offs and collections. |
| You have accounts that have been open for five or more years. | You have too many installment loans, such as car loans and college student loans. |
| Your credit balances aren't close to your card limit. | Your credit card balances are too close to your card limit. |
| You have few or zero delinquencies of 30+ days. | You have delinquencies of more than 30 days. |

# Sudden unknown credit score change

A sudden unknown change in your credit score is a red flag. For example, you may apply for a loan and be turned down because your credit score is too low. You review your credit report to determine why your score has dropped suddenly. You discover that your report has credit accounts you didn't open and several are more than 30 days delinquent. Let the lender know that some of the information on your credit report is inaccurate and that you're going to file a dispute to resolve the issue.

During tough economic times, your score may change because the lenders change practices, restrict your account, or turn you down for credit.

You must dispute the inaccurate information with the credit agency from which the lender received your credit report. You need the report number. When you go online to dispute the information, follow the links to *dispute online.* (All three agencies have the link on their Web sites, usually under the heading Personal Solutions or Services.) When you click Personal Solutions, one of the subheadings that appears on the Personal Solutions page is Dispute Online. Click the heading, and it takes you to the dispute form with directions on how to complete the form.

A sudden change, usually a drop in your credit score, is most likely caused by having too many accounts with several that are delinquent for more than 30 days. Dispute inaccurate information immediately so that you can get the issue resolved before it escalates even farther.

A *fraud alert* tells the credit bureaus that you've been the victim of identity theft. You report the alert to one bureau and per the Fair and Accurate Credit Transactions Act (FACTA), it then reports it to the other two bureaus. You use a dispute to question any wrong information on a particular bureau's credit report. To dispute information, you must first have a current report from the bureau with which you're disputing the information.

You are entitled to free reports reflecting corrections of any items you have disputed.

To place a fraud alert on your report, do the following. For more detail, see Chapter 2.

✔ Contact your local police and file an identity theft report.

   To file an initial 90-day fraud alert, you do not need a police report.

✔ Place a fraud alert on your credit report.

✔ Check your other accounts to see whether any of them have been tampered with as well.

✔ Close any accounts that have been tampered with.

✔ Choose a new personal identification number (PIN) and get a new ATM card.

## Looking for consistency

When you review your report, look for consistency in the information outlined in Table 5-4.

| Table 5-4 | Information on Your Credit Report That Should Be Consistent |
|---|---|
| *Credit Report Information* | *File a Dispute If Inconsistent or Inaccurate* |
| Personal profile | Your name, current and previous address, any other names listed, birth date, current and previous employers |
| Credit summary | Account information |
| Public records | All information |
| Credit inquiries | Hard inquiries, soft inquiries |
| Account history | Accounts information |
| Credit score | Up or down? Do you know the reason? |

## Pulling your credit report together

Your credit report is an effective weapon in the war against identity theft. You can look to the report for an early warning that someone is helping herself to your good name and credit. Table 5-5 summarizes the telltale signs that you're a victim.

| Table 5-5 | Telltale Signs That You're a Victim |
| --- | --- |
| *What to Look For* | *Where to Find It in the Credit Report* |
| Credit accounts you didn't know you had (such as car loans) | Credit Summary |
| Hard or soft credit inquiries you didn't make | Credit Inquiries |
| Credit cards you didn't open | Credit Summary |
| Addresses you've never lived at | Personal Information |
| Sudden changes in your credit | Credit Score Report (a separate report not in the credit report) |
| Public records judgments | Public Records |

# Disputing Your Credit Report

You've found information that you want to challenge. How do you do it? Well, the three credit bureaus have online dispute forms. Figure 5-8 shows a sample of Experian's online dispute form. Figure 5-9 explains disputes and has a hyperlink to the online dispute form. Notice that on the dispute form, you have a space to include your credit report number, and you must include your SSN.

When you file a dispute, you need to include a credit report number from a personally ordered report that's no more than 90 days old.

At the bottom of the dispute form is a notice to let you know that it's a crime to obtain a credit report for anyone else; you may dispute information only on your own report. Refer to Figure 5-9 for the terms and conditions.

You can also view the status of your dispute online. The form is essentially the same as the one shown in Figure 5-9, but at the top, instead of saying Request a dispute, it says Check the Status of Your Dispute. The credit bureaus have 30 days to respond to your dispute.

**Figure 5-8:**
Sample
online
dispute
form from
Experian.

**Request a dispute**

You must have a current copy of your Experian personal credit report in order to use this service. If you have a copy, please enter the report number listed at the top of the report. If you do not have a report number that you received within the last 90 days, order a current copy of your personal credit report.

*Experian does not and will not disclose the personal information you provided to us in connection with this service to any third parties for any purpose unless required by law or for internal audit purposes without specifically indicating such disclosure to you and informing you of your choice to prohibit such disclosure. For more information see Privacy.

Please fill in the following information. This information will be used only to verify your identity for security purposes in order to allow you access to your online credit information.

*Report number

*State

*Social Security number

*ZIP code

**Terms and conditions**

🛈 **You must agree to the statements below to dispute information in your credit report:**

☐ I agree to the terms and conditions.
☐ I certify that I am disputing information on my own personal credit report.
☐ I understand that it is a federal crime subject to incarceration and/or monetary penalties to obtain a personal credit report for someone other than myself.

**Figure 5-9:**
Experian
terms and
conditions
for disputing
your credit
report.

**Terms and conditions for disputing**

When you use our online services, you are certifying that you understand and agree to the following conditions:

- Experian is regulated by the federal Fair Credit Reporting Act and state laws pertaining to credit reporting. We cannot remove accurate information or information verified as accurate from your credit report.

- Because we use security measures to protect your privacy and to safeguard your information, we may not always be able to provide online delivery of your credit report. You may order your report by calling 1 800 311 4769 or by writing to us at PO Box 9600 , Allen, TX 75013. You may dispute information by calling 1 800 493 1058 and entering your personal credit report number.

- All information you provide while using this service must be accurate and true.

- Once an item has been verified by the credit grantor, you may not dispute the same item again without providing additional relevant information.

- Be sure to **save** or **print** your credit report to avoid having to initiate another session, which will result in an additional fee. To print or save your report, select the **Print your report** link in the Credit Report Toolkit and use your browser's **Print** or **Save As** feature from the File menu. Refunds will not be issued for successful online deliveries.

- For your protection, if you are inactive (have not clicked on an item or refreshed the page) for a period of 20 minutes, your session will conclude and you will be logged out.

- You must LOGOUT or close your browser when you have finished viewing your report to assure the privacy of your credit information.

Finally, you have a form to check the results of your dispute. The form is essentially the same one used for checking the status of your dispute with two notable differences. The first is, the heading of the form says View the Results of Your Dispute, and a box is added just to the right of the box for stating an investigation ID number. The credit bureau gives you the investigation ID number when you check the status of your dispute.

Possible responses you might receive from a credit reporting agency include no response, a rejection (based on your dispute being deemed frivolous or on you manipulating the system), or a letter informing you that an investigation has begun. For more possible responses and other information, go to the following Web site:

```
www.creditinfocenter.com/repair/fixrspnd.shtml
```

# Part III
# Being Smart with Your Sensitive Information

The 5th Wave          By Rich Tennant

"Their fatal mistake was getting involved with MSN.com's home page building option. It's so easy. It's irresistible. They included a photo of them holding the stolen credit cards next to the car they bought with a fraudulent loan application, a list of their favorite places to shoulder surf, identities they'd like to use again..."

## In this part . . .

$B$eing discreet in public can actually go a long way in protecting your identity. The important personal information you discard can come back to haunt you in a big way if you don't destroy it before tossing it. This part gives you the rundown on prevention, from keeping your personal information safe to watching what you say and do in public.

# Chapter 6

# Keeping Tabs on Your Personal and Business Information

. . . . . . . . . . . . . . . . . . . . . . . . . . . . . . . . . . . . . . . . . . .

*In This Chapter*

▶ Determining where your personal information hides

▶ Ensuring that your online accounts are safe

▶ Keeping personal information accessible but safe

▶ Preventing paper from becoming a problem

. . . . . . . . . . . . . . . . . . . . . . . . . . . . . . . . . . . . . . . . . . .

*I*n this chapter, I tell you about the ways to keep your personal information safe. When you understand the vulnerabilities with your mail and online accounts for bill paying and banking, you can prevent them from falling into the hands of an identity thief.

# Discovering Where Your Personal Information Hides

Your personal information can be found in more locations than you probably realize. Table 6-1 outlines some of the locations your personal information is located. The table is not all-inclusive, but it gives you a good idea of where personal information is commonly stored.

| Table 6-1 | Where Information Can Be Found |
|---|---|
| *Type of Information* | *Where It's Found* |
| Your address | Driver's license, your mail, your personal checks, your employer's personnel records, medical records, auto registration, government records, business records, utility bills, mortgage information, credit applications, the white pages of the phone book (if you have a listed number), post office change of address card, and other records such as church, volunteer, school |
| Your name | Credit card receipts, your mail, W-2s, driver's license, online accounts, your employer's personnel records, medical records, auto registration, government records, business records, utility bills, public records, and credit applications |
| Your SSN | W-2s, some direct deposit paycheck stubs, annual Social Security statement, government records, your employer's personnel records, your driver's license number (in some states), credit applications, student ID numbers (at some universities), Medicare cards, military IDs, and medical records |
| Your date of birth | Driver's license, online sites (such as http:// anybirthday.com) and other sites that ask for your birthday, government records, credit applications, school records, vaccination records, promotional items (such as a store credit card) |
| Checking account numbers | On your checks, account statements, business records, and credit applications |
| Your credit card account number | Credit card receipts in some businesses, account statements, online pay services, business records, credit applications, all the companies you do business with by using a credit card, lease agreements for rental cars, trucks, and apartments |

Nowadays people often meet and talk with their friends and share experiences at online networking sites, such as Facebook, Twitter, and MySpace. You need to be careful about how much personal information you post online. The more you post, the easier you make it for the thief posing as a friend to get your information and steal your identity. The best advice I can give you is to keep your personal information offline. Of course you wouldn't put your Social Security Number (SSN) online, but what about

✔ Your date of birth?

✔ The city where you live?

✔ Your cellphone number?

✔ Your name? A pseudo name?

Do you give the information to those who you've befriended you on a private chat page? The personal networking pages aren't the only pages where you need to be careful with sharing personal information; the same logic applies to professional networking pages. You can post a resumé, but you don't need to include any personal information, such as your home address. Prospective employers can contact you initially by e-mail.

I'm not saying don't network — even I network — however, I am cautioning you to use the same discretion online that you'd use when meeting friends in public, new or old. You don't share your SSN, your birth date (not right away, anyway), your full name, and so on. Be wary of someone who asks too many personal questions while networking. If you feel uncomfortable, you have a problem. Go with your gut feeling and listen to your intuition; these feelings are often correct.

Here are some simple rules to follow when networking online:

✔ **Do not post personal information on public pages.** Things to NOT include are

- Date of birth (DOB)

- SSN

- Address (including the city where you live)

- Full name

- Pictures of yourself

✔ **Be careful who you allow to see your personal pages.**

- This is true especially for those whom you meet online because people are out there who use the Internet to prey on other people.

- Keep your circle of contacts on your personal page to those who you know in real life and not just from the Internet (but still be careful).

✔ **Be skeptical of anyone you just met (especially online) who attempts to get too close.**

- If this person claims to be a friend of one of your friends, verify it.

- If this person asks too many questions that makes you feel uncomfortable, do not give them any information.

✔ **Avoid answering questions about schools you attended, what year you graduated, or even your pet's name.** Answers to these questions can help someone figure out your year of birth or the answer to security questions you choose in case you forget your password(s).

✔ **Avoid making family connections on social networking sites.** Doing so provides too much information — like your mother's maiden name, your place of birth, and so on — that potential identity thieves can use to get other information about you.

## The important info on the documents you receive

You receive various documents every day. Some are sent by mail, some are handed to you, and others arrive by e-mail. Many of these documents contain information that's useful to an identity thief.

Awareness is your first line of defense against identity theft. Being organized and keeping track of the statements and reports you receive is important if you're to protect yourself against identity theft. Consider the following:

✔ **Credit card statements:** Your credit card statements have your name, the credit card company's name and phone number, your address, sometimes the entire account number, and credit limit printed on it. The thief can also request a change of address and have the bills come directly to her, although most banks confirm a change of address with a follow-up telephone call or letter.

Your credit card statements list all your purchases and payments for the last month's billing period. By checking your statements regularly, you can determine whether someone else is making charges on your card. Generally, you have 30 days from the date of the written or online statement to notify the financial institution about any charges that are questionable.

✔ **Bank statements:** Bank statements have the account numbers and balances, your name and address, and the name of your bank. The checking account statement has information about your account activity and, if you choose, all the canceled checks that have been paid by the bank in your name are enclosed with the statement. Use your bank statement as a tool in detecting identity theft. Review the account at least monthly (or online daily/weekly) so that you know immediately whether any withdrawals you didn't make are posted. Watch for small charges that may go unnoticed, especially if you didn't make the charge.

✔ **Paycheck stubs:** Paycheck stubs for direct deposit have personal information on them, including your name, address, rate of pay, and your employer's name. Shred the stubs before you discard them if you do not want to keep them.

✔ **Investment statements:** Your 401K statements have a great deal of information, including your name, address, account number, balance, and the name of the company that's managing the account. IRA accounts may contain your SSN. If you have an account with a stockbroker, the quarterly statements have the same information as an IRA or 401K. Keep the first statement after you opened the account, and then keep two to three years of current statements and shred the rest. The reason to keep the current year's statement is to check that your money isn't leaving the account without your approval or knowledge. Don't just throw your investment statements away — they contain too much personal information.

✔ **Social Security statement:** On an annual basis, those of us who are 25 or older receive an account statement from the Social Security Administration. This statement has your SSN as well as your DOB, address, and current balance with the projected amount you will receive if you work until you are 62 or 65. Because these are annual statements, you can keep more of them. They aren't bulky, so you can keep them all until retirement if you like, but keeping the most current 20 years' worth is probably sufficient. At minimum, you should keep them to compare numbers year to year.

✔ **Tax information (W-2s, interest accounts, 1099s, and so on):** These are the most vulnerable tax documents because they have the most information. They have your name, your address, your employer's name and address, your pay for the year, and your SSN. Tax information is useful to identity thieves because the form has your (and your spouse's) SSN, your home address, place of employment, pay rate, and so on — which can all be used to assume your identity. Keep copies of your tax returns for at least five years in a locked file cabinet or safe. This helps minimize theft.

If you are filing by using Turbo Tax or another online tax service, make sure that you have installed — and updated as necessary — virus and firewall protection on your computer. (See Chapter 11 for more about these and other electronic safeguards.) When you send the completed documents, make sure that the site has a secure connection. To do this, look for a lock at the bottom-right corner of the screen. If the lock is locked, the transmission is secure. If you don't see a lock, check with the site to find out whether it uses SSL (Secure Sockets Layer) or another form of secure connection before you transmit the completed form with all your personal information.

In addition to statements, many folks receive the following documents by mail:

- ✔ Preapproved credit card offers
- ✔ Driver's license renewal forms
- ✔ Utility bills
- ✔ Direct deposit paycheck stubs
- ✔ Government and military correspondence and benefits statements
- ✔ Vehicle registration
- ✔ Insurance policies, such as car, home, life, medical, and so on
- ✔ Blank checks for your personal checking account

These documents have personal information, and they come in the mail — which is vulnerable.

## *Finding your information online*

Finding your information online isn't that difficult. All you have to do is access public records Web sites, and you can find some information. If you own a house, for example, the address, parcel number, the mortgage company, the amount borrowed to purchase, the purchase price, and the taxes paid or owed on the property are all on file at the county clerk's office. Table 6-2 outlines where personal information can be found online.

# Problems with my mail

*Mail napping,* stealing mail to get information about someone to be used for monetary gain, is one way the identity thief can get his hands on your mail and consequently your personal information. In 2007, the United States Postal Inspection Service handled 2,909 fraud complaints and made 1,236 arrests for mail theft; as a result of the investigations, 1,118 people were convicted.

It's hard to say whether this is just the tip of the iceberg. For every mail thief caught, several more may still be out there preying on the mail. Even with the good records of the Postal Inspection Service, parts of the country are experiencing volume thefts. These thefts occur in Tucson and Phoenix, Arizona, parts of California, and parts of Texas. The thefts include mail trucks, collection boxes, apartment mailbox panels, co-op mailing racks, and neighborhood delivery and collection units. The mail is stolen to get your checks, credit card applications, and bank statements.

Protect your mail: Don't leave it in the box overnight or for extended periods of time — not even in a locked mailbox. Be stingy and keep all your mail for yourself! Place your outgoing mail in a blue United States Postal Service mailbox or at the post office.

| Table 6-2 | Where You Find Personal Information Online |
|---|---|
| **Personal Information** | **Where to Find It** |
| DOB | Sites like `http://anybirthday.com`, public records. |
| Your name | Online directory lookup, such as `http://anywho.com`. All you need is a published phone number, name, or address. |
| Real estate owned | Public records county clerk's office. |
| Previous and current addresses | Record search Web sites, such as `http://completedetective.com` and www.anywho.com. You need a first and last name. |
| Your name, DOB, SSN, address, account numbers, balances, and more | Your online investment accounts. |
| Your name, address, and account numbers | Your online banking accounts. |
| Criminal and civil court records | Public databases. |
| Public records | Numerous public records databases are online, as well as numerous virtual directories, genealogy directories, and school directories. |

Web sites exist where you can pay a fee to obtain information about yourself. The number of searches you request determines the amount of the fee. You can search criminal records, the county clerk's office, and so on. All you need to do is type in your SSN, DOB, name, and address. The site searches through public records for criminal convictions, civil suits, bankruptcies, and so on. Keep in mind that thieves can search this information, too. If your report contains errors, you may not be able to get the information removed, especially if you paid for the background check yourself. If you were turned down for a job as a result of errors, you can request that the erroneous information be corrected.

Some companies charge $9.95 per month to remove information about you from the Internet. Some sites charge considerably more. I haven't used any of these companies, so I can't comment on how effective they are, but you can try one if you feel the need. To locate these companies online, search for *remove my internet info*. The results will feature information that is both good and bad. You can also search for complaints against a company by going to the Better Business Bureau (BBB). The information you find can help you make a decision on whether to use the company's services.

The Fair Credit Reporting Act (FCRA) governs access to financial records, so the search Web sites can't run financial inquiries. The FCRA requires your permission to run a credit and financial check. You sign a form to grant permission to a prospective employer, car dealership, or mortgage company to run a credit and financial check. Without the form, they can't legally run a check. The FCRA also requires that if derogatory information appears in the report, you receive a copy so you can contest its contents. Chapter 2 discusses recent changes to the FCRA.

## Accounts you have online

In this Internet age, having accounts that are managed online is commonplace. Using your computer to manage your accounts is fast and easy. The accounts that you may have online include the following:

- ✔ Bank accounts (savings and checking)
- ✔ Accounts for your bill paying service
- ✔ Insurance (homeowners, auto, life, and health)
- ✔ Investment accounts, such as 401K, mutual funds, and others
- ✔ Individual accounts with online merchants
- ✔ Services like PayPal

Any account you can access online has the potential to be compromised. To access the account, you generally use a PIN (personal identification number, or password). Sometimes the PIN is all numeric, and sometimes it consists of alphanumeric characters.

The danger with online accounts is having a weak PIN, a weak password (or one you need to write down), or weak security on your computer. After an identity thief figures out your password or PIN, he can access your accounts as easily as you do. The thief can also call and pretend to be you by answering questions, such as your DOB, your mother's maiden name, and so on, and have the password and username changed to her own. Today when changes are made in user and password accounts, you receive an e-mail (in the e-mail account you cited when you signed up for the account) about it. Most banks allow you to set a verification password on your account so changes can only be made with that password and not by identifying the caller through personal information. Money can be withdrawn from the account or moved to other accounts; the accounts can be closed out.

The most secure combination of characters for a PIN or password is a combination of letters, numbers, and special characters (at least six characters long), such as TGIF29#$!.

## Checks, receipts, and other papers you generate

For someone who lives in a "paperless" society, I bet you still generate a great deal of paper. For example, you generate checks, ATM receipts, credit card purchase receipts, and debit card purchase receipts, to name just a few. How you treat the important paper you generate either makes you more vulnerable or less vulnerable to identity theft. Table 6-3 highlights the paper you generate.

| Table 6-3 | Paper You Generate |
| --- | --- |
| *Action* | *You Generate* |
| Use your debit card | A receipt, with date and balance |
| Use your ATM card | A receipt with your balance at your bank or branch of your bank |
| Write a check | Check with your signature |
| Use your credit card | In some businesses, a receipt with your full card number, name, and card expiration date |
| Complete a loan application | Copy with all your personal information, including your SSN |

Shred, rip into tiny pieces, or cut into tiny pieces all the documents you generate that contain your personal information before you discard them. Don't make your information easily available to the identity thief; become a hard target by practicing prevention. The best defense is shredding.

## Government documents

If you look in your wallet, you'll probably find at least one government document — your driver's license. You may be surprised to find how many government documents you have, and the importance of each, when you see the following list:

- ✔ **Driver's license:** In addition to your driver's license number, your driver's license contains your name, address, eye color, hair color, height, weight, and your birth date. You show it to police officers even when you aren't driving and at airports to pass through security checkpoints. Your driver's license is usually requested when you purchase merchandise by personal check. In fact, the cashier often writes the driver's license number on the check.

Because your driver's license contains so much personal information, cut up the old one into little pieces that can't be put back together. The ID thief can make up a phony driver's license with your details to open an account in your name, use your stolen personal checks, or cash fake checks in your name.

✔ **Birth certificate:** Your birth certificate proves that you are a U.S. citizen. It contains your mother's maiden name; your father's name; the city and state you were born in; and the time, day, and year you were born. You need a birth certificate to get a passport, state ID card, and so on. To be safe, store your birth certificate in a locked — and fireproof — file cabinet or safe-deposit box.

✔ **Passport:** Your passport is also an important document. It has your picture, full name, and address, and it proves that you're a U.S. citizen. You show your passport when you travel abroad. You show it to customs when you arrive in another country and upon return to the U.S. Your passport can be used by terrorists or other criminals attempting to gain entry into the country. If your passport is lost domestically, it can be sold to someone else and used to establish citizenship. Store your passport in a safe-deposit box or locked — and fireproof — file cabinet.

✔ **Auto registration form:** The auto registration form has your full name and address on it as a proof of ownership. The ID thief can use your name and information to purchase an automobile, and your name and maybe even your address will appear on the auto registration. When you leave your car, be sure to lock it!

✔ **State ID cards:** State ID cards identify people who don't have a driver's license. In addition to your ID number, it contains your name, address, and birth date.

To open a bank account at most banks, two forms of ID are required; one is a current (unexpired) driver's license or a current passport, and the other is typically either a birth certificate or an unexpired credit card.

As I discuss in Chapter 1, don't leave your mail overnight, even in a locked mailbox. Also be careful where you mail your important documents from. For example, the post office is safer than the mailbox at your home or apartment. Vigilance is important to make yourself a hard target. Thieves will go after the easy target rather than the hard one because there are enough easy ones to go around.

# Keeping Your Information Safe but Available

Store your personal information so that it's secure from theft but easily accessible by you. The information needs to be handy for you to access but difficult for the identity thief.

## Software to help keep your information safe

When you store the information on your PC, protect it with the following:

- **Antivirus software:** This software scans your computer for *viruses* (programs that intend to harm your computer system) and then removes them from your machine. You usually end up with a virus (or a *worm* or a *Trojan horse*) when you open a seemingly innocent e-mail attachment that in fact harbors the little devil. Two popular antivirus programs are Norton AntiVirus and McAfee VirusScan. Most new computers come with some sort of antivirus software preinstalled.

- **Firewall:** A firewall heads off destructive programs at the pass. You can use the options that come with your firewall software to restrict applications with inbound and outbound access to your computer and the Internet. Norton and McAfee offer firewall software at a reasonable price.

- **File encryption:** Encrypting the files you store on CD and on your PC is the best way to secure them electronically. PGP is a company that produces encryption software, which is available for personal use. I use PGP encryption for e-mails and find it easy to use. Check out PGP here:

  ```
  www.pgp.com/products/desktop_home/index.html
  ```

- **Password-protection:** Be sure to protect sensitive documents with a password.

- **Spyware protection:** This safeguard prevents spyware from being installed on your computer. Most virus protection software provides spyware protection. Spyware protection software, like the virus and firewall protection, must be up-to-date to be effective. If you don't keep it updated, it is useless.

An easy way to be sure that your protection is updated is to use automatic updates.

For more information about the safeguards listed in the preceding bulleted list, see Chapter 11.

## Tips to keep your information safe

In addition to using software, you can use the following tips to protect your information:

✔ You can store files on a CD and lock the CD in a fire-rated safe that's either tethered to a secure anchor or heavy enough to prevent it from being taken easily from your house.

✔ You can store a copy of a CD in a bank safe-deposit box.

✔ Do not store your personal information on a Web site or in e-mail files. E-mails can be captured and read by anyone. Web site links in e-mails are used to get the recipient to divulge personal information that's captured by the identity thief.

✔ Be careful about storing personal information on your laptop hard drive. If the laptop gets stolen or lost, the information will be lost or compromised. Use some form of encryption to protect the data on the hard drive.

✔ Know the Web sites and companies you purchase merchandise from and make sure that they use Secure Sockets Layer (SSL) or some other form of encryption to transmit personal data.

✔ Be wary of any Web sites that ask for personal information before you can access their site. The Web site owners may be using a legitimate marketing tool, but you need to consider what they do with the information that they collect. Is the information sold? How secure is the server where they're storing all the information they collect about you? When you're at legitimate sites, you can take security warnings with a grain of salt — especially if your virus, spyware, and firewall protection are all up-to-date. The scammers will use phony alerts on legitimate Web sites to get you to buy their virus protection, spyware, and so on. When you give your credit card to make the purchase, the number is stolen.

Read the Web site owner's privacy policy before you give them any personal information. The privacy policy lets you know how they'll treat the information they collect. The privacy policy gives you the opportunity to opt out if the Web site owners are going to share the information with anyone else.

## Accessing your information

No matter how you store personal information — either online or on hard copy — you need to be able to access the information easily. Here's a simple plan to help you ensure that you can access your information when you need it:

- ✔ Make a list of all your credit account numbers, issuing company names, and contact information. Do the same thing for your bank accounts and investment accounts. Also keep a record of the current balances, your Social Security card, and your birth certificate. Keep copies of your tax returns, as well.

- ✔ Put the hard copies of the list in a safe location — a fireproof safe or a bank safe-deposit box. If the information is on a CD, keep the CD in a safe location.

- ✔ If you need the information, you now have it in one place — no need to panic when you need it.

When you update the information, make sure that you destroy any hard copies before you discard them. You don't want this information to fall into the wrong hands.

# Knowing When to Hold 'Em, When to Fold 'Em, and When to Shred 'Em

If you live in a paperless society, why do you generate so much more paper than you did 20 years ago? The answer is simple: With computers, you can easily produce documents. And what's better than documents? I'll tell you what — *more* documents! Some of the paper generated is important, however, and you must know what to keep, where to keep it, and for how long.

## What to keep

Table 6-4 provides a quick guide for you to use when considering which documents to keep. The list after the table provides more detail on each item.

| Table 6-4 | Documents to Keep | |
|---|---|---|
| *Document* | *Where to Keep It* | *How Long to Keep It* |
| Cancelled personal checks | Safe place, such as a fire-rated file cabinet | Checks relating to taxes for five years |
| Bank statements | Fire-rated file cabinet, or encrypted CD if you do online banking | Six months for checking and one year for savings accounts |
| Investment and security accounts | Fire-rated file cabinet or encrypted CD | For as long as you have the account open or until you file your taxes |
| Credit card statements | Fire-rated file cabinet | At least two months. (You have 30-60 days from date of billing to report fraud or suspicious transactions.) |
| Mortgage loan documents, monthly statements | Fire-rated file cabinet | For as long you as you have the mortgage and for interest paid for tax purposes |
| Deeds to property | Fire-rated file cabinet or bank safe-deposit box | For as long as you own the property |
| Vehicle purchase loan agreement | Fire-rated file cabinet | Until the loan is paid |
| Vehicle pink slips | Fire-rated file cabinet | For as long as you own the vehicle |
| Insurance policies — homeowners, life, auto | Fire-rated file cabinet, bank safe-deposit box | For as long as you own the policies |
| Social Security card | Fire-rated file cabinet | Indefinitely |

Here are some additional points to keep in mind:

✔ Personal checks that are needed as a receipt for tax purposes should be kept with your tax records. Keep these records kept in a fireproof file cabinet. Keep the tax returns there as well. The checks and tax returns need to kept for five years as required by the IRS.

✔ Bank account statements for your personal checking account need to be kept for at least six months to compare to the next month's statement. The account statement can be kept in a fire-rated file cabinet.

✔ Your savings account statements need to be kept for at least one year to check the balance in the account. If the account is an interest-bearing account, as most are, you'll receive a tax statement of how much interest was paid for the year from the bank at the end of the year to file with your tax return. The copy of this document needs to be kept with your tax return.

✔ Investment account statements need to be kept for as long as you have the account. This is a good way to track your balance from quarter to quarter.

I use my statements for comparison and I review them. Reviewing the account statement frequently is an excellent way to see whether someone has been siphoning money from your account — which means that she has your account number and information.

The best place to store account statements is in your file cabinet drawers. These files are helpful for reviewing the account activity and for making decisions on whether to move the money to another account. I file quarterly account records from my securities and investment accounts in a large loose-leaf binder by date for reviewing ease.

✔ Keep your credit card statements and receipts for the current two months. The receipts are used to reconcile your statement and to make sure that you made all the charges that appear on the statement. If you didn't make any of the charges, now is the time to dispute them with your credit card company. (You have 90 days from the date of the statement to dispute a charge.)

✔ Keep paycheck stubs from direct deposit by your employer. If you don't keep them, they need to be destroyed before being discarded. If you keep the stubs, keep them in the file cabinet with your tax returns and then destroy them before discarding.

✔ Any mortgage documents, deeds, or lease agreements need to be kept in a fireproof storage box at home or the safe-deposit box at the bank. These documents need to be kept for as long as you own or rent the property. The mortgage payment book and slips need to be kept, as well as any statements showing the account activity. Any rent receipts you receive, as well as the cancelled checks, need to be kept as a record of payment. When you move and the documents are no longer needed, destroy them before discarding.

✔ Vehicle purchase agreements and loan papers need be kept in the fireproof file cabinet. This is true whether the vehicle is new or used. If you purchased the vehicle from another private party, keep the sales agreement. When you finally pay off the loan on a vehicle purchased, be sure to file the pink slip in the safe-deposit box. The pink slip needs to be kept and transferred to the new owner when you sell the vehicle. The loan papers, however, can be destroyed and discarded.

✔ Vehicle and homeowners insurance policies should be kept in a safe-deposit box or locking fireproof file cabinet. The information contained in the policy coverage statement is important. So when you discard the old policy, destroy it before you throw it away.

✔ Life insurance policies contain personal information and need to be kept locked in a fireproof file cabinet or a safe-deposit box. Destroy outdated policies before you discard them.

## *Best practices for destroying what you don't keep*

I talk a great deal about destroying the documents you want to discard that contain personal information. Any documents containing personal information need to be destroyed before being discarded to prevent your personal information from falling into the wrong hands.

Dumpster diving, as I cover in Chapter 1, is a real threat. You may think that no one would go through dirty, smelly garbage cans, but they do because it works. They find personal information and use it to steal your identity. The good news is that heading off thieves at the pass is as simple as destroying your documents before you discard them. Here are the best ways to do it:

✔ **Shred the documents.** Shredders are the best and most effective method for destroying documents. Some of these shredders are actually powerful enough to shred credit cards. You can purchase a shredder at discount department and office supply stores.

The best shredder to purchase is a *criss-cross shredder,* which makes the documents look like confetti and not just like strips. The long strips can be pieced together, and the personal information can then be read and used.

After you shred the documents, place the contents into a plastic bag and put the bag in the bottom of your garbage can.

Make sure that you follow the safety directions and precautions in the manufacturer's instructions to avoid mishaps.

✔ **Use a permanent marker to mark out personal information and then tear up the documents.** The next best way to destroy the unwanted documents is to take a permanent marker, mark out any personal information, and then tear up the document.

Don't just mark out the personal information with the permanent marker and leave it at that; also *tear up* the document into *small pieces* before discarding. This way, you ensure that the document doesn't yield any information to an identity thief.

✔ **Tear or cut up the documents into small pieces.** Tear or cut the documents if you don't have a shredder. Make sure that you tear or cut the documents into small pieces so they can't be taped back together easily.

✔ **Cut up the expired or cancelled credit cards and driver's licenses.** Cut up those expired credit cards and driver's licenses. Don't put them in the trash in one piece, or you only invite trouble. Cut the cards and driver's licenses into tiny pieces that can't be taped together easily. Don't throw them away without cutting them up so the card number can't be used by any one else to make purchases on the phone or online. For a demonstration that shows how to adequately cut up your card, go to

```
www.creditcards.com/credit-card-news/video-cutting-up-
          a-credit-card-1457.php
```

Destroy documents that contain personal information that you don't want to keep. This helps to keep you from becoming a victim of identity theft.

# Chapter 7

# Watching What You Set on the Curb

*T*he important personal information you discard can come back to haunt you in a big way if you don't destroy it before tossing it. Before you throw away any document with your name on it, think about what the consequences would be if it fell into the wrong hands. This chapter outlines the issues you may face if you don't destroy various types of documents before discarding them, including credit card statements, bank account statements, utility and cellphone bills, cancelled checks, and old driver's licenses.

## Protecting Your Mail

Your mailbox (and garbage can) contains a bonanza of information for the identity thief. You need to pay attention to what's in your mailbox. By following the simple tips in Table 7-1, you can help protect your mail from falling into the wrong hands.

| Table 7-1 | Tips to Protect Your Mail |
|---|---|
| *Ways to Improve Mail Security* | *Result* |
| Use a locked mailbox. | Your mailbox is a harder target. |
| Don't put outgoing mail in a curbside box. | Your mail isn't available easily. |
| Don't leave your mail in the mailbox overnight. | Your mail won't be mail napped. |

*(continued)*

---

### Table 7-1 *(continued)*

| *Ways to Improve Mail Security* | *Result* |
|---|---|
| Have your personal check reorder sent to bank. | Your blank checks won't be stolen. |
| Notify the post office of a change of address immediately. | Your mail will stay with you. |
| Mail bills at the post office, use a specified U.S. Postal Service mail collection box, or hand to a letter carrier. | Your checks won't be stolen and washed. |
| Report missing mail to the post office. | Your bills will come only to you. |
| Have your local post office hold your mail while you're on vacation or otherwise away from home for an extended period of time. | Your mail will be anxiously and safely awaiting your return. |

---

A raised mailbox flag means that mail is in the curbside box to be picked up. The flag was raised to let the mail carrier — and everyone else, including identity thieves — know that outgoing mail is in the box. So placing anything at the curbside mailbox to be picked up, especially those bills with personal checks and credit card statements enclosed, isn't a good idea. On the other hand, leaving delivered mail in the box for an extended period of time isn't a good idea either. How long should you leave delivered mail in the curbside box? For as short a time as possible. In other words, retrieve your mail as soon as you can. You don't want to give the identity thief any more opportunity than necessary to steal your mail; when you're not home, have a trusted neighbor remove the mail from the box.

## Watching What You Throw Away

Your garbage cans hold a treasure trove of personal information. You throw away valuable personal information every day, and if you're like most of us, you probably don't even give it a second thought. Before reading this book, you probably didn't even own or plan to buy a shredder.

*Dumpster diving* isn't an Olympic sport, but you wouldn't know that by the enthusiasm its participants have for scavenging for personal information in your garbage. The thieves are looking for preapproved credit card applications and the part of your credit card statement that you discarded without shredding or tearing. There they are: your bank statements with account numbers and balances, mixed in with last night's spaghetti. Wow, look over there, your cancelled checks you tossed because you don't need them for tax receipts. You get the idea. You must destroy the documents that contain your personal information before discarding them.

If you don't shred, it isn't dead. Don't leave any morsels for the identity thief to help him in his quest to steal your identity and live life to the fullest at your expense.

Destroy expired credit cards before you discard them. Throwing away expired credit cards without destroying them will only come back to haunt you later. The identity thief only needs your name, card number, and expiration date to order stuff online or on the phone. The three-digit security code is on the back of the card, and the identity thief will have this as well.

You also need to destroy your expired debit card to prevent the identity thief from getting your card number and name.

## *Monthly credit card statements*

When an identity thief enters a dumpster or for that matter, garbage cans in front of your house, she has a competitor — the neighborhood cat. In the mix of the food stuff and other things is your credit card statement, perhaps a little stained with coffee grounds or tomato sauce, but still legible. The only problem is that the thief needs to wrestle the paper away from the cat that's crouched on it (and probably feasting on a half-eaten tuna fish sandwich). The fight is worth it to the identity thief, though, because the gain outweighs the unpleasant experience.

You may be thinking, "Why would anyone choose to go through someone's stinky, dirty garbage?" The payoff keeps them coming back for more. For the identity thief, finding the personal information you discard that's legible enough to use to her advantage is the reason. Your credit card statements have just the kind of information the identity thief seeks. The thief will use the information from the statement, or she'll sell it to someone else.

For an identity thief, finding your monthly credit card statement is like striking gold. Your credit card information can be used to buy anything he desires, and the best thing for him is that he knows he doesn't have to pay for it. In most states, you're responsible for zero of the unauthorized charges on your credit card if you report the fraudulent charges immediately upon receiving your monthly statement. However, you still need to review all the charges on the statement and dispute those you didn't authorize. To dispute the unauthorized charges you need to contact the credit card company and tell someone there which charges you're disputing on your bill. Prevent the theft in the first place by shredding your paid credit card statements before throwing them away.

Shred your preapproved credit offers and credit card statements before you discard them. Here are some additional tips to help protect your credit from theft:

✔ When you pay your credit card bill, don't write your full credit card account number on the Memo or For line on the check; write only the last four digits. The credit card company knows the rest of the numbers. This helps protect your account number from prying eyes because a number of people will handle the check in the credit card company as well as your bank.

✔ Destroy the cancelled check before discarding it. If you discard the check without destroying it, you may inadvertently distribute your credit card account number or, at minimum, your checking account number and signature. For more information about discarding cancelled checks, see the section "Cancelled checks" later in this chapter.

## *Monthly checking account statements*

The identity thief is after all sorts of treasures in your trash. For example, your monthly checking account statement. Just think of the information that's on that statement — your name, address, account number, bank name and address, and your balance.

The account information can be used to make counterfeit checks to drain your account. With the information from your discarded statement, the identity thief can open a new checking account in your name and write bad checks on the account. The checks are *bad* because the identity thief puts only enough money in the account to open it, so when checks for purchases are written on the account, non-sufficient funds (NSF) exist to cover the checks. Because your name is on the account, you're the one who appears to be writing the bad checks. You find out about the problem when you write a check at the grocery store, and they tell you they can't accept your check.

Stores use check-guarantee companies to get reports on checks that the bank sends back stamped NSF, known as *returned checks*. By helping merchants identify customers who are passing bad checks, the check-guarantee companies help the merchants minimize their losses.

The check-guarantee companies also protect the customer. For example, when you notify the companies that checks have been lost or stolen, they alert retailers for you. In addition, you can request a consumer report from an agency, such as SCAN (Shared Check Authorization Network). SCAN isn't a credit bureau; it's a consumer-reporting agency that's governed by the Fair Credit Reporting Act (FCRA). You can dispute inaccurate information on your SCAN report just as you can credit bureau information.

## Savings account statements

Savings account statements need to be shredded; otherwise, don't place them in the trash. The savings account statement contains information — such as your name and address, account numbers, and even a balance — that identity thieves could use to help them in their quest to obtain your identity. The name of your bank is also on the statement (with the bank's phone number). Even if the thieves can't access your account with the information on the statement, it's enough to let them know how much money you have. They'll find other ways to access your account, especially if it will yield a great payday!

## Utility bills

Among the papers and various stuff you find in the trash are the Detach for Your Records parts of your utility bills. This part of the bill has your name, address, and account number on it. Utility bills — telephone, water, garbage, and electric to name a few — are used as proof of address to open accounts at the local bank in your name. The identity thief can put them to good use if you don't shred them before you discard them. Don't give identity thieves the chance to use your discarded utility bills for their gain and your pain. Shred or tear up the part you're going to throw away.

## Cellphone bills

Cellphone bills have the appearance of not being something you need to think about when you're taking precautionary measures to prevent you from becoming a victim of identity theft, but consider the following: Cellphone bills have your name, address, account number, and cellphone number all right there on the bill stub that you're given to keep for your records (and, if you're like most everyone, you promptly discard). An identity thief can use your bill stub as proof of address to open a bank account in your name. To protect yourself, shred or tear up your cellphone bill before you discard it. With just your phone number, you can become the victim of slamming or scamming; to find out more, go to

```
www.ftc.gov/opa/1998/07/cramming.shtm
```

## Old tax returns

Your tax returns have your address, SSN, employers' names and addresses, how much you make, bank accounts, stock account information, and so on. Never discard old tax returns without shredding them first. A tax return that isn't shredded is the mother lode of all finds for an identity thief. You'll be the identity thief's best friend, and you won't even know it until the bills roll in and the collection agencies start to hound you.

Throwing out old tax returns without shredding them will definitely cause a great deal of pain for you for a long time. To prevent having a mess to clean up, shred it.

## Cancelled checks

Most folks simply throw cancelled checks (ones they don't need for tax purposes) in the trash. Most of the time, people discard checks without tearing or shredding them. The checks contain important information, however, such as your name, address, account number, and the name and address of your bank.

To the identity thief, the information contained on the checks is what's important — not the actual checks. The identity thief can use your account information to make counterfeit checks to either clean out your account or to write bad checks in your name. The thief can also order stuff online by using your checking account information like a debit card, except that the money for the item purchased comes directly out of your checking account.

If you aren't going to keep all your cancelled checks, destroy them before you throw them away. Another option is to have your bank hold your cancelled checks for safekeeping and not send them to you with your monthly statement. You must pay a fee to have your bank hold your checks, and the fee varies from bank to bank. To find out whether your bank offers the check safekeeping service, call the phone number listed on your checking account statement.

## Expired driver's licenses

Before you toss your old driver's license in the trash, destroy it. I don't mean cut it in half; I mean totally destroy it like you would your old credit card.

Your driver's license number can be used to make a counterfeit license with your name and address. To prevent counterfeiting, most states issue driver's licenses that have holograms or offset photos of the licensee on them. To see the hologram, however, you need to remove the license from the wallet picture window. Most businesses don't ask a person writing a check to remove the license; they just quickly jot down the license number on the check. If a license isn't checked closely, an identity thief can get away with cashing counterfeit checks by using the counterfeit license.

Some shredders are strong enough to shred a driver's license or credit card, thus keeping them from falling into the waiting hands of the identity thief. If you don't have a shredder, cut the old driver's license into small pieces so that it isn't worth the effort to put it together to read your date of birth and driver's license number.

If you notice judgments for parking tickets or other DMV fines, you may want to order a copy of your DMV driving record. There is usually a small fee to order the printout.

# Old credit and debit cards

Your old credit and debit cards contain important information even if they're expired. These cards should never be tossed without cutting or shredding them. By cutting them up, I mean cutting them into several small pieces and putting them in different trash cans; don't just cut them in half or in a few large pieces that can be put back together easily. The magnetic stripes have information, such as the cardholder name, card number, address, and so on. Don't risk it; be safe and shred your old cards.

# Hotel key cards

A great deal of debate has been going on about whether hotel key cards contain personal information on the magnetic stripe on the card. *Computerworld* magazine did a study on the hotel key myth to find out whether the keys actually contain personal information, such as your name, address, and in some cases, your full credit card number, that identity thieves could use to steal your identity. The staffers at the magazine had a magnetic card reader maker attempt to read the data on 100 cards from major hotels. Even with state of the art high-tech scanners, the cards were unreadable. The reason for this is that each hotel uses a unique code (known as the *facility code*) and no two facility codes are alike so the cards can't be read by any other hotel's reader. You need the particular reader that can read the facility code for that particular hotel. Read about the study here:

```
www.computerworld.com/s/article/107701/It_s_Just_the_Key_
            to_Your_Room
```

## Debunking myths

Amazing how myths get started and take on a life of their own. Snopes.com is a Web site you can visit to find out whether what you're hearing is an urban myth. Other Web sites debunk urban myths as well. To find them, type **urban myths** in your Web browser's search box.

So the bottom line is this: If you feel uncomfortable, don't leave the key in the room and take the key with you when you check out. Some hotels charge nominal fees ($3 to $5) for unreturned keys to cover the costs of replacing the card. The fee is small enough, so if you are insecure about the card being returned with your information on it, you can just take the card and pay the fee.

When you get home, make sure you check your credit card statement closely for any charges you don't recognize after or during your visit to the hotel. This helps make sure no one got your card number from the hotel key — especially if you lost the key and had to get another one from the front desk.

The real issue with hotel keys that's proven correct is that thieves have copied stolen credit card numbers (from other sources) onto the stolen hotel keys' magnetic stripes. These cards can then be used to purchase only gas — because the magnetic stripe is the only thing that's read during the purchase at the pump. Obviously the hotel key/credit card can't be used to make purchases in a store because it still looks like a hotel key and doesn't have the credit issuer's logo on it. If the thieves don't get the security code on the back of the card, they may not be able to order anything on the Internet or on the phone.

If you do take the hotel key (either unintentionally or on purpose), destroy it before discarding it. Destroying it means shredding it or cutting it into little pieces — not just cutting the card in half. Whether the key contains your personal information isn't the issue; you always need to be safe by being alert and taking the necessary precautions.

# Chapter 8

# Practicing Discretion in Public Places

*I*n this chapter, I tell you why it's important to watch what you say about your personal information in public places, how to choose and use an ATM, and the importance of keeping your credit card receipts. I also show you how to keep your personal checks from being counterfeited or stolen, the smartest ways to hang on to your wallet or purse, and how to avoid shoulder-surfing thieves.

## Carrying Minimal Personal Information

This is an easy secret: The less personal information you carry, the less personal information an identity thief can steal from you. The following sections discuss some simple measures you can take to prevent your important information from being stolen.

### Do not carry your Social Security card

Don't under any circumstances ever carry your Social Security card in your wallet or purse. Lose your wallet or purse — or worse, have it stolen — and you lose your Social Security card. Your Social Security Number (SSN) is an important identifier in society; the number can be sold or used by anyone when she has your card.

The only times you need to carry your Social Security card is when you start a new job (so that the Human Resources department can photocopy it) or when you apply for government benefits. After you return home from your first day at a new job or after you apply for those government benefits, take your Social Security card out of your wallet or purse and place it in the fireproof safe where you keep your other important documents for safekeeping.

Be stingy with your SSN. Nobody but the government can require you to reveal your Social Security Number. Others — such as utility companies for opening a utility account — can deny you service if you don't reveal your SSN. You don't have to give your SSN to any business that asks for it, except when completing a credit application or for verification purposes your first day on a new job.

If you suspect or know that someone is using your SSN to get a job, contact the Social Security Administration at www.ssa.gov and the IRS at www.irs.gov (to avoid tax problems). On the other hand, if someone is using your SSN to get credit, the Social Security Administration can't fix your credit, and I suggest that you follow the steps I outline in Chapter 2.

You can see whether someone is using your SSN to get a job by checking your Social Security statement. You can order a statement online or contact the nearest Social Security Administration office and request one. In addition to any statement you request, a statement is sent to you annually.

Memorize your SSN, and you won't have a need to carry your Social Security card. Problem solved!

Still I find that people do carry their Social Security card with them in their wallet or purse. The other day, I was in line next to a woman making a purchase at a store; she pulled out her debit card and — to my surprise — right next to her driver's license was her Social Security card! Not a smart move. If her purse is stolen (or even lost), all her personal information — driver's license with her address and birth date and her SSN — is right there for the taking.

I repeat: There is no reason to carry your Social Security card with you other than the first day on a new job. The information is used to verify that you have a right to work in the U.S. and to fill out the forms for tax purposes (W-2). Be vigilant about protecting your identity!

## Memorize your bank ATM PIN

Choose an ATM personal identification number (PIN) that you can remember easily. This way, you don't need to write it down. Writing down your PIN defeats the purpose of having a PIN. Writing down your PIN and carrying it in your wallet or purse with your ATM card is an especially bad idea. If your wallet or purse is stolen or lost, you lose your PIN and possibly your money as well.

When you choose a PIN, don't use your birthday, your children's or spouse's birthday, your SSN, your address, and so on. These numbers are too easy to guess. Try instead the last four digits of a friend's phone number (not your own!) or a special date that isn't your birthday.

Protect yourself. Don't make it easy for would-be thieves to steal your hard-earned money. Memorize your PIN so that if you lose your ATM card, you can rest easy knowing the card is useless to anyone else.

Change your PIN at least annually and any time you think your password has been compromised. I know — remembering all the passwords, PINs, and so on is difficult. But when you choose a PIN or password, select something that's easy for *you* to remember but is hard for someone else to guess. The PIN should be at least eight characters long with a combination of letters in upper- and lowercase as well as symbols. Some online Web sites will not accept a password that doesn't meet their standard of using lower- and uppercase letters with symbols. Some symbols will not be accepted in some systems, so be sure to follow what is acceptable.

For banking and other online financial purposes, use a different username and password than what you use for your social networking accounts. Why make it easy for the thief?

## Carry one credit card

Look in your wallet or purse. How many credit cards are in there? You probably have several cards in your wallet, and even some you forgot you were carrying and haven't used in a long time. So right now, stop reading and take out all the extra credit cards in your wallet. You'll be glad you did.

Carrying more than one credit card only compounds your problems when your wallet or purse is stolen or lost, so just don't do it. Take retail store credit cards, for example. The only time you need to carry a retail store credit card is when you're going to that store. In fact, most retail stores now accept the major credit cards, so how many different cards do you really need? The fewer cards you have, the less you have to worry about if your wallet or purse is stolen or lost.

You're striving to become a hard target, which means that you're practicing prevention. If you carry less personal information, you'll be a harder target. If someone does get your wallet, he won't have as much personal information about you as he does about the other person who was nice enough to carry all his credit cards at one time.

# *Carry personal checks only when necessary*

Carrying your personal checks everywhere you go isn't the best idea. I realize that at times, you need to purchase something on the spur of the moment and having your checks with you comes in real handy. But losing your blank checks can be a drain on your checking account balance if someone finds and uses the checks to help themselves to your money. Consider some alternatives, such as using cash or the one major credit card that you carry in your wallet or purse.

If you do lose your blank checks, contact someone at the bank immediately and have her freeze your account to cover outstanding checks written on the account. You may need to open a new account.

After you write a check, make sure that you only tear out the one you just wrote and not the next one along with it, which is blank. Giving a blank check to someone could be a problem for you, depending upon the honesty of the person to whom you unknowingly hand the blank check.

Minimize your exposure by carrying your personal checks only when you know you'll need them. The less often you carry your personal checks, the less chance you have of losing them or having them stolen.

Here are some other tips for keeping your checks secure:

- ✔ Do not put your driver's license number or SSN on your checks.

- ✔ Make sure that you can account for all your checks — used, unused, and void.

- ✔ When you pay by check, be aware of your surroundings while you write and sign the check. If someone looks over your shoulder, she can easily memorize your name and address and the name of the bank where you have your account.

- ✔ Be careful with the check registers that are a carbon of the check you just wrote. If you lose the register, the information in the carbon can be a problem. The carbon in the register has the check number, account number (for most banks), bank name, and your signature (often blocked out by a black box). Keep these check registers in an especially safe location when shopping.

- ✔ When you void checks, destroy them before you discard them, and do not forget to record in your register that check number XYZ has been voided and the date you voided it.

Lately, I've noticed women carrying checkbooks in their wallets. Most women's wallets have a place for a checkbook. Although it's convenient to carry your checkbook, it isn't a good idea. If the purse is stolen, so is your checkbook. Keeping your checkbook in your car isn't a good idea either. By all means, carry your checkbook if you intend to make purchases; but don't carry it when you go dancing or to the amusement park to ride the rides. On vacation, carry traveler's checks rather than your personal checkbook. With the widespread use of debit cards, you really don't need to carry your checkbook.

# The Walls Have Ears and Eyes

Identity thieves have no dignity. They'll stop at nothing to get your personal information, even if it means looking over your shoulder while you're at the register, eavesdropping on your wireless phone conversations at the mall, monitoring the use of public Wi-Fi connections, or even setting up fake, free connections. Don't let these bandits get the best of you. The following sections show you how to defend yourself against these crimes.

## Shoulder surfing

*Shoulder surfing* isn't the latest water sport craze to hit the beaches of Southern California, and it has nothing to do with the real sport of surfing. *Shoulder surfing* describes the art of looking over the shoulder of another person to see what he's doing.

Shoulder surfing got its start in airports, bus stations, and train stations. Thieves would record the phone credit card numbers of those unsuspecting victims who were using a public phone to make telephone calls. How it works is that the person may be standing alongside you, pretending to use the adjacent pay telephone, but what she's actually doing is watching you punch in your phone credit card number and PIN. The person doing the shoulder surfing doesn't have to be directly behind you or even next to you; he can be in direct line of sight looking through a camera with a zoom lens to record the punching in of the numbers. He then writes down the number and sells it to others for their use.

These days, shoulder surfing is used to capture your PIN when you use your ATM and key in your PIN. With the advent of camera cellphones, it's easier than ever to fetch your account and PIN.

So what can you do? Here are two easy ways to help protect your identity:

- ✔ **Protect your keystrokes from plain view when you key in your PIN.** You never know who's watching even a short distance away, so block their view with your body.

- ✔ **Check whether the ATM slot looks like someone tampered with it.** You can usually see cracking or some other telltale mark, or your card won't go into the slot easily. If you see anything like this, *don't use the ATM.*

Beware of this sophisticated trick: Some thieves will actually place a camera close to the keypad, usually in the deposit envelope holder. The camera sits in the bottom of the holder and is aimed at the keypad to capture your keystrokes. In addition, they modify the place where you insert your ATM card. They place a portable reader in the slot, which reads your card number and then displays a message stating that the ATM isn't working.

## *Be careful what you say*

Cellphones are in widespread use today. You can hear people talking on their phones everywhere. I don't know what the deal is, but people think you need to talk loudly into cellphones, and consequently, you can plainly and clearly hear one side of the conversation.

Now, if the person using the cell is ordering something, you can hear him give his credit card type, number, expiration date, and name. All that a thief needs to do is write down the information and *voilà,* she has a credit card to use to order stuff on the phone. You also sometimes hear someone giving his SSN over the cellphone in a public place. This is not a good idea at all.

Conversations between you and someone who's with you in a public place can also be overheard, so be careful what you discuss about your personal information. Discussing personal information in public places just isn't a good idea if you want to be a hard target.

Think of your personal information as sensitive information that if discovered, may help someone assume your identity. The walls have ears — you never know who's listening and trying to pick up personal information to use to his advantage. There was a saying during World War II, *loose lips sink ships.* The phrase makes perfect sense in the prevention of identity theft.

# Keeping Track of Important Things

If you've ever lost your wallet or have had a credit card number stolen, you know what I'm talking about here: Big trouble, big pain in the neck. The sections that follow provide some tips for managing those pesky receipts and preventing them from falling into the wrong hands. You also get the rundown on what to do if your wallet goes missing.

## Checking credit card receipts

Look at the credit card receipt you just signed. Does it have your full credit card number, name, and expiration date printed on it? The law has changed and only the last digits will be printed on all copies of the credit card receipt in the near future. But for now, those receipts contain all the information an identity thief needs to wreak havoc with your credit.

Here are some ways to safeguard your information:

- Don't leave your copy of the credit card receipt behind at the register. The receipt has too much information on it.

- Don't throw away your receipt in a trash can near the area where you just used your credit card. Keep all your receipts so that you can reconcile your monthly bill and then shred them before you throw them away.

- Don't leave the receipt you signed on the table in a restaurant. Make sure that your server picks it up before you go.

- Beware of *skimming*. This activity occurs mostly at restaurants. The waiter has a small handheld device that he swipes your card through. The device captures the data off the magnetic strip on the card. The data contains enough information that can be transferred to another magnetic strip of a counterfeit card, which can be used fraudulently. If possible, make sure that your waiter doesn't perform this activity with your card.

- When you review your receipt, make sure that no one around you can read it along with you, especially if the receipt has your full credit card number and expiration date printed on it.

## Choosing a safe ATM

When you're going to use an ATM, choose it carefully. Here are some tips for choosing and using an ATM:

- Use an ATM that's both familiar and comfortable to you.

- Scope out the area before you approach the ATM. If you feel uncomfortable for any reason, move on.

- Have your ATM card out and in your hand as you approach the ATM.

- Check out the ATM. Look for any signs that the machine has been tampered with. For example, if attachments are protruding from the card slot or keypad, or if the screen is blank, find a different machine.

- Avoid using ATMs that have messages attached saying that the instructions for use have changed; banks don't post such messages directing you to use a specific ATM.

- Observe other people using the ATM and notice if they're having difficulty. That may be an indication of trouble.

- Make sure that the area around is well-lighted at night.

- Be aware of your surroundings. Watch the person next to you or behind you.

- Use your body to hide what you enter on the keypad.

- Take your receipt with you. Do not throw it away in the trash cans near the ATM.

- Don't forget to take your ATM card from the slot.

- Avoid using non-bank ATM machines; they can be set up to collect card and PIN numbers.

- Check your bank statement for withdrawals by ATM to make sure you made them. With online banking, you can check as soon as you get to a secure computer.

- Never check your bank balances or do any online banking from a public computer.

## *Losing your wallet or purse*

Losing your wallet or purse is a pain in the neck. If you lose it, you have some work to do. Do the following:

- Take an assessment and think of what was in your wallet or purse. Keep a list of what you carry to refresh your memory if your wallet or purse is lost or stolen.

For a checklist that can help you remember and document all the things you carry with you, check out this site:

```
www.idtheftcenter.org/artman2/publish/v_fact_sheets/
        Fact_Sheet_104.shtml
```

✔ Take out all your credit card contact numbers you've stored in a safe place and begin calling them. Tell your creditors that you had your wallet stolen or lost your driver's license.

✔ Contact someone at the DMV in your state and let her know you lost your driver's license.

✔ Contact someone at your bank and tell him to cancel your ATM card and issue a new one.

✔ If you were carrying checks, contact the bank and freeze your account.

If you lose your wallet or purse, take action immediately — don't delay. As soon as you realize your wallet or purse is gone, get to work. Follow the actions that I outline in the preceding list. The sooner you do, the less damage will be done.

# Ordering Stuff by Phone

To order stuff by phone, all you need to provide is the name on your credit card, the card number, and the expiration date. Most companies that take phone orders also ask for the security code on the back of your credit card. For Visa, MasterCard, and Discover card, this is a three-digit number on the back of the card; for American Express, this is a four-digit number on the front of the card. This provides some level of security that wasn't utilized several years ago. For someone to use your credit card to order merchandise, he needs the security code. This means he needs to have your card in his possession or to know the security code.

This goes for small purchases and large purchases alike. For added security, some businesses ask for the three- or four-digit security number on the back of the card, but your signature and your photo ID aren't verified. This purchasing scenario is ideal for an identity thief who's using stolen credit cards.

When you place a phone order, you need to know the company — don't call a company you're not familiar with — and you need to check your monthly statement. Problems occur when you don't follow the simple rules of knowing who you're ordering stuff from and not checking your monthly card statement. Don't order anything from unsolicited callers offering a service or product, especially if you'd be making an impulsive purchase.

Always get an order or confirmation number and the name of the customer service rep that helped you. Also record the date and time you placed the order. This way, you have a fallback if something goes kerflooey with your order.

When you order stuff by phone, guard your privacy. Don't use a cellphone or place the order in a public place. It's too easy for someone to eavesdrop on your call and capture your credit card information.

CASE STUDY

# Mike's story: It happened to me

My wife and I used my credit card to order a Turbo Cooker that was advertised on TV several years ago. We received the product a few weeks later as expected, but when our monthly credit card statement arrived and we checked it like we always do, we noticed several charges on the statement we didn't make.

I contacted someone at the card company and told her that we didn't make the charges and we wanted them removed from the statement. The card company removed the charges. But then the next month's statement had new charges from the companies again. I called the phone number that was next to one of the charges and told someone there that I didn't authorize any charges from their company and wanted the charges removed from our card. I also called the card company and talked to someone in the fraud department. She said that she was familiar with the company making the charges, and she would take care of it. On the next month's statement, the charges were removed.

The company advertising its product on TV was legitimate, but one of the people answering the phone or processing the calls wasn't so trustworthy. The card number was probably provided to the company making the unauthorized charges on our card for a fee.

We were lucky because we check our monthly credit card statement religiously. Some companies that make unauthorized charges are banking on the fact that most people don't check their monthly statements, and therefore, their charges aren't disputed immediately, if at all.

I've ordered other things by phone and haven't had any problems. Ordering stuff by phone isn't inherently unsafe, but you do need to be vigilant and check your monthly bill to make sure that it contains only charges you authorized. If charges appear that you didn't authorize, dispute them immediately.

The company selling the product we purchased hired a firm to take the calls and place the orders, which is how the problem occurred. The person taking the information may not have been honest and made a few extra bucks selling credit card information. The other possibility is that the company taking the calls didn't shred the order forms and then someone did a little dumpster diving, found the credit card numbers, and used them.

The moral to the story is to check your monthly credit card statement every month. You never know when your card will have charges you didn't make. When you check your credit card statement monthly, you can catch these unsolicited charges and get the issue resolved quickly with the credit card company.

# Part IV
# Arming Yourself against Potential Identity Theft

**The 5th Wave**                    By Rich Tennant

"Oh, that's Jack's hobby corner. He's made some wonderful blank checks, Social Security cards, driver's licenses, that sort of thing."

# In this part . . .

In this part, you find out what help is available to you in the identity theft battle. For instance, government agencies and online companies help keep you from becoming a victim or help you if you already are one. This part also explains common scams and methods that identity thieves use; know the scams so that you can avoid them.

# Chapter 9

# Avoiding Loss of Your Identity: Online Services That Can Help

*In This Chapter*

▶ Researching identity theft protection companies

▶ Comparing costs and services among various companies

▶ Discovering the benefits of an identity theft prevention company

▶ Resolving disputes

*I*n this chapter, I discuss the companies that claim they can help prevent identity theft. Numerous prevention services are out there, and in this chapter, I look at several large companies and outline the services provided by each. Also, I show you the benefits of hiring a company to safeguard your identity. Finally, I look at how the companies address client disputes. Other companies provide similar services, but LifeLock, ID Watchdog, Identity Guard, Truston, and TrustedID are the most prominent in the field.

## Sizing Up Identity Theft Protection Companies

An identity theft protection company does just that — helps protect you against identity theft — but it also helps you recover your good name should you become a victim. How do you know what company will ensure that you get what you want? A good place to do some research is at the Better Business Bureau (BBB) Web site:

    www.bbbonline.org

The BBB has a rating system that can help you decide what identity theft company you want to deal with. When you go to the site, click the For Consumers link. Then type in a description of the business (in this case, type **identity theft protection**) and choose your state from the drop-down list. You see the companies that fit the description you typed. To the right of the company's name, click the View BBB Report button to see information about that company. In the following list, I describe the highlights of what you see:

- ✔ **BBB Accredited Business logo:** If you see this logo associated with a company, you know that company supports the BBB's services to the public. This means the company makes a good effort to resolve customer complaints.

- ✔ **An alphabetic rating (A–F):** This rating displays in the center of the page. To the right of the rating, click the Rating Explanation link for more information about how the BBB evaluates companies.

- ✔ **Company Profile:** Here you find out how old the company is, where it's located, who its contact person is, and so on.

- ✔ **BBB Comments & Analysis:** This box contains further information that the BBB has chosen to share with consumers beyond the ratings.

- ✔ **Complaint Closing Statistics:** Near the bottom of the company's page is a box containing stats on how many (and what type of) complaints against the company have been filed and whether the company has resolved the complaints.

The ratings on the BBB site for companies range from A (good) to F (bad). If a company has an F rating, the BBB doesn't recommend you do business with them. A word of caution here is necessary: Think long and hard about signing on with a company that has an F rating.

So what do the ratings mean? Well, the ratings are based on customer complaints and how the company responds to those complaints. Customer service is a major source of complaints. Are you getting the services? Does the product perform according to what was advertised? How does the company address your complaint when you call or write it and are all the complaints about customer service? If the complaints to the BBB are unresolved or go unanswered, you may want to consider moving on and avoiding that company.

To find the rating for each company:

1. **Go to the BBB Web site and click the For Consumers link.**

2. **On the page that appears, click the For Consumers link (yes, again, this time in the upper-left corner) and then click the Check Out a Business or Charity link.**

3. **Type in information about a particular company in the new screen that appears.**

   Under Search Results, you see a list of companies that matched your criteria.

4. **Click the View Report link to see more information.**

Table 9-1 has information about five identity theft companies so that you can compare them side by side. When an account is *administratively closed,* the BBB closed the open complaint because the business did not respond or when the BBB asserts that the business made a reasonable effort to contact the complainant to resolve the complaint but was unsuccessful and the complainant did not respond.

| Table 9-1 | BBB Ratings for Identity Theft Companies | | | |
|---|---|---|---|---|
| *Company* | *BBB Accredited Business?* | *Number of Resolved Complaints* | *Number of Cases Closed Administratively* | *Overall Rating* |
| LifeLock | Yes | 45 | 0 | A+ |
| ID Watchdog | Yes | 58 | 5 | A |
| TrustedID | Yes | 9 | 1 | A |
| Identity Guard | Yes | 128 (in four years) | 0 | A+ |
| Truston | Yes | 0 | 0 | A- |

By using the BBB and other independent sources, you can gather enough information on whether you want to do business with a particular company. Be careful to make sure you're getting unbiased, truly independent business ratings. This is also true for any business, not just for identity theft prevention companies. Researching the identity theft prevention companies helps you make an informed choice. The last thing you want to do is pick a company that says it'll protect your identity and then come to find out that when you need that company, it's not there for you.

# Identity Theft Prevention Services

In recent years, companies have stated that they'll help keep you safe from identity theft for a fee. These companies provide guarantees that if you become a victim while a client, they'll offer various remedies. Five of these companies are LifeLock, ID Watchdog, TrustedID, Identity Guard, and Truston — the ones I discuss in the earlier section, "Sizing Up Identity Theft Protection Companies." The companies' services are based on the premises that they monitor your credit report, alert you if any changes occur to it, and place a fraud alert on it.

But just what are the services provided by these companies? It all depends. Although many of these companies provide similar services, the services do vary from company to company as does the type of company. For example, if preventing the theft of your identity is important to you, choose a company that provides the service. Some companies help guide you through the process to recovering your identity if you're a victim but may not actually provide prevention services. Although today, most provide recovery and prevention as a bundled service.

Numerous service providers are out there, and I don't have enough room in this book to review them all, so here I review the same five I discuss earlier.

*Note:* You don't need to use any of the companies that I discuss in this chapter. The services these companies offer are in line with the industry standards.

The following list describes the most common services offered by identity theft protection companies:

- ✔ **Credit monitoring:** The company establishes a baseline with a snapshot of where your credit report is at in a given time period. After you approve the report, the company then monitors changes in the credit report with the baseline report. These companies monitor credit reports on a monthly basis. This is not a fraud alert; it is routine monitoring of your credit reports.

  This is similar to what the credit bureaus provide except you have one place to get all three monitored instead of going to each bureau and paying for the service or opting for all three by one bureau.

- ✔ **Fraud alerts:** Due to a recent court decision, the identity theft prevention company cannot place a fraud alert on your credit report; only you can do that.

  For more information, go to this site:

  ```
  http://phoenix.bizjournals.com/phoenix/
          stories/2009/08/24/daily87.html
  ```

- ✔ **Credit freezes:** I discuss the freeze, or *credit lock,* in detail in Chapter 2. For the credit freeze, you don't need to be a victim; however, it's free to victims. Non-victims have to pay to place the freeze, and to thaw the freeze, they have to pay again.

✔ **Repair/recovery:** The companies also provide you with repair services and a warranty guarantee of their services if you become an identity theft victim while subscribing to their prevention services. The credit bureaus also provide similar services. Generally, they help with the paperwork to file with the creditors, credit bureaus, and so on.

✔ **Guarantee:** Some provide a guarantee saying they'll pay for any losses you sustain if you become a victim. Usually a limit is applied to the dollar amount recovered. Make sure you read and understand the fine print to find out exactly what's covered by the guarantee.

The dispute process is outlined in case you have an issue with the company's services. In most cases, disputes are resolved through mediation (arbitration) rather than lawsuits. (See the "Reviewing Dispute Resolution Methods" section, later in this chapter.)

✔ **Blogs/e-newsletters:** These services keep you informed about what's occurring on the identity theft front and the latest tools that the thieves are using to attempt to steal your identity.

✔ **Identity theft resources:** Sites such as www.privacyrights.org/identity.htm, www.idtheftcenter.org, and www.identitytheft.org will also provide timely information about identity theft trends and so on. The better informed you are about the current trends in identity theft, the more knowledge you'll have and the more power you have to prevent you from becoming a victim.

Although I give you the information you need to make an informed decision of whether to use a company's services, make sure to do your homework and research any company you're thinking of doing business with. After you have your questions answered, you can make a good decision that will help give you peace of mind.

Some companies require that you provide copies of your IDs, a power of attorney, and other sensitive documents as soon as you become a member. Others request those documents only if you have a case opened with an advocate after you're a victim of identity theft, and they maintain a strict document destruction policy to safeguard your information. Just as you should question others who maintain sensitive documents, closely examine what information these companies want to access and their hiring practices. Do they have complete background checks? Do you have the direct phone extensions of the people you talk to so you can call them directly? You'll be relying on this company at a time when you're stressed, emotional, and feeling violated. Make sure upfront that you feel comfortable that it's trustworthy.

## Staying on top of your credit with monthly alerts

Monthly alerts keep you posted on what's going on with your credit. However, most monitoring services will notify you in an e-mail alert that your credit has changed within 24 hours after it's occurred. If you don't get 24-hour e-mail alerts when your credit changes, you may not want to use that service provider. This is important because being notified monthly — even though it's better than nothing — is a long time to go without knowing that major changes have occurred in your credit. I discuss how to read credit reports in more detail in Chapter 5; it's important for you to know how to interpret your credit report. When you know what to look for, you'll better know how to determine if incorrect information is on the report that you need to dispute.

*Note:* You're likely to get a lot of false alerts, depending on the program. Often small changes end up sending notifications to you. These changes, such as 123 SE Main Street to 123 S.E. Main St., don't necessarily indicate identity theft. Other companies have attempted to compensate for this by lowering the sensitivity. Unfortunately, that means that early signs of identity theft might not be caught. The bottom line is that there's no substitute for monitoring your own credit report.

A company that provides identity theft protection is different from one that provides restoration help. A restoration company guides you through the process if you become a victim. The restoration company will help with the forms that need to be filed, help you keep a log of what has been done, and so on.

# Comparing Costs and Services

Identity Theft Labs (www.identitytheftlabs.com), a contracted affiliate of a handful of identity theft companies, is a group of individuals who evaluate the services provided by LifeLock, TrustedID, ID Watchdog, Debix, and Identity Guard. The group, which claims to bring an unbiased view of the companies to consumers, associates itself only with those companies whose services it endorses. When you go to the Web site, you see a table comparing the top-four identity theft prevention companies; Debix isn't in the table and hasn't been reviewed. The Unbiased Reviews row contains a link for each company; clicking the link takes you to a Web site with more information about that company and its service.

Although Identity Theft Labs didn't review Truston, it's an alternative that provides identity theft prevention/repair. As I explain earlier in this chapter, Truston is a BBB-accredited business.

There's no such thing as 100-percent security or prevention, so if a company claims 100 percent, don't sign up with it even if it's in writing. Read the guarantee closely and you'll probably find a loophole because no company would guarantee 100-percent protection from identity theft.

All the service providers that offer identity theft prevention or protection usually charge a monthly or annual fee for their services. The monthly service fees charged by each company are different depending on the services. In Table 9-2, I look at the fees for these services. Some companies offer one service and one fee. Other companies offer a choice, but the price doesn't vary too much.

The costs for services pale in comparison to the cost of becoming an identity theft victim. Table 9-2 has the breakdown for each of the five companies I discuss in this chapter. In the sections that follow, I give a brief rundown of the services offered by each.

Keep in mind, the monthly costs are for illustrative purposes; some of the companies require an annual contract, so the amount is paid in full for the number of years based on the plan you select. The more years you sign up for, the lower the annual cost, but you're locked in to the contract terms. Other companies request full payment upfront for the plan you select.

**Table 9-2    Identity Theft Prevention Companies Cost Comparison**

| Company | Web site | Annual Cost | Monthly Cost |
| --- | --- | --- | --- |
| LifeLock | www.lifelock.com | $99.00 | $9.00 |
| ID Watchdog | www.idwatchdog.com | $179.95 | $19.95 |
| TrustedID | www.trustedid.com | $84.15 | $7.01 |
| Identity Guard | www.identityguard.com | 179.88 | $17.99 |
| Truston | www.mytruston.com | $120.00 | $10.00 |

## LifeLock

The LifeLock service has two options — monthly at $9.00 or $99.00 for the
year. LifeLock (its Enrollment page is shown in Figure 9-1) offers the following
services:

- Proactive identity theft protection
- Reduction of credit card offers (these are the ones sent in the mail or by
  e-mail)
- $1 million service guarantee
- Recovery services

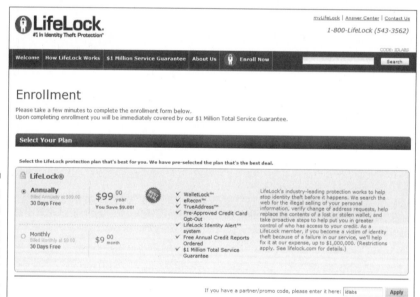

**Figure 9-1:**
LifeLock
offers a
special
price if you
sign up for
a year.

## ID Watchdog

ID Watchdog (shown in Figure 9-2) offers several plans to choose from:

- Monthly plan at $19.95 per month
- Annual plan at $179.95 for ID Watchdog Plus

✔ Annual plan at $259.95 for ID Watchdog Plus and Snapshot

✔ Three-year plan at $466.92 for ID Watchdog Plus

✔ Recovery services

**Figure 9-2:**
ID
Watchdog
protects
consumers
through
monitoring
and
detection.

## TrustedID

TrustedID offers the following services (see Figure 9-3):

✔ IDFreeze is $189.99 billed annually in one installment for the family plan. The individual plan is $99.00 and is billed annually in one installment.

✔ CreditLock (www.creditlock.com) has various membership packages.

✔ Data Breach Response Services (contact for quote); usually for businesses, not individuals.

✔ A blog with information and updates about identity theft.

✔ Recovery.

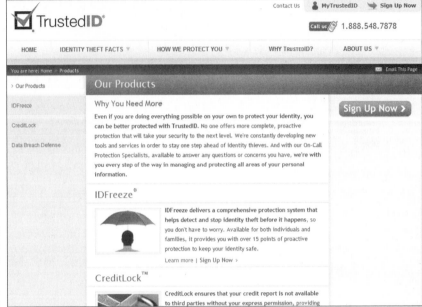

**Figure 9-3:**
TrustedID
offers family
and individ-
ual plans.

# *Identity Guard*

Identity Guard has a FAQs page (see Figure 9-4), which can answer a lot of question as you get started with a identity theft protection company. This one offers three plans:

✔ A $9.99 plan that offers the following services:

- Credit reports, scores

- Quarterly credit updates, Internet surveillance

- Resource center of information about identity theft

✔ A $14.99 plan that offers all the services of the $9.99 plan plus three-bureau monitoring

✔ A $17.99 plan (called Total Protection) that offers all the services of the two previous plans plus these two additional services:

- Computer security suite

- Public records update

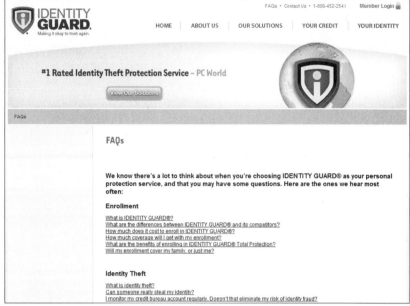

**Figure 9-4:**
Find more
informa-
tion at the
Identity
Guard FAQs
page.

# Truston

As I mention earlier, Truston hasn't been reviewed by Identity Theft Labs; however, it is BBB accredited and worth discussing. Truston has individual subscriptions, but the bulk of what the company does is market its services for other major players, such as credit card companies, banks, and so on, who then provide the service to their clients. Truston provides similar services as the four that Identity Theft Labs reviewed.

Truston is an online service (see Figure 9-5) in which you can sign on through a portal — *MyTruston.* To sign up, sensitive information isn't required. Truston also has an advantage over other identity theft prevention companies because it sends reminder e-mails to do certain things such as what to do next in the recovery process. Truston also provides reminder e-mails to ensure all paperwork and tasks are completed if you become a victim. If you become a victim, this helps you stay on task and not miss any important documentation. Truston takes you through a step-by-step process, which takes the complexity out of what to do if you've been a victim.

**Figure 9-5:**
Truston
doesn't
require you
to provide
sensitive
information
when you
use its
services.

Truston offers the following services:

- ✔ **Credit reports:** Ensures you receive your three free credit reports annually.

- ✔ **Identity theft recovery services:** Sends reminder e-mails to ensure that steps are followed and completed.

- ✔ **Prevention services:** Sends out credit bureau fraud alerts, freezes your credit report, stops preapproved credit card offers, and stops telemarketing calls.

- ✔ **Fraud alerts:** Reminds you to place a fraud alert on your credit reports if you have been a victim. Reminds you to set up checking account fraud alerts with Chex Systems.

- ✔ **Database:** Saves all your information — such as who was contacted and when — in a database. Contact information is not saved. Not saving personal information is a good thing because it's one less place that has your personal information.

# Uncovering the Benefits of an Identity Theft Prevention Company

The benefits of subscribing to the services provided by identity theft prevention companies is definitely cheaper than becoming a victim of identity theft. According to a report published by the BBB and the Javelin Strategy & Research identity theft fraud survey in 2004, the average cost per individual victim is $5,686. None of the companies charge more than that for their services. So what are the benefits for using an identity theft prevention company?

Usually when you find out you're an identity theft victim, considerable damage has been done already to your credit and reputation. Therefore, you need to find out whether someone is using your identity to obtain credit as early as possible to minimize the damage. The best solution is to prevent you from becoming a victim in the first place.

Even though someone monitors your credit reports and places fraud alerts or freezes on your report, that does not guarantee that you will never become a victim. What those actions do is ensure that certain tasks are done and certain prevention tools are put in place to help *minimize* your exposure. That's the payoff for paying a yearly or monthly fee for the service. In the following section, I look at how each company addresses disputes it may have with you or any other client.

What can you do? You can place a freeze on your credit report. This can be done whether you're a victim of identity theft or not; however, depending the state you live in, you may incur a cost for the credit freeze for each bureau to place that freeze on the report and to remove it if you are not a victim. The credit freeze can be an issue if you intend to make large purchases with credit. If you plan to do so, hold off placing the freeze until the purchases are complete to save you time and money.

You can pay for credit monitoring from one of the three credit bureaus. If you choose to do this, make sure you opt for the three-in-one credit report, or whatever the bureau uses to monitor all three credit bureau reports at once. By monitoring all three reports, you can get a complete picture of what's happening. Remember, not all creditors report to all three bureaus due to the cost. With monitoring, the bureau will send you an e-mail alert when any changes occur on your credit report within 24 hours of the change. Some also send a quarterly report regarding whether there are any alerts and how many.

You can and should monitor all your financial statements — credit card, bank statements, IRA, and so on — *every month*. You do this to make sure that your financial information hasn't been compromised.

# *Reviewing Dispute Resolution Methods*

When you're collecting information to make a decision about which company to use for protecting your identity, review its policies for addressing disputes. You can find this in the Terms and Conditions or Terms of Use page of a company's Web site. To continue with sign-up, you likely need to accept the terms and conditions or terms of use. You've probably seen similar terms on other Web sites and, like most everyone else, probably don't read them and just click the I Accept button and move on. In this case, you need to read the terms and conditions — in fact, print them so you have them for future reference — to know the company's dispute and cancellation policies. Each company has its own methods for handling disputes. In this section, I briefly outline the dispute resolution methods used by the same five companies I discuss throughout this chapter: LifeLock, ID Watchdog, TrustedID, Identity Guard, and Truston.

# LifeLock

LifeLock uses arbitration to resolve disputes that may arise with its clients. At the top of the home page, click the About Us tab to go to the About LifeLock page. On the left side of the page, click the Terms and Conditions link below the About LifeLock heading. The Terms and Conditions page appears. Scroll down to the Arbitration section, which describes what the current process is to dispute a claim. When you read this section, note the following:

- ✔ You agree to the LifeLock dispute process.
- ✔ All disputes are settled confidentially in Maricopa County, Arizona, which is where LifeLock's corporate office is located.
- ✔ All disputes are addressed by using the American Arbitration Association's (AAA) rules for consumer-related disputes.
- ✔ The parties mutually agree to the selection of the arbitrator.
- ✔ When the consumer and the company can't agree to an arbitrator within 30 days of the notice, the AAA selects an arbitrator.
- ✔ The arbitration hearings are to take place in one day with both sides present supporting evidence. A decision of findings is made within 15 days from the conclusion of the hearing.
- ✔ The decision of the arbitrator is final and binding on both parties.
- ✔ LifeLock will pay for the arbitration. Any other expense will be paid by the party that incurred the expense.
- ✔ You can appeal the decision to any state or federal court.

# ID Watchdog

At the bottom of ID Watchdog's home page is an About Us link, and below that link is the Terms & Conditions link. When you click the Terms & Conditions link, you're taken to the Terms and Conditions page (makes sense, right?). Scroll down to the Dispute Resolution Process section, which involves three steps:

1. Negotiation.

   If you or ID Watchdog has a dispute, both parties agree to a ten-business-day resolution after being notified of the dispute by e-mail or telephone.

2. Mediation.

   If negotiation fails, you move to mediation. ID Watchdog uses the AAA to initiate a phone mediation from Denver, Colorado. This takes place within 15 business days of a failed negotiation.

3. Agreement to Arbitrate.

   If the dispute can't be resolved within 30 days of a failed mediation, an arbitration hearing occurs in Denver, Colorado, at the AAA offices. Both parties attend the arbitration hearing, either in person or by telephone.

If both parties agree to arbitrate as outlined in the agreement, they give up their rights to litigate the claim in court.

# TrustedID

TrustedID calls their terms and conditions *service terms.* To access these terms, find the About Us link at the bottom of Trusted ID's home page. Scroll down the page and click the Service Terms link. This takes you to the Terms and Conditions page. Scroll to the Entire Agreement section at the bottom of the page and read the last paragraph of the section. This is the section that outlines dispute resolution. The following is a summary of the paragraph:

✔ TrustedID uses rules set forth by JAMS (Judicial Arbitration & Mediation Services), which is similar to AAA (American Arbitration Association), to settle disputes. Find out more about each at their respective Web sites:

   ```
   www.jamsadr.com
   www.adr.org
   ```

✔ If the parties can't agree to an arbitrator within 15 days, JAMS will appoint one.

✔ The hearing is to take place in San Francisco, California.

✔ Both parties can seek litigation in the U.S. federal courts located in the Northern District of California.

# Identity Guard

Identity Guard's Terms of Use link can be found at the bottom of the home page. When you click the link, you're taken to the Terms of Use page. Scroll down to the Choice of Law section and read it, especially the part that's in all capital letters. The following is a summary of what the dispute process is for Identity Guard:

✔ The arbitration is binding on the parties and will be held in Washington, D.C.

✔ Identity Guard and you can't consolidate or join any other claim or action in arbitration with any claim or action. In other words, no class action claims.

✔ You agree to accept the laws of the Commonwealth of Virginia and waive the right to laws in your own or other jurisdictions.

✔ Both parties can seek litigation in the U.S. federal courts located in the Commonwealth of Virginia.

# Truston

Truston doesn't collect personal information, it doesn't have a service agreement for you to sign, and you can cancel the service at anytime. Therefore, no terms and conditions are posted on its Web site.

The services are activated and maintained by the user; Truston provides the database for you to track and protect your identity yourself. Truston provides reminders for you to complete the tasks.

# Chapter 10

# Becoming Familiar with Identity Thieves' Scams and Methods

*In This Chapter*

▶ Avoiding scams to get your personal information

▶ Knowing who is asking for your personal information

▶ Catching on to identity thieves' tactics to scam you

*B*ecause identity thieves will stop at nothing to get your personal information, you must maintain a vigilant attitude in thwarting their efforts. Lots of scammers are out there, trying lots of scams on lots of unsuspecting people. I don't want you to be unsuspecting; I want you to be suspicious because being suspicious can save you a lot of heartache and money. To that end, I use this chapter to detail common scams, and I provide a section specifically discussing the methods scammers use to snare victims.

## Being Stingy with Your Personal Information: Don't Give It Out Freely

Identity thieves will stop at nothing to get your personal information. Your best protection is to be aware of your environment and guard your personal information. The following sections offer some guidance to keep you safe.

### Who's calling?

Thieves often call folks and say that they're from a bank or a credit card company. The thief on the phone goes on and asks you for your full name, date of birth, Social Security Number (SSN), and credit card number. Don't fall for these telephone scams, which fall into the category of *social engineering*.

Thieves use a number of scams, and they vary the themes daily. So before you leap and give the person on the other end of the phone the personal information she wants, ask why she needs the information and tell her you'll get back to her after you check out her story. If you don't feel comfortable, don't give the info.

A new trend is to use phone number caller ID spoofing. *Caller ID spoofing* is when a company, person, or so on uses a phone number that doesn't originate from the actual calling party's phone. Numbers like 000-000-0000 display on your caller ID screen. The displayed number may also say Out of Area. Don't answer any number that has all zeros in the caller ID display — it's a spoofed number or is at least being hidden from you. Be suspicious of why someone, or some company, would want to hide his phone number by displaying all zeros.

Other calls display as Private or Unknown Number. People choose these options for various reasons so when they call you, you don't know who's calling until you answer the phone. I don't answer any calls from unknown or private numbers, and I rarely accept calls from numbers I don't recognize.

You can see how thieves can use the call spoofing and private or unknown caller technologies to work their scams. They can easily be anonymous so you don't know who's calling. When you answer, they can scam you with whatever scam, which is usually to get personal information, financial information, and so on.

To be safe, ask for a callback number. If the number came up on your phone's display, search the phone number online at a Web site such as www.anywho.com. If the caller won't give a callback number, hang up — especially if the number's blocked or is displayed as Private or Unknown with no number displayed.

I recommend getting on the Do Not Call Registry. You can register online at www.donotcall.gov.

Give personal information over your landline telephone only to someone that *you* call. This way, you know who's on the line. Just don't give personal information over the telephone in a public place or on your cellphone. If you have only a cellphone (and no landline), be careful what information you provide over the cellphone, especially if you did not initiate the call. Finally, do not give any personal information if you are in a public place on a cellphone even if you initiated the call.

# Phishing out a thief

"Back in the day," as my kids would say, an identity thief would collect the needed information the old-fashioned way — dumpster diving, picking up discarded credit card receipts, rummaging for carbons of credit card receipts, stealing wallets and purses, and eavesdropping.

Today, everyone has the Internet. The Internet contains a wealth of information at your fingertips, and its ease of use makes it a great tool for an identity thief to find those essential numbers (SSN, birth date, personal identification number [PIN], and so on). Identity thieves even use the Internet to have potential targets come to them. For example, have you ever received a spam e-mail asking you to verify some personal information? This technique is *phishing*.

Here's how phishing works: The e-mail, which claims to be from a reputable source, such as your bank or credit card company, requests that you click a link and go to its Web site to make sure that your information is correct. When on the site, you're asked to provide personal information to verify the company's records. Your name, credit card number, the card's expiration date, SSN, date of birth (DOB), and so on is requested. This technique is called *phishing* because the person perpetrating the scam is throwing a *line* or *net* to see who bites. Don't fall for it.

I received one of these e-mails shortly after using an online payment company. The e-mail said that my account would be deleted if I didn't provide the information requested. I didn't have an account with the company, and the timing of the suspect e-mail was actually coincidental and random. (The e-mail message started by saying, "Dear Customer, your account needs to be updated" — it wasn't personalized.) I didn't reply to the message; I just deleted it. However, enough people must answer the e-mail to make the scam successful; otherwise, identity thieves wouldn't use it. Typically, the scam is used for a short period and then the thief shelves it until the media hype and warnings about it die down. Then they use it again with a slightly different message.

Here is a good Web site that provides information on e-mail scams: www.scamdex.com. In the following sections, I detail some of the phishing scams you're likely to encounter. Having some knowledge of these scams can help you avoid falling victim to them.

### Nigerian phishing scam

The old Nigerian letter scam (named as such because the scam originated in Nigeria) is also being perpetrated online, with a different spin, but the scam is the same: An e-mail states that the sender has a large sum of money he wants to transfer out of whatever country he's sending the e-mail from. What he wants you to do is help him move the money to your bank account, and he'll pay 20 percent or more of the amount for your help. Of course, he sucks you in with the lure of millions of dollars. He asks for your bank account number and the bank routing number so he can transfer the money. After he gets the account number, he cleans out your bank account, and you end up with nothing.

Another similar scam is when you are selling something and advertise it on eBay or Craigslist. The buyer says that he will send a cashier's check for more than the amount you have listed in your ad. You think that's pretty good. After all, who wouldn't want more than expected? What the scammer wants you to do is cash the cashier's check, keep the amount for the item and shipping, plus a little extra, and then send the difference back to the buyer. The only problem is, the cashier's check is no good, so when the bank finds out, you're out all the money plus the item.

Don't fall for a scam like this even it sounds plausible; it isn't. Don't give anyone your account number. My advice is *do not* correspond with these thieves; just delete the e-mail. I get these e-mails once in awhile, and I just delete them. These e-mails are spam, and you are not being targeted directly because the e-mails are sent out to large numbers of people at one time.

I get several of these e-mails in my Hotmail account and very few on my other e-mail account. Most of the time, the sender gets my name wrong, and these e-mails go to my junk mail folder. Here's an actual e-mail I received the other day. I have not edited the message; this is exactly how it looked when I received it:

> Dear, Friend,
>
> I am Mr. So-and-So, Managing Director, Barclays Bank Plc, London, United Kingdom. I am writing about an opportunity in my office that will be of immense benefit to us both.
>
> On January 11, 2000, a German estate tycoon, the late Mr. Andreas Schranner, deposited £10,000,000 (British pounds sterling) under our portfolio management department for a period of two (2) years, and the deposit matured on February 18, 2002, with over 100-percent growth, which amounted to a total of £20,520,000 (British pounds sterling).

Upon maturity, a routine notification was sent to his forwarding address, all to no avail. We made several attempts to contact him but without responses. After a month, another reminder was sent to him from my desk, and evidently, I discovered from his contract employers that Mr. Schranner died in the Air France Concorde Flight 4590 plane crash on July 25, 2000. Upon further in-depth investigation, I discovered that he died with his wife and entire family, as all efforts to trace members of his neither family nor relatives proved futile. You can read more about the crash by visiting this site: `http://news.bbc.co.uk/1/hi/world/europe/859479.stm`.

Mr. Schranner has long passed away, and since his death, none of his next of kin or relations has come forward to claim this money as the heir. He died without informing anybody about these funds, which have since matured, and the rollover on the funds has also expired. This sum of ₤20,520,000 (British pounds sterling) is still in my possession in my bank — lifeless and unnoticed — because there no one will ever claim these funds. All materials, immaterial documents and certificates relating to the funds, are also in my possession.

Against this backdrop, I propose you to stand in as the next of kin to the late Mr. Andreas Schranner. The banking laws and guidelines stipulate that at the expiration of eight (8) years, such funds will be transferred into banking treasury as unclaimed funds. The money will be approved into your account and subsequently, we shall share in the ratio: 60 percent for our bank and 40 percent for you as gratification for assistance rendered. I will visit your country for the disbursement, according to the percentages indicated earlier after this money gets into your account.

Let me crave your indulgence in portraying sincerity toward this matter as trust stands to be our watchword in this transaction. Our assurance is that your role is risk-free to accord this transaction the legality it deserves. With all modalities in place, we are certain in actualizing a hitch-free funds transfer without any impediments. My position with this bank already guarantees the swift execution of this project. We'll discuss much in details when I do receive your response. Kindly signify your willingness to assist by sending me a message for further procedures relating to this transaction.

The thief doesn't ask for bank account information at first; after you correspond with him, he'll ask for the info to make the transfer. This e-mail offered me a 40 percent cut for my assistance. Now you can see how thieves prey on people's greed. The conversion of ₤20,520,000 (British pounds sterling) is equivalent to $33,406,438 (U.S. dollars). The amount he'd give you is $13,362,575. Sounds great doesn't it? All you have to do is give him your bank account information or deposit a bogus check into your account. Tempting? Remember: Nobody gives you something for nothing.

### Other phishing scams

Be alert to e-mails that are sent to you about job offers for jobs you didn't apply for. Remember: If something sounds too good to be true, it is! Don't be duped into taking one of the jobs even if you're unemployed. Do your homework and check out any company at which you're interested in applying for employment. Following are some common phishing scams:

- **Work-from-home scam:** These are the e-mails claiming that you can earn thousands working from home. All you have to do is send the thief some money to get the information so you can get started. Some work-from-home programs are legitimate. Check out work-from-home companies with the Better Business Bureau (BBB) or the FTC. Also, perform an online search for *scams*.

- **Overseas check-cashing scam:** The thief asks via e-mail whether you'll cash overseas checks so that the funds will be in U.S. dollars. This is basically a scam to take your money. Here's how it works: You're the money manager or accountant for the company. The thief claims it's easier to have all the funds in U.S. currency, so she asks you to give her your bank account so she can directly deposit a check in your account. But she has no checks, and guess what, she cleans out your bank account. If she sends you a check, it's usually fraudulent and you're stuck for the full check amount because it was deposited into your account. How can you tell whether the offer is a scam? Here are some things to watch for:

  - *Bank account numbers:* Legitimate employers don't ask for that information.

  - *SSN:* All employers will eventually ask for a SSN, but be careful. Don't be so eager to give your SSN, especially for an unsolicited job offer in your e-mail.

  - *Driver's license:* Although two forms of identification are needed when you start a new job, the employer doesn't ask to scan your license before an employment offer is made. The reason for the identification is to verify citizenship.

  - *Spelling and grammatical errors.*

  - *Red flags:* For instance, Monster.com lists words that tip off fraud. These include *package-forwarding, money transfers, wiring funds, eBay* unless the ad is an eBay job posting, *PayPal* unless the ad is a PayPal job posting, and *Foreign Agent Agreement.*

✔ **Reshipping merchandise scam:** The thief offers for you to work as a shipping clerk (or whatever title she assigns to the job). Your job is to repackage and reship the merchandise to places overseas. The reason she gives for repackaging and reshipping is that it's easier to ship the merchandise. The real reason for doing this repackaging and reshipping is that the items are purchased with stolen credit cards and when the items are repackaged and shipped, they're hard to trace. However, the stolen property is shipped to your address and you're the one that'll be on the hook when law enforcement knocks on the door with a search warrant for stolen property. This scheme has been shown on NBC's *Dateline.*

✔ **FDIC (Federal Deposit Insurance Corporation) phishing scam:** You receive an e-mail that appears to originate from a financial institution, a government agency, or another well-known/reputable entity. The message describes an urgent reason you must verify or resubmit personal or confidential information by clicking a link embedded in the message. The provided link appears to be the Web site of the reputable entity, but in phishing scams, the Web site belongs to the thief.

When on the fraudulent Web site, you may be asked to provide your SSN, account numbers, passwords, or other information used to identify the consumer, such as your mother's maiden or your birthplace. After you provide the information, the thief can access consumer accounts or assume your identity.

Recently e-mail phishing scams have claimed to come from other federal government agencies, such as the IRS and FBI. In the e-mail, the scammer asks for personal information under the guise that it's official business and you must comply. The government agencies *do not ask* for your personal information in e-mails. These e-mails get you to give up your personal information by using the fear tactic that if you don't comply, you'll be in trouble with the agency and could be prosecuted for a crime. The e-mail phishing perpetrators use spam mail to reach as many e-mail accounts as possible in the hopes of hooking some unsuspecting persons. Become educated about e-mail phishing scams so you don't fall prey to these thieves and lose your identity and hard-earned money.

Going online is an easy way to check out a company. You can just Google the company's name or search for *phishing* to read up on scams at other sites. The BBB offers advice to job seekers as well as info on reshipping and package-forwarding job schemes.

Never give anyone personal information when it's solicited in an e-mail unless you know the party that's asking for the information. Be careful when completing an online survey, especially if it asks for personal information of any kind.

---

# Homeland Security scam

In a scam that surfaced recently, the Patriot Act and the FDIC are being used fraudulently to get your personal information. Here's how the scam works: An e-mail is sent stating that the Secretary of the Department of Homeland Security has advised the FDIC to suspend all deposit insurance on your bank accounts because of suspected Patriot Act violations.

The e-mail goes on to say that all deposit insurance will be suspended until your personal identity, including bank account information, can be verified. The FDIC has distributed an alert stating that the e-mail is fraudulent and further warns that clicking the link in the e-mail may activate an Exploit-URLSpoof.gen virus.

The FDIC has set up an alert repository at alert@fdic.gov that you can use to report receipt of one of these e-mails.

## They're from the government

The government doesn't ask you for information in a public way, such as in an e-mail. If it needs to collect information — especially if you're suspected to be in violation of something like the Patriot Act, as I describe in the sidebar "Homeland Security scam" — a subpoena or search warrant is needed.

Table 10-1 gives you an idea of some of the information the government has about you. Most of the information is collected as a matter of record keeping, such as birth certificates, property tax rolls, real estate owned, and so on.

| Table 10-1 | Government Information |
|---|---|
| *Document* | *Level of Government* |
| Birth certificate | County and state |
| Driver's license number | State |
| Your address | Federal, state, and local |
| Real estate owned | County |
| SSN | Federal (IRS) |
| Criminal records | Federal, state, and local |
| Financial | Federal, state, and local |
| Property taxes rolls | County |
| Income tax documents | Federal, state, and local |
| Vehicle registration | State |
| Passport | Federal |

You provide the information in Table 10-1 when you apply for a driver's license, passport, or Social Security card, purchase property, record property, or commit criminal offenses for which you've been convicted — things along those lines.

Most of the documents in Table 10-1 are considered public records, and anyone can get access to them. Some documents, such as your birth certificate (in some states), SSN, tax information, and financial records, are not public. Even the government needs to obtain a subpoena or search warrant before it can examine your financial records.

# Why financial information?

Your financial information is the key to your identity, and you need to protect it. Ask yourself this question: Why does that business need my SSN anyway? You need to be suspicious of anyone asking you for financial information.

If someone asks for your financial information in an e-mail, something isn't right. Any financial institution you've done business with knows your financial information. If someone there wants to update your files, he won't request the information to be updated via e-mail. If you've done business with that company in the past, you probably know its Web site address, and the institution would need to provide that link in an e-mail message.

To know whether the link to the Web site launches a real site, look for the VeriSign logo. The logo indicates that the site is authentic.

When you feel comfortable with a site and are going to perform a transaction of some kind, look for the lock at the bottom-right corner of your browser window before you complete a form or an application. Make sure that the lock is locked. This way, you know that anything you transmit is encrypted. If you don't see the lock or there isn't another indication that the information is going to be sent encrypted over the Internet, *don't provide the information.*

# Bank examiner scam

The phony bank examiner scam has been around for a long, long time. This scam must be effective because every now and then, you hear about someone being victimized by it.

Here's how the scam works: Someone poses as a bank examiner or a bank officer. In a phone call, the thief tells the victim that she's a bank officer where the victim has an account. Because of a computer glitch or some other problem, the bank must verify some information. The caller then asks the victim about his account balance, any recent activity, and so on. Next, the scammer tries to determine whether the victim lives alone and if the phony bank officer is successful in obtaining the needed information, the caller thanks the victim and tells him she'll call back if any problems occur.

The scammer calls back after a brief period of time and asks the victim again for assistance in catching a dishonest teller the bank suspects of stealing from customers' accounts, including the victim's account. The victim is asked to withdraw a large sum of money from his account and turn it over to a *bank examiner*.

The scammer posing as a bank examiner tells the victim that a *dummy* account has been set up in his name for the transaction. Assurances are made that the account that's been set up is fully insured, and the victim won't lose any money to the dishonest teller. The victim then withdraws the agreed upon amount.

The scammer uses scare tactics to convince you to help. She tells you that your bank account is being drained, and if you don't act soon, you'll have no money left in the account — the crooks will have it all.

A meeting is then arranged between the victim and the phony bank examiner, and at the meeting, the victim is told by the phony bank examiner that the money actually came from the *dummy* account and not the victim's account — and the money is needed as evidence. The phony bank examiner gives the victim a receipt for the money. The victim never sees the money or the phony bank examiner again.

In another variation of the scheme, the phony bank examiner asks that the victim withdraw the money and mark the bills. The money is given to the phony bank examiner, who says she'll re-deposit the money to see whether the teller in question alters the deposit slip. The victim's money and the phony bank examiner are never seen or heard from again.

A bank examiner or a law enforcement officer would never ask you to use your own money in any investigation. Besides, financial institutions never involve their customers in their investigations.

The old tried-and-true bank examiner scheme is still perpetrated today because it works, and fraudsters or con artists will use whatever works to separate you from your money. This scheme is usually perpetrated against elderly Americans; they're most vulnerable because they're easy to convince and often fall for the scheme because they want to help.

Most scams work because they play to the victim's trusting nature. Know the telltale signs of a scam so you just hang up the phone when you hear it. If it sounds too good to be true, it's probably a scam of some kind.

# A Method to Their Madness: How Identity Thieves Suck You In

As I've said time and time again, identity thieves will stop at nothing to get your personal information. That means you have to be proactive to thwart their efforts and to protect yourself. In earlier sections of this chapter, I outline ways to be careful while doing business over the phone or the Web and also how to recognize popular scams used by identity thieves. In this section, I discuss the general tactics that scammers use. Scams are constantly changing, evolving, and becoming more sophisticated, but identity thieves tend to continue using the same methods over and over again. If you can recognize these methods, you can avoid the scam — even if it's one you aren't familiar with — and save yourself from becoming a victim.

Popular means of attack that identity thieves use include preying on your

- ✔ **Emotions and dreams:** This attack includes offering you free or easy money in the form of prizes, lottery winnings, and fake inheritances.

- ✔ **Fear of being hurt:** This attack comes with a threat to hurt you either financially (e-mails that are supposedly security alerts from your bank and so forth) or physically.

- ✔ **Need to feel accepted:** Some people feel that they do not fit in. When someone comes along and makes them feel like they are wanted, they fall prey to the scammer.

- ✔ **Fear of authority:** In this attack, the thief poses as the IRS, Homeland Security, and so on. See the "Homeland Security scam" sidebar and the "Other phishing scams" section, both earlier in this chapter, for more about this type of scam.

- ✔ **Curiosity:** Here you're enticed with current events, gossip, or supposed pictures of yourself online.

- ✔ **Dream of love:** The old online dating scam.

- ✔ **Dream of a good career or car:** Thieves send you e-mails requesting your resumé or job applications for identity theft or a great deal on a car (an unbelievable deal when you're buying/selling a car, usually involving a wire transfer).

In addition, this list highlights a few general red flags that need to raise your suspicion:

- ✔ **Requests for personal information:** The requests might ask for your birth date, mother's maiden name, SSN, account information, driver's license information, or information about habits/location (such as when are you going on vacation or when do you typically leave the house?).

✔ **Sense of urgency or secrecy:** Scams usually try to impress a sense of urgency so you don't have time to check on them or have second thoughts. Others will threaten you if secrecy about the situation is broken. The more you're being pressured to act instantly or give information instantly, the more you need to be suspicious.

✔ **Too good to be true:** If it seems to be too good to be true, it probably is.

Finally, be wary of the following:

✔ **Transactions involving checks:** Even when your bank makes a balance available to you, that doesn't mean the check has cleared completely. Depositing a check, wiring money, or taking out cash can leave you high and dry when the check turns out to be no good.

✔ **Transactions involving wire transfers or Western Union:** This is one of the few ways you can send money and never see it again.

✔ **Suspicious authority figures:** Make sure that you are really looking at the authority figure you think you are. You may tend to see only the uniform and not the face. Look for badge numbers, official vehicles, and other signs of authority. Never be afraid to ask if you can call corporate or headquarters to verify. You may even ask to call 911 for backup, if you're concerned that the "police officer" that pulled you over is a phony.

I leave you with this one last thought: As far as means-of-attack go, think about how many ways there are to contact you. There have been reports of scams by e-mail, text message, fax machine, snail mail, TTY, classifieds, online dating, online auctions, instant messages, social networking, fake UPS drivers, fake census workers, fake BBB representatives . . . .

# Part V
# Safeguarding Electronic Information

## The 5th Wave
By Rich Tennant

"Don't be silly - of course my passwords are safe.
I keep them written on my window, but then I
pull the shade if anyone walks in the room."

# In this part . . .

These days, most people use computers on a daily basis. So much of your personal information is on your computer and online. By following the guidelines I detail here, you can make it more difficult for identity thieves to get any sensitive information about you that's on the Internet. I also show you how to get the most from your computer's security features.

# Chapter 11

# Staying Safe from Online Threats

*B*eing secure online is critical to protecting your identity. Think of all the information that's available about you on the Internet. Years ago, finding out information about anyone took some effort. You had to search public records in person and through other sources. Today, all you need to do is to search the Internet. Just do a Google search on your name and see what comes up. This isn't the only search engine; think of all the others search engines that are available. Think of the sites you visit, especially social networking sites. How much information do you post about yourself, family, and friends? Even if you keep it private, do your friends keep it private? Social networking sites can be dangerous to your personal information.

In this chapter, I first give you a few tips on shopping safely online. Then I discuss in some detail how you can be more secure on the Internet by keeping your antivirus protection up-to-date, by putting security safeguards (such as encryption and spyware blockers) in place, and by devising a security plan.

## Ordering Stuff Online

Purchasing merchandise online is incredibly easy, but you must protect yourself. Here are several tips for safely ordering stuff online by using an online pay service from the HowStuffWorks Web site, `http://money.howstuffworks.com/identity-theft.htm`:

✔ **Use a smart card.** When you use a smart card, the amount of the purchase is subtracted from the balance on the card, just like when you use a debit or credit card. A *smart card* is the same size and shape of a credit card but has an imbedded microprocessor inside the card. This makes the data on the card harder to change or read than magnetic strips do on other cards. On the smart card, the data is imbedded into the card so the card carries the intelligence. Without the reader, the card cannot be read, thus providing tamper proof protection of data on the card.

✔ **Use a one-time use credit card number for online purchases.** This comes from your bank, has a different number than your actual account number, and is good for the single transaction. This prevents you from exposing your credit card number online or through malware you may not be aware exists on your computer.

✔ **Use a stored value card.** This is like a prepaid phone card — you purchase the card with a certain dollar amount, and each time you use it, the purchase amount is subtracted from the balance.

✔ **Use e-wallet software.** This software is secure and allows you to purchase items by letting the merchant's server send a message to your PC. Then you select the card that's defined in your "wallet" to make the purchase.

✔ **Use digital cash.** This is a series of credits you purchase that are stored on your PC. You spend these credits by making purchases over the Internet.

✔ **Use an online payment service.** Through this service, you can set up an account and make purchases drawing from that account.

The most common method for purchasing items online is to use a credit card. The following tips from the HowStuffWorks site helps you make purchasing merchandise on the Internet more secure:

✔ **Use the latest Internet browser.** The browser allows you to navigate the Internet and provides encryption. Encryption scrambles data sent to a server to protect it. When you use the most recent browser version, you're also using the latest encryption version.

✔ **Only use one credit card to make purchases on the Internet.** This way, you can track your purchases and activity on the card more easily. This is a good way to keep a record of all your Internet transactions to help ensure accuracy of your card's charges. If the card is compromised, you can cancel it and get a new one. These days, online sites request the security code to complete the transaction, just as it is for phone orders. Merchants ask for the security code to help protect them from fraudulent charges, and the code also helps protect you because the identity thief has to get the code to complete the transaction.

✔ **Look for digital certificates and the VeriSign logo, which authenticate the Web site you're accessing.** When you click the VeriSign logo, you can be assured that the site is legitimate and not a redirect or a clone.

✔ **Check your e-mail for confirmation from the merchant after you complete a purchase.** Merchants usually send you an e-mail to confirm the order and to tell you when the item will be shipped.

✔ **Read the Web site's privacy policy.** This should let you know that personal information you provide will be kept confidential and not sold or disclosed to others.

✔ **Don't give your password or ID online unless you know who you're dealing with, even if your Internet service provider (ISP) asks for it via e-mail.** This request is a scam and is used by identity thieves to collect personal information.

# Understanding Common Online Threats

You can assess what online threats might plague you by determining what you're going to do with your computer:

✔ **Are you going to search the Web?** Numerous viruses and other malware on the Internet cause major security issues for you and your private information.

✔ **Are you going to gaming sites?** If you're going to gaming Web sites, your computer's security features need to be the strongest possible because these sites are known to have viruses and other malware built into them.

✔ **Are you going to download music?** Downloading music from Web sites is also a security risk, and you need stronger security to ensure that you don't infect your computer.

Eighty percent of legitimate Web sites have malware on them as noted in the report at

```
www.redorbit.com/news/technology/1707131/
           legitimate_Websites_suffer_losses_due_to_malware/
```

So, any Web site is potentially dangerous. Currently the most dangerous Web sites are social networking sites and those that use peer-to-peer downloading applications. Even searches using search engines can be dangerous because hackers use current trends to infect search results.

A red flag that your system is infected is that your computer is running slower than usual. If you aren't sure that your system is infected, take it to a professional to check it (that is, if you don't feel comfortable checking the system).

Common online threats include keylogger software, spyware/adware, Trojan horses, e-mail from unknown sources, and cookies. I describe each in turn in the following sections.

## Keylogger software

The *keylogger* is a program that logs every keystroke you make on your keyboard when typing, which the thief can then see. The main job of the keystroke logger is to capture your user IDs and passwords. When the thief gets your bank user ID and password, he can log on to your bank account. Some banks have added another layer of protection that doesn't let you log in if you're working on a different computer than the one you originally signed up with for online banking.

Keylogger software is generally imbedded in other software and delivered to your computer system with spyware.

## Spyware/adware

*Spyware* is a program that collects information about you without your knowledge. Most spyware isn't dangerous, but some contain viruses and other malware. Some spyware has a greater risk than other spyware programs.

*Adware* serves advertisements to your computer that you didn't consent to having displayed. Most adware is spyware. Adware and spyware are similar to viruses because they can be considered to be malicious in nature.

## Trojan horses

The *Trojan horse* is loaded onto your computer, again without your knowledge, when you open or download a seemingly innocent program. The keylogger, for instance, is imbedded with a Trojan horse.

Trojan horses are used to plant other malware programs on your computer. Some uses are

- ✔ **To hijack your computer and set it up as a zombie for delivering a denial-of-service attack (DOS):** The DOS prevents access to Internet servers because a large number of requests are sent to it at once during the attack.

- ✔ **To hijack your Internet session:** This brings you to the hijacker's bogus site, such as a banking site, to capture your personal information.

## E-mails from unknown sources

E-mail attachments are used to carry viruses; when you open the attachment, the virus is then released on your computer. In some cases, after you open the e-mail carrying the virus, the virus is then sent to everyone listed in your Address Book. E-mail attachments also carry Trojan horses that are activated when you open the attachment.

Don't open e-mail attachments from unknown senders, especially in messages that go to your junk mail account. These messages can often come from unfriendly sources — the type that would send you a virus in an e-mail.

Set up a filter in your e-mail account so unsolicited e-mails go to the junk mail folder and not your inbox. Most e-mail providers, such as Yahoo! and Hotmail, automatically set up mail filters to help you weed out junk mail. This is why some e-mails from people you know end up in the junk mail file until you add them to your Address Book.

Although your antivirus software will scan e-mail attachments for viruses (and some e-mail providers, such as Yahoo! and Hotmail, provide this service with the e-mail subscription), you still need to apply a little common sense when opening e-mail attachments. Before opening an e-mail with an attachment (denoted by the paperclip icon next to the sender's name), ask these questions:

- ✔ **Were you expecting the e-mail from someone you know?** If you answer yes, it's probably safe to open the message.

    However, before you do, determine whether the attachment is important to you. The e-mail could be a chain e-mail that's being passed around from e-mail account to e-mail account, in which case, you don't want to open it. I usually don't open these attachments (even from someone I know) because I'm leery that an attachment that's been passed from person to person might have originated from an unsavory source.

- ✔ **Is this person in your main e-mail address book, and have you received previous e-mails from her?** If yes, you can likely safely open this message.

✔ **Does the description of the e-mail in the subject line make sense to you?** If not, proceed with caution. Your best course of action might be to delete the message without opening it.

✔ **Do you recognize the person's e-mail address (even if you haven't received mail from her before)?** If not, don't open the attachment, and better yet, don't open the e-mail.

## Cookies

A *cookie* is a sample piece of text from a Web site you visited that your browser stores on your computer. These cookies make it easier for the Web browser to open that Web page the next time you visit it. Cookies track where you go on the Internet (for marketing purposes). If you're like me, you don't want to have your Web surfing habits watched by anyone for any reason — good or bad. Because cookies are a piece of text, they aren't executable (a file that opens a program or does something else), which is good news. Here are the two types of cookies:

✔ **Temporary:** Temporary cookies, or *session cookies,* are deleted as soon as you end the session (that is, leave that particular site). Temporary cookies are a way to speed up going to a particular site if you have been there before and they are usually not malicious in nature.

✔ **Permanent:** Permanent cookies are more persistent, are stored on your computer's hard drive, and can be dangerous to your computer because they can be Trojan horses or other malicious programs. Permanent cookies can also harbor viruses.

Permanent cookies were made to keep information you may have entered on a site so that when you return to that site, you can retrieve the information. For instance, when you complete an online job application and return to that site, the cookie allows you to retrieve the information you previously typed; without the cookie, you have to start a new session, and the information isn't available.

Most cookies are harmless, but they're still something to keep an eye on. (At the very least, too many cookies on your hard drive can make your computer sluggish.) Most antivirus protection programs find cookies and then you can delete them from your system. If the cookie is from a site you visit often and the security threat level identified by the antivirus program is really low, you may want to keep the cookie. The decision is up to you, but at least you know that the cookie is on your hard drive.

# *Implementing Security through Windows Security Center*

In the last section of this chapter, I show you how to devise a security plan. You'll have a good start toward outlining one after you identify your computer system's safeguards — and implement others — which I discuss in this and the following section. Computers purchased today come with a one-year subscription to antivirus software and your Internet service provider (ISP) comes with a firewall. Microsoft has a Security Shield program installed in Windows XP and Vista. To access Security Shield, click the Start button, and then choose Control Panel➪Security Shield.

To find out what protection systems you're currently running on your computer, take a look at your computer's Security Center. On Windows 7, click the Start button and then choose Control Panel➪System and Security➪ Action Center. On Windows Vista, click the Start button and then choose Control Panel➪Windows Security Center.

The Action Center/Security Center shows whether your antivirus protection and firewall are running and whether Automatic Updates is on. These updates are from Microsoft and are important to patch any security holes that may be present in the Windows operating system. Automatic Updates ensures that your system is up-to-date and all the latest patches are installed. If you don't use Automatic Updates, you need to check for updates. This can be an arduous task because you don't know when updates are available for downloading. To find the latest updates, go to Microsoft's Web site and check for updates under the Windows version you're running. See Chapter 12 for more about Windows security.

If antivirus protection, Automatic Updates, and the firewall are on, you have some safeguards in place. Like any product or system, some are better than others; later in this chapter, I look at some of the products on the market for antivirus protection and firewalls. Some of the firewall products are free, and you can bundle some with your antivirus protection. Keep in mind, free antivirus protection systems aren't as good as the subscription services you can purchase. Other protective programs you can install on your computer include spyware blockers and a proxy server. I discuss these and others later in this chapter.

Be careful what software you download from the Internet. Some software programs (EXE) are safe to run (or *connect*); other programs could be dangerous to run. If your antivirus protection is up-to-date, when you attempt to download software that's infected with viruses, your antivirus protection lets you know. Your firewall alerts you if an EXE (executable) the firewall rule set doesn't recognize is trying to run; the firewall will ask whether you want to run the EXE. Be wary of any EXE you don't recognize as something your system runs on a regular basis. An example of an EXE that runs daily is the Microsoft updates. The EXE goes to the update Web site for the particular software to search for and gets updates.

If you're using a wireless laptop computer, make sure that you've installed virus and firewall protection as you would on any computer. However, here are several points you need to consider to secure your wireless connection.

- ✔ **Change the default administrator's password.** You do this by clicking the Start button, and then choosing Control Panel⇨User Accounts. In the User Accounts dialog box, click Change an Account, and a new screen appears. Under Pick an Account to Change, you see two choices: Computer Administrative or Guest.

- ✔ **Turn on WPA/WEP encryption.** WPA stands for Wi-Fi Protected Access, and WEP stands for Wired Equivalent Privacy. Encryption scrambles the transmission so it can't be read.

- ✔ **Don't auto-connect to open Wi-Fi networks in your neighborhood.** Doing so can expose your network or computer to security breaches.

By developing and following a security plan, you can help keep your information online safe. The security plan is simple, and I discuss devising one in the section "Devising a Security Plan" later in this chapter.

# Identifying and Implementing Other Security Safeguards

To secure your electronic information, you must know your risks (as I describe earlier, in the "Understanding Common Online Threats" section), but you must also take certain precautions, such as these (this list isn't all inclusive):

- ✔ **Installing and regularly updating antivirus protection on your computer:** You can set up the antivirus software to automatically check for and install updates. What could be easier than that?

✔ **Installing and regularly updating a firewall:** Your ISP provides limited firewall protection, but I strongly recommend that you get another firewall. You can download free firewalls, which I discuss further in the following section.

✔ **Performing regular backups of important files and folders:** This precaution won't keep your system safe, but making backups now can save you time and effort later, in case your computer becomes infected. You don't want to lose important information because you didn't make a backup.

✔ **Using strong passwords to protect your data:** Don't make it easy on thieves. The harder it is for a thief to guess your password, the less likely the thief can get to your information.

I discuss these and other safeguards throughout the following sections.

## Firewall and antivirus software

You can determine whether the firewall and antivirus protection programs are running by going to the Windows Action Center/Security Center (for details, see the section "Implementing Security through Windows Action Center" earlier in this chapter), or you can look at the lower-right corner of your screen (to the left of the clock); this area is known as the *notification area*. The icon for the antivirus and firewall programs appears in this area if they're running. Right-click an icon to see a menu (which might vary, depending on the company), offering you choices, such as

✔ **Home (or Open):** This option takes you to the main software screen. From the main screen, you can navigate through various pages to change settings, to view and set the Automatic Updates schedule, and so on.

For antivirus protection software, you also see a manual-sweep screen so you can sweep your computer for viruses. You can also schedule automatic virus sweeps of your computer in the wee hours of the morning when you aren't using your computer.

Running the sweep while you're using the computer slows down your system, but you can still work if you choose to have the scans done while you're awake. To get to the firewall's main screen, right-click the icon at the bottom right in the notification area. The firewall program works the same way.

✔ **Options:** Provides information of what the options are in the program and what features are available.

✓ **Shut Down:** This link shuts down the program entirely, leaving you with no protection.

✓ **Schedule:** Use this option to schedule automatic scans of your computer.

✓ **Check for Updates:** To make sure that you have the latest version of your virus and firewall programs, see whether the program is set to get updates automatically. Doing this varies, depending on the program you use. To schedule automatic updates, use the following *very general* steps (the steps for your particular software might vary):

1. Click the icon for the program, firewall, or antivirus protection and then go to the main menu.

2. Click the options or updates.

   For my firewall program, I go to the Miscellaneous folder to check for updates.

3. After you arrive at updates or check for updates, whichever language is used, click the link to see whether there are updates available.

   As I state previously, most of the antivirus programs have an Automatic Updates option. The firewall programs, on the other hand, may not have an automatic update feature. The firewall program lets you know whether updates are available and whether you need to manually get them.

4. Download the updates to your computer and then restart it for the updates to take effect.

   For antivirus protection, you don't need to restart your computer for most of the updates.

✓ **Help:** Click to find information about how to do something in the program.

### Buying a firewall program

Having a firewall from your ISP is a good start. But you may want to purchase a firewall from a company that provides your antivirus protection. Or perform an online search for *firewall* and download some free ones. I use *Comodo,* a free firewall program; it works well and is easy to install. All you have to do is download the program and keep the default settings. With Comodo firewall, I haven't had any issues, but prior to using it, I had issues with my computer and had to clean it up even while running an updated antivirus program.

To download the Comodo firewall:

1. **Go to www.comodo.com and then click the Internet Security link under the Popular Downloads on the left side of Comodo's home page.**

   Don't confuse this link with the Internet Security menu on the right side of the page.

You're taken to the Comodo Internet Security-Free Version page.

2. **Click the Free Download button and follow the onscreen directions to complete the download.**

Below the Free Download button are tabs that explain more about the product. These tabs include

✔ **Overview:** Provides an outline of what the program will do.

✔ **Features:** Describes the program's features.

✔ **Frequent Questions:** The typical questions asked by users (with answers), such as

- *Can you install only the firewall or only the antivirus protection?*

  The answer is yes; you can install only the components you want.

- *What's the difference between the Free version and the Pro version?*

  The only difference is that the Pro version also provides TrustConnect total Wi-Fi protection and LivePCSupport. TrustConnect protects your connection to a wireless network. LivePCSupport is the technical services provided by the company. You can call them for technical questions about the product. If you have a wireless system, get the Pro version to ensure that you have a secure connection to the Internet with a Wi-Fi connection.

✔ **Support:** Provides answers to your technical questions about the product.

✔ **Video:** A training video you can watch online to explain how the program works.

### Putting protective programs in the Startup menu

After you determine that you have antivirus and firewall programs to help keep you safe online, make sure that the firewall and antivirus protection is in the Startup menu on the desktop. This is important because you want to these programs running in the background when you start your computer. If the software was installed when you purchased the computer, the software is in the Startup menu, which means that when you start your computer, the firewall and antivirus protections boot up as well.

### Understanding rule sets

When you purchase or download a firewall program, you may want to use the default settings for the *rule sets,* which basically tell the firewall what to block. Anything that isn't in the rule set isn't blocked. A rule set details what you want blocked from connecting to your computer. The rule sets block *packets* (data being sent) and Web site addresses. The default rule sets provide adequate protection for you to surf the Internet.

As you surf the 'Net or if your antivirus software is updating, you get a firewall notification. The notification tells what program, or the site address, that is trying to connect to the Internet, and it asks whether you accept or block the connection. The alerts can come when you surf the 'Net or one of your programs attempts to update by connecting to the 'Net.

If you recognize the program that's trying to connect, accept it; if not, you can block it or go to the firewall's main page to get more information. You can manually block Web sites, but I recommend that you use the default settings unless you're computer-savvy. Otherwise, you could block your Internet connection and other applications that you need to run.

You can block network zones and applications, define accepted applications, view firewall events, and so on.

## Spyware blocker

As I discuss earlier in this chapter, *spyware* is a program that secretly collects information about you. Generally, spyware isn't dangerous, although some spyware contains viruses and other malware. Your antivirus program identifies spyware that's on your computer, tells you the threat level that the spyware poses, and gives you the chance to delete the spyware (and any other issues). To delete the spyware, select the check box next to it and then click either the Delete button or the Quarantine button.

Quarantining renders the spyware harmless. To delete the quarantined spyware permanently, go to the quarantined spyware, click Select All, and then click the Delete button. To read the quarantine log, click the Quarantined Spyware button. I recommend deleting any spyware your antivirus program finds.

You can download adware blocker programs for free. These programs scan your system for adware programs and then you can delete them from your computer. You can have them scan automatically or you can do so manually.

## Proxy server

A *proxy server* sits between you and the Internet and intercepts all requests to the real server (that is, your computer) to see whether it can take care of the request; if it can't, it passes the request on to the real server. Think of a proxy server as someone doing your bidding. For example, if you own any shares of stocks, before the annual stockholders' meeting, you receive a proxy vote request because you have only a fraction of shares and, therefore, don't attend the meeting. After you send the proxy form back with how you want the stockholders to vote, someone places your vote on the issue that goes before the stockholders.

Proxy servers do two things:

- ✔ Improve performance by saving requests for a certain amount of time.
- ✔ Filter requests by preventing access to certain Web sites.

Many companies use proxy servers to restrict access to certain Web sites. Some of these sites contain adult material that's inappropriate for the work environment, and others, such as music or gaming, are restricted to prevent viruses and Trojan horses from entering the network and infecting the servers.

*TrustConnect* is a secure Internet proxy service that encrypts all the data you send over wireless connections, which prevents hackers from accessing your private information.

## Pop-up blocker

A *pop-up blocker* does just that — it prevents pop-up ads and other pop-up banners from constantly appearing onscreen while you're on the Internet. Most Web browsers come with a pop-up blocker. You can toggle the blocker on/off by choosing Tools⇨Pop-Up Blocker (Internet Explorer) or by choosing Tools⇨Options⇨Content (Firefox). Internet Explorer comes with its pop-up blocker already on. Both browsers enable you to set exceptions, and Explorer enables you to choose among High, Medium, and Low settings.

## Backups

Back up important files and folders at least monthly. Some companies provide that service, and even encryption software companies provide backup storage space. Some antivirus protection programs offer backup space as well. This is mainly to back up your operating system configuration, not your files and folders. A lot of your personal information might be contained within important files. Losing the information on your hard drive is a real pain if your computer crashes or your laptop is stolen. Sometimes the data can be retrieved; other times, it's lost forever. So it pays to back up your data.

## Encryption

When storing personal information on your computer in files and folders, encrypt the files and folders just in case someone gets control of your computer. The encrypted files and folders will be useless to him. You may be asking: How does encryption work? Simply put, encryption scrambles the text so that it can't be read without decrypting it — and you need a *key* (or password) to do that.

## The Enigma machine

Encryption has been around a long, long time, and you often hear it stated as a *coded* message. Various types of machines encode messages, and one that comes to mind was used by the Germans during WWII — the Enigma machine. The Enigma machine has three rotors with numbers to represent the 26 letters of the alphabet; the message is typed and when the machine receives it, the three rotors need to be in a certain configuration to decrypt the message. The machine takes the number on the rotor representing the letter of the alphabet and steps up with the other two rotors to scramble the message. The person typing the message can see the letters instead of the corresponding numbers on the front of the machine. This way the writer knows that the secret message was typed correctly.

You can purchase from among several versions of encryption software online. One is such version is Pretty Good Privacy (PGP). To find out more this version:

1. **Go to www.pgp.com.**

   The PGP home page displays.

2. **Click the Products tab and then click PGP Desktop Home.**

The cost of the software is a one-time license $99 fee, which includes one year of free technical support. With the Desktop Home version, you can encrypt e-mails, files, folders, or the entire hard drive. Your key is the most important thing to remember when using encryption software; otherwise, you can't retrieve your documents.

I've used PGP encryption products for e-mail attachment encryption and find them user friendly and effective. The software automatically encrypts e-mails and can also be signed digitally for validating the integrity of the e-mail. PGP Virtual Disk provides backup for files and folders. The data is encrypted and decrypted automatically; you don't need to do anything. This is a far cry from the early days of encryption when the steps to encrypt were done manually and were confusing to implement. Now with the automatic encryption systems, you can easily use encryption to protect your e-mail attachments, files, and folders.

## Passwords

Think about the number of passwords you use to access bank accounts, credit card accounts, mortgage accounts, and so on. Do you use strong passwords? Using strong passwords helps prevent thieves from guessing your passwords by using password-cracker software. The tougher the password, the harder it is to crack.

You'd be surprised how many people use *password* or *passwd* as their login password. You can probably guess that these aren't strong passwords. These passwords are usually default passwords and need to be changed immediately. People use them because they're easy to remember. The following are the ten most commonly used passwords:

| | |
|---|---|
| password | love |
| lust | money |
| private | secret |
| sex | snoopy |
| god | qwerty |

Do *not* use any of these passwords. Most of the password-cracker programs have these passwords in them. I also recommend against using passwords that contain your personal information, such as

✔ Your initials

✔ Your birth date

✔ Your zip code

✔ Your pet's name(s)

✔ Relatives' names

✔ Mother's maiden name

✔ Relatives' birth dates

The only thing protecting you from a potential thief is the strength of your password, so the stronger you make it, the better protected your personal information will be.

Don't have your browser save all your online passwords. When signing in to an account, whether at your bank's site or your favorite online retailer, you might see a Remember Me option (or Save My Password or Keep Me Logged in for 2 Weeks), which can make your information more vulnerable if your system gets compromised. I recommend that you always choose to *not* have your passwords remembered.

### *Understanding authentication and password attacks*

*Authentication* happens when you provide what is necessary to prove you are the legitimate end user. This is done through the use of passwords, PINs, fingerprints, and so on. Here are the three types of authentication:

✔ Something you know (password)

✔ Something you have (a token or a card)

✔ Something you are (fingerprint or hand geometry)

## Beware the social engineer

Social engineering is another way thieves can get your password. A *social engineer* possesses social skills and asks questions to get information she needs to access your systems or accounts. Here's how this works: She e-mails you saying she's from IT and needs your password to fix something in your account. Or she can call you and say she's from IT and needs you to type your password, and oh, by the way, she needs you to tell her what you're typing so she can check something. Don't fall for such schemes. She's very convincing, but guess what, IT never asks for your password; IT can get into your account with administrative passwords. Never, ever give anyone your password even if the reason sounds legitimate because IT won't ask for it.

Another social engineer trick is to ask you about your pets' names, hobbies, and so on because the thief knows that people use them to form passwords; the thief figures it's worth a try. Social engineers prowl social networking sites looking for victims. He'll attempt to befriend you, and after he has, he then starts asking questions that seem innocent. Don't be fooled; he really isn't your new friend but is instead after your personal information. At home, at work, or on the road, don't answer e-mails asking for bank account information so the sender can check something, can change your password, or so on. Banks won't ever ask for account or password information in an e-mail.

Passwords are the weakest of all the authentication methods because people tend to use passwords they can remember and which others can easily guess. The following list describes a few types of password attacks:

- **Brute force attacks:** These passwords are cracked by the thief simply guessing. This is why you only get only three or four attempts to type a password before you're locked out of an account.

- **Dictionary attacks:** These password-cracker programs run every word in the dictionary. When someone uses this attack to run passwords, all dictionary words are flagged. So it's better to not use dictionary words, such as *password, open,* and so on.

- **Password-cracking software programs:** These have some legitimate uses and are available for IT (Information Technology) managers to unlock an account. As you can guess, these are used in an attempt to obtain passwords for financial information and to obtain administrative passwords for a computer system. If the administrative passwords are compromised, the system is also compromised.

### Creating strong passwords

Most of the passwords you use are work related, and the systems you have access to have *password complexity* — certain requirements about the passwords you choose. To meet password complexity requirements, you need to use a combination of the following:

✔ Non-alphabetic characters, such as !, #, %, &, and $

✔ Numbers

✔ Upper- and lowercase letters

Choosing good passwords can make all the difference in securing your personal information. The more effort you put into password selection, the better off you'll be when it comes to protecting your assets. Here are some guidelines for choosing a good (strong) password:

✔ Use at least six characters.

✔ Insert some punctuation.

✔ Insert non-alphabetic characters.

✔ Mix lower- and uppercase letters.

✔ Make up a phrase or a combination of words that are easy to remember.

✔ Don't repeat characters, letters, and so on, such as *ooooo*.

✔ Don't use sequential numbers, such as *123456*.

✔ Don't use your account name as your password.

✔ Don't use all numbers, all punctuation, or all letters.

A password doesn't need to be an actual word; it can be a made-up word or even a passphrase, such as

✔ **iSItTgIfa?:** Is it thank goodness it's Friday again?

✔ **ShMEt$!:** Show me the money!

✔ **iAmLfD!:** I am late for an important date!

Here are some password examples:

✔ **KaTZFi$h%7m#:** This word means nothing, but the trick is to remember it. *Catfish* is spelled using the *$* for *s*. *K* is used rather than *c,* and *z* is added to *Kat.* Three non-alphabetic characters are used, #, %, and $.

✔ **3$oiGsNp:** The password means nothing, but it includes lower- and uppercase letters as well as the number and dollar characters.

✔ **8301LdP:** The password means nothing, but numbers as well as upper- and lowercase letters are used.

I provide these password and passphrase examples only to show you what you could come up with. Do *not* use any of these examples.

No password or passphrase is immune from being cracked, but you owe it to yourself to come up with strong passwords and passphrases. Choose your passwords carefully and change them periodically. How often you change them is up to you, but don't wait too long.

# Devising a Security Plan

This section looks at what makes up a security plan. I cover some basics earlier in this chapter, such as an updated antivirus protection program and an updated firewall (other than the one provided by your ISP).

With the basics and the other safeguards I list in earlier sections, you can develop a checklist for your security plan. Checklists are a good way to ensure you aren't missing any important safeguard. Your checklist will look similar to Table 11-1. You can use this or make up your own. The simpler the checklist, the more likely you'll use it to help secure your computer.

| Table 11-1 | Computer Safeguards Checklist | |
|---|---|---|
| Safeguard | Yes | No |
| Virus protection auto-scans and updates on | | |
| Firewall on | | |
| Windows Automatic Updates on | | |
| Pop-up blocker on | | |
| Wi-Fi (if applicable) on | | |
| Be careful when opening e-mail attachments | | |
| Spyware blocker | | |
| Pop-up blocker | | |
| Proxy server | | |
| Back up files | | |
| Be careful what you download | | |
| Use strong passwords | | |
| Encryption for files and folders | | |

# A word about social networking security

Social networking sites are an issue. Most people don't think they are, but do you have personal information on your networking Web page? You probably do, but you're probably thinking, "I don't have the information visible to the general public." But what about your contacts, friends, and so on? Do they take the same precautions to protect your information that they have access to? They may not intentionally display personal information about you, but it could happen.

Before computers and social networking sites, people networked on the phone or in person. Most people didn't share much personal information other than birth dates, home addresses, and phone numbers — and this occurred only if you were friends. If you were close friends, you might share information about where you work. Today, an explosion of information is on the Internet. Take precautions when using social networking sites; be wary of anyone who wants to be your friend and starts asking too many personal questions. Social networking sites are a gold mine to identity thieves and other predators, so be careful when using them. Make sure that you follow the safeguards recommended by the social networking site's guidelines. And be stingy about divulging personal information to people who want to add you as a friend.

# Chapter 12

# Dispensing Security with Windows XP, Vista, and 7

*I*n this chapter, I discuss what features are available for Windows security. Windows XP and Windows Vista have a Security Center feature, which is where you can find out what security your computer is running and turn on automatic updates. In Windows 7, this feature is called the Action Center.

# Wielding Windows Security Center Tools

Windows Security Center for XP and Vista helps make sure that your computer is safe while on the Internet. The Security Center offers only basic features, but at least you know what firewall and antivirus protection you're using and that the tools are on. Your commercially available firewall and antivirus protections have their own update systems, which I talk about in Chapter 11.

I recommend you set your virus protection programs to update automatically. My virus protection updates frequently without interfering with my using the system. Firewall programs, on the other hand, do not get as many updates as the virus protection systems, so most do not have an automatic update feature. However, the firewall program will still let you know when updates are available, or you can manually check.

In this section, I show you how to access the Security Center and what settings you can manage from there.

# *Accessing the Security Center*

To go to the Windows Security Center for XP and Vista and discover what protection is on, follow these steps:

**1. Choose Start⇨Control Panel.**

The Control Panel appears, as shown in Figure 12-1.

**Figure 12-1:**
You can access the Security Center through the Control Panel.

**2. Double-click the Security Center icon.**

The screen shown in Figure 12-2 appears, listing three security features:

- *Firewall:* Protects your computer by blocking unwanted programs from accessing your computer.

- *Automatic Updates:* This feature automatically scans for updates.

- *Virus Protection:* Helps protect your computer from unwanted programs that cause problems with your computer.

If On appears to a feature's right, it's on (sounds obvious, right?).

**3. Click the On down arrow to find more information about the Virus Protection feature.**

Figure 12-2 shows the virus protection information, including that the virus protection is on and what software is in use.

Virus protection is important to protect your computer. Information Technology (IT) doesn't tell you whether your virus protection is up-to-date. Ensure that it's up-to-date by setting your virus protection to update automatically.

**Figure 12-2:** Checking up on your computer's security features.

4. **Click the down arrow next to Firewall and Automatic Updates to see more information about these features.**

   As shown in Figure 12-3, this computer has at least one firewall installed that is currently on. Unfortunately, the feature doesn't tell you whether your firewall is up-to-date.

   Below the information is a note about how running more than one firewall can potentially cause problems. Two firewalls running simultaneously can conflict with each other and cause your Internet connection to fail.

   Figure 12-4 shows the information available for the Automatic Updates feature. Turn on Automatic Updates and keep your computer safe by automatically installing *patches* (fixes for known vulnerabilities to an OS). Microsoft sends out patches when they become available. When the operating system isn't patched and up-to-date, vulnerabilities can cause security breaches.

Click to hide information

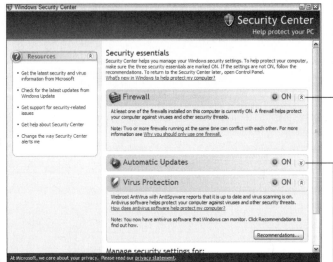

**Figure 12-3:**
Click a
feature's
down
arrows
for more
information.

Click to see more information

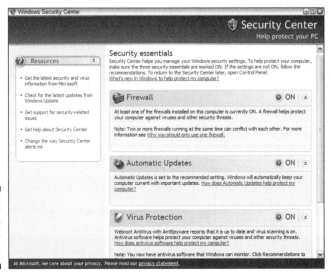

**Figure 12-4:**
Always
update
automatically.

## Managing security settings

The main Security Center screen has a Manage Security Settings For section (see the bottom of Figure 12-2), which lists the following items: Internet Options, Windows Firewall, and Automatic Updates. I discuss each of these in the following sections.

### Internet Options

When you click the Internet Options link, the Internet Properties dialog box appears, as shown in Figure 12-5.

**Figure 12-5:**
The Internet
Properties
dialog box.

The Security tab is the default tab that appears. In the Select a Zone to View or Change Settings section are four icons: Internet (highlighted; this zone is for Internet Web sites except those in the Trusted or Restricted zones), Local Intranet, Trusted Sites, and Restricted Sites.

In the Security Level for this Zone section, select a security level. You can choose from three settings, and each setting provides a different level of security:

✔ **Medium:** Prompts you before downloading potentially unsafe content. Will not permit unsigned Active X controls to be downloaded. (Look at Figure 12-5 to see the Medium security setting for the zone.)

✔ **Medium-High:** This is the default setting and is appropriate for most Web sites. Prompts you before downloading potentially unsafe content. Will not permit unsigned Active X controls to be downloaded. (Figure 12-6 shows the Medium-High security settings for the zone.)

✔ **High:** If you select the High security level, you may not be able to get to the Internet. This setting provides the most secure connection by implementing the maximum safeguards and disabling less secure features. (Figure 12-7 shows the High security settings for the zone.)

I recommend that you use the Medium-High setting (the default). You will find that by using this setting you can surf the Web without much difficulty. The Medium setting may not provide enough protection, and the High setting may cause issues when surfing the Internet.

**Figure 12-6:**
Medium-
High
security
settings.

After you choose the level of security you want, click the Apply button and then click OK; the settings are saved.

If you click the Custom Level button in the Security Level for This Zone area, the Security Settings – Internet Zone dialog box appears, as shown in Figure 12-8. This dialog box allows you to set the security features for the three levels I mention previously. By setting security manually through this dialog box, rather than by choosing Medium, Medium-High, or High, you can pick what features you want to disable. The level and default settings are best when you aren't comfortable working with computers. If you have some expertise, you can use the Custom Level settings to choose your desired security features.

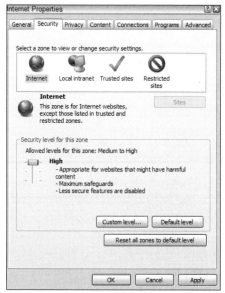

**Figure 12-7:**
High
security
settings.

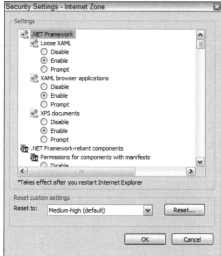

**Figure 12-8:**
The Security
Settings –
Internet
Zone dialog
box.

## Windows Firewall

In the Manage Security Settings For section in the Security Center (refer to Figure 12-2), click the Windows Firewall link to open the Windows Firewall dialog box, as shown in Figure 12-9, with the General tab displayed.

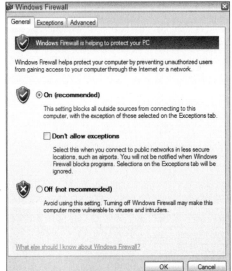

**Figure 12-9:**
The
Windows
Firewall
dialog box.

You can use this dialog box to see whether the Windows Firewall — and any other firewall you've installed — is running. The General tab has two main settings:

✔ **Green shield with a check mark:**

- *On (Recommended):* The firewall is on.

- *Don't Allow Exceptions:* For use in public networks, such as in airports, which are less secure connections. Windows Firewall will not notify you when it blocks programs.

✔ **A red shield with an X and an Off option.** If the firewall is off, the Off option is selected and your firewall isn't running. This isn't a recommended practice because your computer is vulnerable.

Windows has a new version of the firewall product. This version's stronger, but be careful about running two firewalls at the same time. They could cause a problem, and you may not be able to access the Internet.

I recommend that you run your own firewall. You can purchase one or use a free one such as Comodo, which I discuss further in Chapter 11.

The Windows Firewall dialog box has two other tabs: Exceptions and Advanced, which I discuss in the following sections.

### Exceptions tab

Figure 12-10 shows the Exceptions tab. Notice that you can select certain applications to allow them access to your computer, or you can deselect them to deny access.

- ✔ **Add Program:** Click this button to add programs to the exceptions list. Programs you may add are those that may need to check for updates, such as virus protection.

- ✔ **Add Port:** Click this button to open a port through the firewall. I recommend you use this feature judiciously to prevent an inadvertent opening of ports. When a port is open through the firewall, *any* traffic can come through the firewall. So be careful adding ports.

- ✔ **Delete:** Click this to delete all exceptions that are checked.

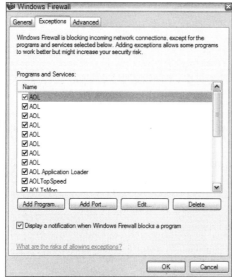

**Figure 12-10:** Windows Firewall blocks everything unless you mark exceptions here.

### Advanced tab

Figure 12-11 shows the Advanced tab.

This tab includes the following four sections:

- ✓ **Network Connection Settings:** When you click Settings, the screen in Figure 12-12 appears with two tabs:

  - *Services:* If the check box in this list is selected, that service has access to your computer. You can see the list of services in Figure 12-12.

  - *ICMP:* Click this tab to see the various Internet Control Message Protocols (as shown in Figure 12-13). You can select the protocols you want your computer to accept. Be careful what you allow, especially if you don't know what the protocols do. Better to have your firewall default setting address the protocols that could be problems.

  - *Services:* If the check box in this list is selected, that service has access to your computer. You can see the list of services in Figure 12-12.

  - *ICMP:* Click this tab to see the various Internet Control Message Protocols (as shown in Figure 12-13). You can select the protocols you want your computer to accept. Be careful what you allow, especially if you don't know what the protocols do. Better to have your firewall default setting address the protocols that could be problems.

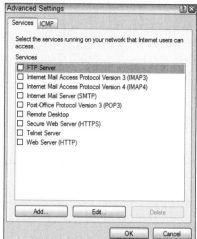

**Figure 12-12:**
Choose
which
services
Internet
users can
access.

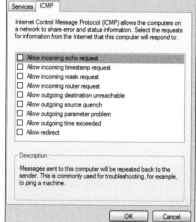

**Figure 12-13:**
Choose
which
protocols
your
computer
will
respond to.

✔ **Security Logging:** Click the Settings button (refer to Figure 12-12) to see the Log Settings screen. You can choose to log dropped packets or successful packets. You can name the log under the Log File Options box.

When you click the Save button, the log file saves using whatever you name it.

✔ **ICMP** (Internet Control Message Protocol): This is used to send messages over the Internet.

✔ **Default Settings:** This section allows you to go back to the default settings, as shown in Figure 12-12.

## *Automatic Updates*

Automatic Updates is the bottom link in the Manage Security Settings For area of the main Security Center screen (refer to Figure 12-2). When you click that link, the Automatic Updates dialog box (as shown in Figure 12-14) appears. Here you can set times for Automatic Updates to run. Run these during times when you aren't using your computer because this usually takes up computer resources and causes your computer to run slowly.

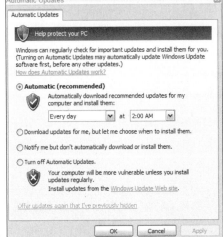

**Figure 12-14:**
Options
in the
Automatic
Update
dialog box.

When the updates are loaded, restart the system so that the automatic updates schedule will take effect automatically. When the download completes, the computer will restart automatically. To avoid disruption, set Automatic Updates to run in the middle of the night. I also recommend that you set Automatic Updates to search every day to be sure you have the latest updates installed on your computer.

As you can see in Figure 12-14, the Automatic Update process options are

- ✔ **Automatic (Recommended):** If you select this option, you can set the frequency and time from the drop-down lists provided. After selecting this option and setting the schedule, you don't have to think about it again.

- ✔ **Download Updates for Me, but Let Me Choose When to Install Them:** If you select this option, you have to remember to install the updates manually.

- ✔ **Notify Me but Don't Automatically Download or Install Them:** If you select this option, you have to remember to both download and then install the updates.

✔ **Turn Off Automatic Updates:** I don't recommend. If you select this
option, you need to check for updates by going to the Microsoft Web
site and then download and install any that you find.

# Windows Defender

Windows Defender is a spyware blocking program that finds and eliminates
spyware. The software is free for Windows XP, but you have to download
it from Microsoft. Windows Defender is included with Windows Vista and
Windows 7. Figure 12-15 shows Windows Defender in XP (which looks the
same in Vista).

**Figure 12-15:**
Windows
Defender in
Windows XP.

To access Windows Defender for Windows Vista and Windows 7, choose
Start⇨Control Panel and then click the Windows Defender icon. For Windows
XP and Server 2003, load it into your startup menu so that Windows Defender
comes up automatically. To load Windows Defender into the startup menu,
just follow the download screens as you would when you download any
program. The download places a shortcut on the desktop that's available
when your system boots up. Windows Defender doesn't run on Windows
2000 because the release was before its completion.

As shown in Figure 12-15, across the top of the screen are four buttons:
Home, Scan, History, and Tools. I discuss these in the following sections. At
any time, you can click the question mark button for help.

The XP version of Windows Defender does look significantly different from the Windows 7 version. The Windows 7 version does affect the performance of your computer while running a scan more than the XP version.

# Home

The Home screen is the program's main screen where you can determine whether any unwanted software is running on your computer (refer to Figure 12-15). At the bottom of the screen, you can see when the last scan ran on your computer and when more scans will be performed (if you have the scans set to scan your computer automatically). As you can see on this screen, it's scheduled to scan at 2:00 a.m. daily. Finally, you will see that the real time protection is on.

# Scan

The Scan button allows you to manually scan your computer for spyware. You can set the program to have Windows Defender scan automatically according to a schedule. This is from the Tools button, which I discuss in the "Tools" section, later in this chapter.

# History

To see a history of scans completed on your computer, click the History button (see Figure 12-16). Here's where all the problems are logged from the completed computer scans.

When you join Microsoft Spynet, any software that Windows Defender detects is sent to Microsoft to review where the software came from, actions you applied or Windows Defender applied automatically to rid your system of the spyware, and whether the actions were successful — including quarantining or removing the software from your computer.

Near the upper-right corner are two links:

 ✔ **Allowed Items:** Items that are permitted on your computer. Defender does not monitor them unless you remove them from the list. Click the Allowed Items link to see the Allowed Items log. Allowed items are those programs and files you choose to permit even though Windows Defender determined that they might be a threat to your computer.

✔ **Quarantined Items:** Click this link to see the quarantined items of completed scans, as shown in Figure 12-17. Here you can see the quarantined spyware by your computer scans and take action for the quarantined software.

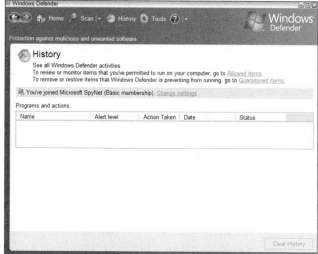

**Figure 12-16:**
The History button gives the lowdown on Windows Defender activities.

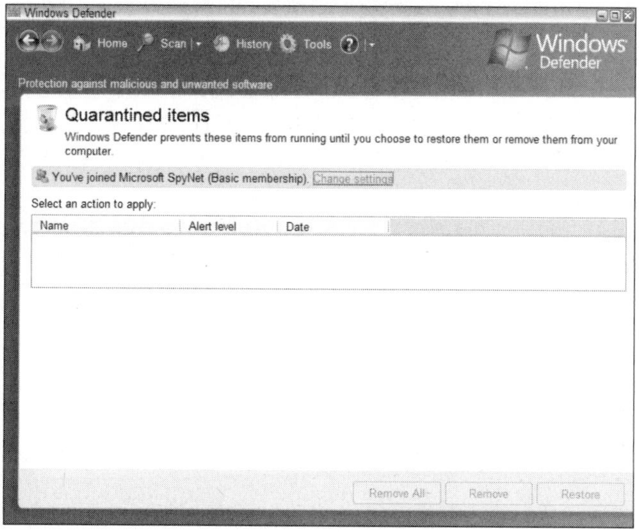

**Figure 12-17:**
When Windows Defender finds something suspicious, Defender logs it in the Quarantined Items list.

# Tools

When you click the Tools button at the top of Windows Defender, the Tools and Settings screen appears, as shown in Figure 12-18.

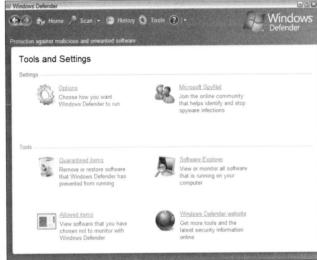

**Figure 12-18:**
Windows
Defender
spyware
blocking
tools and
settings.

Your choices here are Settings (Options and Microsoft SpyNet) and Tools (Quarantined Items, Allowed Items, Software Explorer, and Windows Defender Website). In the following sections, I talk about each choice in turn.

## Options

Click the Options link (refer to Figure 12-18) to see the Options screen shown in Figure 12-19. Here you can set up a schedule for automatic scanning in the appropriately named Automatic Scanning section. Use the Frequency, Approximate Time, and Type drop-down lists to set your options. The figure shows the system set in Quick Scan mode (which scans areas of your computer that are higher risk, such as programs you are running when the scan is performed). Full Scan mode scans your entire system.

In the Default Actions section, you set the default Windows Defender display options that govern what Windows Defender does when it detects a malicious or an unknown program. For each alert level, Windows Defender can provide a recommendation based on the definition for the program, ignore the threat, or remove the program. You select the choice for each risk level and they range from the default setting to ignore, remove, or quarantine the item.

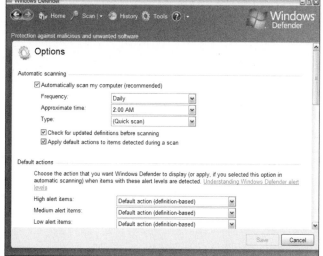

**Figure 12-19:**
Use these
options
to set
automatic
scanning
and default
actions.

Following the Default Actions section is the Real-Time Protection Options section (see Figure 12-20). I won't bore you by listing every single one here. Real-time protection is just that. It's done in real time; that is, right now, and on a scheduled basis. Real-time protection alerts you when spyware and other potentially unwanted software attempt to install themselves or run on your computer. It also alerts you if programs attempt to change important Windows settings. If you select the Use Real-Time Protection (Recommended) check box, the default settings for this category are provided. If the box is not checked, you will not have Real-Time Protection turned on.

The Advanced Options section is shown at the bottom of Figure 12-20. Here you can set what you want Windows Defender to scan. The boxes in this section are checked by default. I recommend that you leave these boxes checked.

Below the Advanced Options section (and not visible in Figure 12-20) is the Administrative Options section. Here you determine who can access the Windows Defender program to make changes.

### Microsoft SpyNet

Microsoft SpyNet is the other link in the Settings section on the Tools and Settings screen (refer to Figure 12-18). Microsoft SpyNet offers two memberships: basic (default) or advanced. Both are free. With advanced membership, you can monitor software for changes, and Defender alerts you when changes occur. Basic membership doesn't perform those tasks. Some personal information may be sent to Microsoft, but Microsoft doesn't use the information to identify or contact you. This is applicable to both the basic and advanced membership settings.

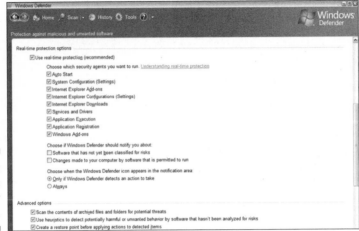

**Figure 12-20:**
Windows
Defender
options.

### Quarantined Items and Allowed Items

The Quarantined Items and Allowed Items in the Tools section on the Tools and Settings screen (refer to Figure 12-18) essentially show you logs listing the spyware captured during a scan. You can then decide to allow or delete the spyware. See the "History" section, earlier in this chapter, for more details.

### Software Explorer

Software Explorer is a tool (the link is found in the Tools section on the Tools and Settings screen; refer to Figure 12-18) that ensures you're running software that won't damage your computer. The Software Explorer tool (see Figure 12-21) lets you know what software runs on your computer; it gives you the software manufacturer's name, the size, the file path, the file location, whether it shipped with the Windows operating system, and so on. If the software isn't legitimate, this tool flags it. You can then decide to remove or disable the software from your computer. (Sometimes, legitimate software is flagged, so you'll want to review what's flagged before removing it.) A classification also lets you know whether the software has permission to run on your system. You can then make the choice whether to run it.

Software Explorer isn't used in Windows 7 because Microsoft says it had nothing to do with spyware, and therefore caused confusion for the home users.

### Windows Defender Website

Click the Windows Defender Website link (in the Tools section on the Tools and Settings screen; refer to Figure 12-18) to find information about Windows Defender and get the latest updates.

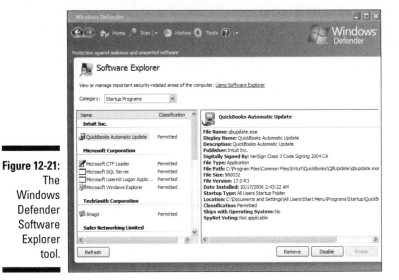

**Figure 12-21:**
The
Windows
Defender
Software
Explorer
tool.

# Engaging User Account Control in XP and Vista

Managing user accounts is important to maintain computer security. Adding new users can create problems especially if you have a guest account enabled. I recommend that you don't enable the Guest Account feature in Windows XP or Vista. The reason for my recommendation is that someone can use the guest account to log on to your computer by setting his own user name and password.

## Managing user accounts in XP

To locate the user account management tools in XP, do the following:

1. **Choose Start⇨Control Panel.**

2. **Click the User Accounts icon, as shown in Figure 12-22.**

   The User Accounts screen appears (see Figure 12-23).

   On the User Accounts screen are three tasks (Create an Account, Create a New Account, and Change the Way Users Log On or Off), which I discuss in the following sections.

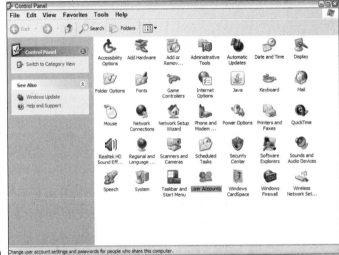

**Figure 12-22:**
Access the User Accounts icon through the Control Panel.

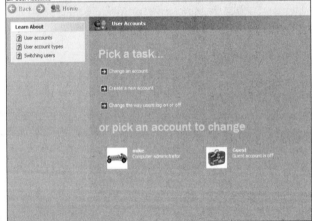

**Figure 12-23:**
Choose a task in the User Accounts screen.

### Change an account

When you click the Change an Account link on the User Accounts screen (refer to Figure 12-23), two account options appear: the administrator's account and the guest account (as shown in Figure 12-24). You can have more than one guest account on your computer.

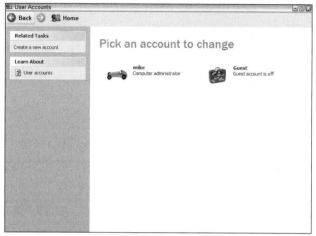

**Figure 12-24:**
Choosing an
account to
change.

When you click one of the accounts, a new screen appears. Click the administrator's account icon, and the screen in Figure 12-25 appears where you can make changes to the account. Only the administrator can get to this account to make changes after the accounts are set up on your computer since it is password protected.

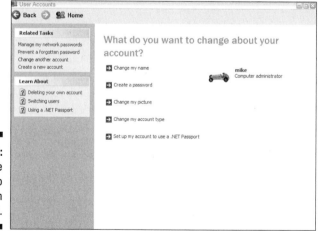

**Figure 12-25:**
Choose
what to
change in
the account.

Under Change My Account Type, you have only two choices: computer administrator or limited. The computer administrator has full rights to make changes to the systems settings, set up user accounts, and so on. Limited users cannot make changes to the system or add other users.

Click the Set Up My Account to Use .NET Passport option to have online conversations with friends and family, create your own personal Web pages, or sign into .Net Passport–enabled pages. .NET-enabled pages allow you to sign in with the same password for all Web sites that require a user ID and password. When you sign up for .NET, you need to use only one password.

The second user account command is for the guest account (refer to Figure 12-24). When you click the Guest icon, a screen similar to what's shown in Figure 12-26 appears. As you can see, this lets you decide whether to turn on the guest account. I recommend that if you do not need the guest account, do not activate it. Why create a security hole for no reason?

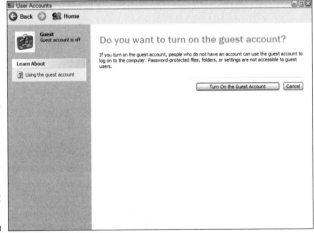

**Figure 12-26:** Decide carefully whether to activate the guest account.

### Create a new account

In Figure 12-23, notice the Create a New Account link. If you click this link, a screen similar to what's shown in Figure 12-27 appears. This screen allows you to set up another account. After you name the new account, click the Next button to display a new screen, as shown in Figure 12-28. Here you can pick the account type from two choices:

✔ **Computer Administrator:** Has control to add or delete users, download software, install software from a disk, and so on.

✔ **Limited:** Users that are limited can access only their own programs and cannot add or delete users. Limited users also cannot add programs or software.

**Figure 12-27:**
Name
the new
account and
click the
Next button.

**Figure 12-28:**
Choose
what type
of account
the new
account
will be.

### Change the way users log on or off

Click the Change the Way Users Log On or Off link (refer to Figure 12-23) to arrive at the choices in Figure 12-29. You can choose a welcome screen or a fast user switching screen. These screens are what the user — you or someone you've given permission to log on to your computer — sees when he logs on. After you make your choices and click the Apply Options button, the system saves your options.

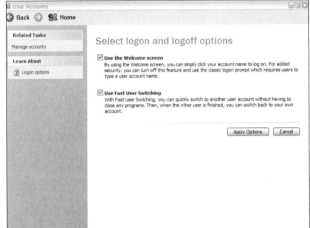

**Figure 12-29:**
Make your choice and click the Apply Options button.

## Managing user accounts in Vista

To manage user accounts in Vista, choose Start⇨Control Panel and then click the User Accounts icon. Follow the commands to accomplish the tasks you want to manage user accounts. The User Account Control (UAC) is a management tool for managing accounts in Windows Vista. You can disable this function if you choose to do so. To add a new account in Vista, follow these steps:

1. **Choose Start⇨Control Panel⇨User Accounts.**

2. **In User Accounts, click the Add or Remove User Accounts button.**

3. **Click Create a New Account button and then add an account name.**

4. **Select the account type — Standard or Administrator — and then click the Create Account button.**

5. **Click the Password Hint button to add a password to the account you just added and then type the password twice.**

6. **Click the Create a Password button.**

   That's it — you added a new user account with a password to your system.

In Windows 7, the UAC tool is also used to manage user accounts. The windows are different than they are in Vista, but the concept is the same and the various screens guide you through how to work with user accounts. The UAC management tool is something you may not need if you don't have a number of users on one computer in your home.

# Windows 7 Security

Windows 7 security uses two tools that I discuss earlier in this chapter: the Security Center and Windows Defender. Windows XP and Vista use the Security Center for monitoring the firewall, automatic updates, and virus protection. Windows 7 uses the Action Center to monitor the firewall, automatic updates, and virus protection. The symbol for the Security Center is a shield with four colors (red, green, blue, and yellow).

I recommend that you purchase a copy of a commercially available antivirus protection program. You can also download free spyware protection programs that minimize your exposure to spyware. Most commercially available antivirus protection programs also screen for spyware. After installing the protective programs, be sure to set them up for automatic updates. I discuss this topic further in Chapter 11. You access the Action Center and other Windows 7 security features through the Control Panel.

## Turning off alerts

The User Account Control (UAC) feature alerts you if changes are made to any user accounts or added software. In Vista, dialog boxes appeared whenever you tried to install software. Most thought this was an annoyance. However, it does serve a purpose: It lets you know that changes are being made to your system via added software. Whether you want to keep the software is for you to decide.

In Windows 7, you can turn off the alerts if you have administrative rights to your computer. According to Microsoft, you'll be protected anyway from malicious software. In my humble opinion, it's better to be notified if something changes or attempts to change on your system than have a false sense of security that nothing happens to your computer and that you're practicing safe Web surfing habits. Issues crop up daily when you're on the Internet, so having alerts pop up is a small price to pay to ensure that your system is secure from Internet malware.

# Windows Firewall

Windows 7 has its own firewall as a part of the security features, but it may not be compatible with the firewall you're running. Before you install a commercially available firewall, check with the manufacturer to find out whether its product will turn off features of the Microsoft firewall. The firewall may not and you will have issues with the two firewalls conflicting with each other.

Running two firewalls may not work, and your system may not permit Internet access because the firewall rule sets may conflict with one another. (A *rule set* tells the firewall what to block.) If the firewalls are configured correctly, you can run two firewalls, but I don't recommend this for a novice user.

# Finding other security features

Windows 7 has another new security feature — *BitLocker.* BitLocker gives you the option of encrypting your portable storage devices so if they're stolen, no one can access the information. You can choose a passphrase to encrypt the data on the portable device. BitLocker appears as a separate icon for the service and in the Control Panel, too.

To change security settings, go to the Control Panel and depending on the task you want to complete, click an icon to access the information to make the necessary changes. The screenshots may change from Windows XP, Windows Vista, and Windows 7, but the screenshots earlier in the chapter can help you in using the settings you desire to protect your system and your personal information.

# Part VI
# Taking Back Your Good Name

The 5th Wave                    By Rich Tennant

©RICHTENNANT

OAKDALE NURSING HOME

"She says the breaking and entering and drag racing charges are a result of Identity Theft. Maybe, maybe not. Cover me while I question the other gang members."

# In this part . . .

*I*f you discover that you're a victim, don't panic. You *can* reclaim your identity. In this part, I take you through the process of filing reports, filling out forms, closing compromised accounts, and opening new ones.

# Chapter 13

# Starting the Process of Reclaiming Your Identity

*I*n this chapter, I guide you through the paperwork necessary to regain your good name and credit if you've been a victim. Doing paperwork isn't the most exciting exercise, but in the case of identity theft, doing the work is important and will help you in the long run.

## Filling Out the Initial Reports

Completing the initial reports is the first step in regaining your identity. The first report is the police report. For this report, you must be persistent because some jurisdictions may not be as responsive as others to identity theft cases. Next in the process is to place a fraud alert on your credit report.

### Placing a fraud alert on your credit report

The fraud alert requests creditors to contact you before opening any new accounts or making any changes to your existing accounts. As soon as the credit bureau confirms your fraud alert, the other two credit bureaus are notified automatically to place fraud alerts. You have to request that the reports be sent to you. The credit bureaus do not automatically send you the reports. You do, however, get confirmation letters from each bureau that the fraud alert has been placed on your credit report. The letter contains a confirmation number and a phone number to call to order reports.

Here's the contact information for each credit bureau's fraud division:

Equifax
800-525-6285
P.O. Box 740250
Atlanta, GA 30374

Experian
888-397-3742
P.O. Box 1017
Allen, TX 75013

TransUnion
800-680-7289
P.O. Box 6790
Fullerton, CA 92834

You don't need a copy of your credit report. All you need to do is call. The credit bureau will send you a copy of your credit report when you place the alert.

## Reporting the crime to law enforcement

Because identity theft is a crime, you need to file a report with law enforcement where you live. Contact one of the various local enforcement agencies, such as city police, sheriff's department, county police, and town or village police. They'll let you know whether you have the right jurisdiction for reporting the crime; if you don't, they'll tell you which one to contact and provide you with the contact information.

For most jurisdictions, you can contact the local law enforcement agency by telephone or online to file the report. When you do so, you're given a report number. You need to send this report number to your creditors along with your completed theft affidavit.

## Completing an ID theft affidavit

The theft affidavit is found on the FTC Web site under Identity Theft at www.ftc.gov. You must send the copy of the police report and the completed affidavit to all your creditors. The following is the process for completing the theft affidavit:

✔ To fill out the form, you must download and print it; you can't complete the form online. Included in the instructions are the addresses for all three major credit bureaus.

✔ You can notarize the form in the space provided. You aren't required by law to have the form notarized. Some businesses don't require the form to be notarized, but doing so may persuade them to accept the form as more credible. *Note:* You may have to pay a fee to have the form notarized.

✔ Some creditors want you to complete their own dispute form. Call them to find out whether they require you to fill out a separate form and then follow up the phone request in writing. Send the letter Certified Mail return receipt so that you have a record of the request. There are spaces to fill in the police report information, including agency report number, the name of the officer or person taking the report, and the e-mail address of the agency.

✔ The affidavit has a documentation checklist that includes a valid government-issued picture identification card, such as a driver's license, state-issued identification card, or passport. The last item in this section is proof of residency during the time the event or disputed transaction took place.

✔ The affidavit has a chart where you can list all the accounts that were opened fraudulently with the address of the company where the account was opened, the account number, type of account (for example, auto loan, credit card, or mortgage), the date it was opened, and for what amount. Send the chart to the credit bureaus as a part of the affidavit. The chart is also a valuable tool for you to track what contacts have been made and their responses.

✔ You must send the affidavit to the fraud department of each creditor, bank, or utility that provided the identity thief with unauthorized credit, or purchases and services. Some companies have their own dispute forms; they'll send them to you after they receive your affidavit. Still other companies don't accept the affidavit and will only accept their own dispute form and a police report, but you won't know until you send it to them.

Figure 13-1 shows the sections of the report from the Federal Trade Commission Web site.

After you complete the form, send it to one of the credit bureaus and have a fraud alert placed on your credit file. The credit bureau you send it to automatically notifies the other two bureaus to place a fraud alert on their files.

Figure 13-2 shows a sample Fraudulent Account Statement. In the form, notice the creditor's name and address in the first box of the table, and then the account number, type of account, the date the account was opened (or credit card was issued), and finally the amount in the account.

Name _____ Phone number _____ Page 1

### ID Theft Affidavit

**Victim Information**

(1) My full legal name is _____
      (First)      (Middle)      (Last)      (Jr., Sr., III)

(2) (If different from above) When the events described in this affidavit took place, I was known as

_____
(First)      (Middle)      (Last)      (Jr., Sr., III)

(3) My date of birth is _____
      (day/month/year)

(4) My Social Security number is_____

(5) My driver's license or identification card state and number are_____

(6) My current address is _____

      City _____ State _____ Zip Code _____

(7) I have lived at this address since _____
      (month/year)

(8) (If different from above) When the events described in this affidavit took place, my address was

_____

      City _____ State _____ Zip Code _____

(9) I lived at the address in Item 8 from _____ until _____
      (month/year)      (month/year)

(10) My daytime telephone number is (____)_____

      My evening telephone number is (____)_____

**Figure 13-1:** Theft affidavit. (Continued on the following pages.)

## How the Fraud Occurred

**Check all that apply for items 11 - 17:**

(11) ❏ I did not authorize anyone to use my name or personal information to seek the money, credit, loans, goods or services described in this report.

(12) ❏ I did not receive any benefit, money, goods or services as a result of the events described in this report.

(13) ❏ My identification documents (for example, credit cards; birth certificate; driver's license; Social Security card; etc.) were ❏ stolen ❏ lost on or about _____.
                                                              (day/month/year)

(14) ❏ To the best of my knowledge and belief, the following person(s) used my information (for example, my name, address, date of birth, existing account numbers, Social Security number, mother's maiden name, etc.) or identification documents to get money, credit, loans, goods or services without my knowledge or authorization:

Name (if known) _____          Name (if known) _____

Address (if known) _____        Address (if known) _____

Phone number(s) (if known) _____        Phone number(s) (if known) _____

Additional information (if known) _____     Additional information (if known) _____

(15) ❏ I do NOT know who used my information or identification documents to get money, credit, loans, goods or services without my knowledge or authorization.

(16) ❏ Additional comments: (For example, description of the fraud, which documents or information were used or how the identity thief gained access to your information.)

## Victim's Law Enforcement Actions

(17) (check one) I ❏ am ❏ am not willing to assist in the prosecution of the person(s) who committed this fraud.

(18) (check one) I ❏ am ❏ am not authorizing the release of this information to law enforcement for the purpose of assisting them in the investigation and prosecution of the person(s) who committed this fraud.

(19) (check all that apply) I ❏ have ❏ have not reported the events described in this affidavit to the police or other law enforcement agency. The police ❏ did ❏ did not write a report. *In the event you have contacted the police or other law enforcement agency, please complete the following:*

**(Agency #1)** _____          (Officer/Agency personnel taking report) ____

(Date of report) _____          (Report number, if any) ____

(Phone number) _____           (email address, if any) ____

**(Agency #2)** _____          (Officer/Agency personnel taking report) ____

(Date of report) _____          (Report number, if any) ____

(Phone number) _____           (email address, if any) ____

### Documentation Checklist

Please indicate the supporting documentation you are able to provide to the companies you plan to notify. Attach copies (NOT originals) to the affidavit before sending it to the companies.

(20) ❑ A copy of a valid government-issued photo-identification card (for example, your driver's license, state-issued ID card or your passport). If you are under 16 and don't have a photo-ID, you may submit a copy of your birth certificate or a copy of your official school records showing your enrollment and place of residence.

(21) ❑ Proof of residency during the time the disputed bill occurred, the loan was made or the other event took place (for example, a rental/lease agreement in your name, a copy of a utility bill or a copy of an insurance bill).

## DO NOT SEND AFFIDAVIT TO THE FTC OR ANY OTHER GOVERNMENT AGENCY

Name _____ Phone number _____ Page 4

(22) ❑ A copy of the report you filed with the police or sheriff's department. If you are unable to obtain a report or report number from the police, please indicate that in Item 19. Some companies only need the report number, not a copy of the report. You may want to check with each company.

### Signature

I declare under penalty of perjury that the information I have provided in this affidavit is true and correct to the best of my knowledge.

_____     _____
(signature)                                           (date signed)

**Knowingly submitting false information on this form could subject you to criminal prosecution for perjury.**

---

Name _____ Phone number _____ Page 5

## Fraudulent Account Statement

**Completing this Statement**

- Make as many copies of this page as you need. **Complete a separate page for each company you're notifying and only send it to that company.** Include a copy of your signed affidavit.
- List only the account(s) you're disputing with the company receiving this form. **See the example below.**
- If a collection agency sent you a statement, letter or notice about the fraudulent account, attach a copy of that document (**NOT** the original).

**I declare (check all that apply):**

❑ As a result of the event(s) described in the ID Theft Affidavit, the following account(s) was/were opened at your company in my name without my knowledge, permission or authorization using my personal information or identifying documents:

| Creditor Name/Address (the company that opened the account or provided the goods or services) | Account Number | Type of unauthorized credit/goods/services provided by creditor (if known) | Date issued or opened (if known) | Amount/Value provided (the amount charged or the cost of the goods/services) |
|---|---|---|---|---|
| Example Example National Bank 22 Main Street Columbus, Ohio 22722 | 01234567-89 | auto loan | 01/05/2002 | $25,500.00 |
| | | | | |
| | | | | |

**Figure 13-2:** Fraudulent Account Statement.

# Taking Care of Compromised Accounts: The First Steps

When you discover that your accounts have been compromised, follow the steps in the following sections to stop their misuse. Waiting doesn't help your cause. As soon as you find out that some of your accounts have been compromised, check all your accounts. For more details, see Chapter 14.

## Call your credit card company

Take out your contact sheet of credit card companies (see Chapter 6). The contact information you need, including account numbers and the credit card phone number, should be on your list.

Call your credit card company and let them know that you've been the victim of identity theft. Keep a journal listing the person you spoke to when you called, the date and time, and a summary of the conversation for your records. For a sample journal see Table 13-1. You can use Microsoft Excel to make your journal, or you can use a table in Microsoft Word — it doesn't make a difference as long as you include the information I list in the sample.

Make sure that you record all the information on the form in the Fraudulent Account Statement section (refer to Figure 13-2). Then follow up your phone conversation by sending a copy of your completed Fraudulent Account Statement form for that credit company.

| Table 13-1 | | Sample Journal | | |
|---|---|---|---|---|
| Company Called | Person's Name | Date/Time of Call | Conversation Summary | Dispute Form |
| | | | | |
| | | | | |
| | | | | |

If you're disputing fraudulent charges on your credit card, tell the card company and follow up the conversation in writing, using the Fraudulent Account Statement, as shown in Figure 13-2.

Keep copies of everything you send to any creditors. Send all correspondence to any creditors Certified Mail return receipt and keep the return receipts for your files.

## Call your bank

After you realize that you've been a victim, don't forget to call your bank. You should have the contact information on file (see Chapter 6). Ask your bank to freeze your accounts if you see evidence that they've been compromised.

For checking accounts, the bank will want to know which checks you have outstanding. A quick look at your check register should provide the information you need. The accounts may need to be closed and new ones opened. If your checks are lost or stolen, for example, the person(s) using your checks can drain your account in short order. To get more details about personal checks, see Chapter 6.

Chapter 14 contains specifics about closing compromised accounts, and Chapter 15 contains instructions for opening new ones.

If you're a victim of identity theft and feel that one or more of your bank accounts have been or will be compromised, close the accounts and open new ones.

Choose a new PIN (personal identification number) for your new ATM card. Don't use the old one in case it's been compromised, as well.

## Ask for fraud dispute forms

The Federal Trade Commission (FTC) has an ID Theft Affidavit form (see the section "Completing an ID theft affidavit"), but some creditors have their own dispute forms and may not accept the FTC ID Theft Affidavit form. You must ask whether they have their own form and have them send it to you.

On the form, enter the information about your conversation, using the information in the sample journal in Table 13-1. If the creditor has its own form, mark the Dispute Form column with Yes. You already recorded the date of the call in your journal; this date will serve as the date you requested the dispute form, as well.

The credit bureaus have their own dispute forms, too. Chapter 5 shows a sample dispute form from Experian. You simply order the form online. Remember that you need a current credit report number, no older than 90 (Equifax is 60) days, to file a dispute.

Don't get bullied into paying for charges you didn't make on accounts you didn't open. Stand your ground. After you file the dispute or theft affidavit for the fraudulent accounts and charges, you don't have to pay the disputed charges, and the charges can't be given to a collection agency, per the Fair and Accurate Credit Transactions Act (FACTA).

# Getting Straight with the Government

If you are a victim of identity theft, you need to let the government know. Filing a complaint with the FTC will help your case. The FTC reports the theft to the appropriate law enforcement agency, as well. The FTC does not investigate the crime of identity theft.

## Filing a complaint with the Federal Trade Commission

The Federal Trade Commission (FTC) has a complaint form on its Web site, www.ftc.gov. Clicking the Identity Theft link (in the Quick Finder section) takes you to the information shown in Figure 13-3. If instead you click the Consumer Protection tab (at the top of the FTC site's home page), you're taken to the Bureau of Consumer Protection page, shown in Figure 13-4. From there, you can file a complaint by clicking the File a Complaint tab, which takes you to the page shown in Figure 13-5.

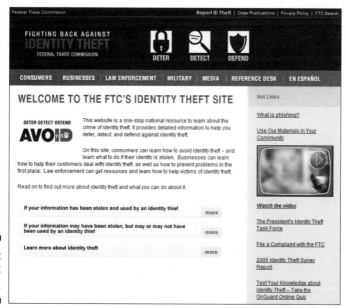

**Figure 13-3:** The FTC Web site.

On the right side of Figure 13-5 is a link that will take you to the Complaint Assistant. When you're ready to file your complaint, click the link, and you're taken to the first step of the complaint process, as shown in Figure 13-6. As you answer each question, the next question automatically appears.

**Figure 13-4:** Access the Bureau of Consumer Protection through the FTC Web site.

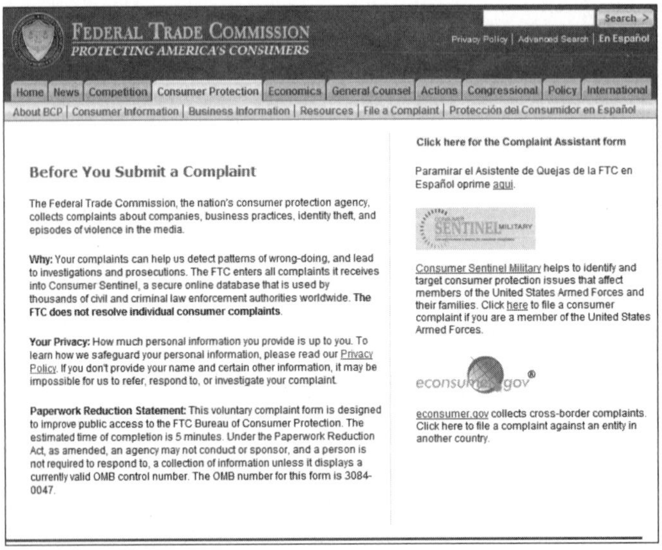

**Figure 13-5:** Read all the pertinent information before filing your complaint.

**Figure 13-6:** The FTC's Complaint Assistant takes you through the process of filing a complaint.

> FTC Complaint Assistant
>
> Step 1
>
> **Step 1: Let's Get Started**
>
> Welcome to the FTC Complaint Assistant. So that we can properly record your complaint, you will first be asked to answer a series of questions. After answering these questions, you will have the opportunity to provide us additional details regarding your complaint in your own words.
>
> **Is your complaint or concern regarding identity theft?**
>
> ○ Yes
> ○ No

The FTC doesn't resolve individual identity theft issues, but the complaints do help the FTC investigate fraud that sometimes leads to law enforcement action.

## What to do if your SSN has been used to get a job

The Social Security Administration (SSA) doesn't help consumers fix their credit problems. They will help, however, if someone other than you uses your Social Security Number (SSN) to get a job. To get help from the SSA, visit its Web site at www.ssa.gov, as shown in Figure 13-7. On the left, click the Report Fraud, Waste or Abuse link, which takes you to the page shown in Figure 13-8. Here you find links to forms and more information.

### Protecting your SSN

As I discuss in Chapter 8, when it comes to your SSN, you can never be too careful. Take these precautions:

✔ Always protect your SSN; don't give it out freely.

✔ Never carry your SSN in your wallet or purse.

✔ Make sure that you secure your personal records at home to prevent a thief from finding your SSN.

✔ After your application for credit has been completed, request that only the last digits of your SSN appear on any copies and ask that the original application be destroyed in your presence.

**Figure 13-7:**
The SSA
Web site.

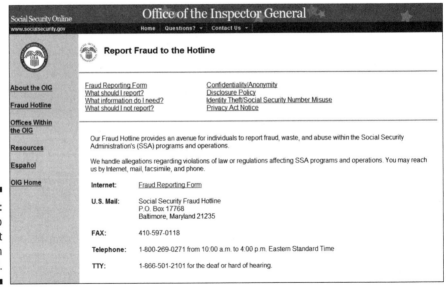

**Figure 13-8:**
How to
report a lost
or stolen
SSN card.

# Tools

In this section, I briefly describe a couple of tools you can use to help you in the battle against identity theft. These tools are in place because both the state and the federal government recognize the problems that identity theft causes and that it's a fast-growing crime in the U.S. and has been for the last several years. In recent years, financial crimes, including identity theft, have gotten a lot of media attention and legislators felt compelled to address the growing problem. So use the tools that are here for you.

### Government laws

Knowing the government laws can help protect you. Federal and state governments have laws in place to help protect you from identity theft. One such state law is the credit freeze (see Chapter 2), which is free if you've been a victim of identity theft. At the federal level, you can get annual, free credit reports from each credit bureau. Fraud alerts are free and can be extended from 90 days to 7 years with a police report. I discuss this government tool in the following section.

### Fraud alert

I discuss fraud alerts in detail in Chapter 2, but remember that they're a tool that can be used to help you if you've been a victim of identity theft. Fraud alerts can also be used to help if your mail was stolen like mine was. The fraud alert is then deployed as a preventative measure, which it was in my case. A fraud alert is an effective tool to help you in the fight against identity theft.

I placed a fraud alert on my credit reports when my mail was stolen several years ago. The alert was for 90 days and covered all three bureaus. I did so as a precaution and used the police report number to place the alert. I wasn't a victim of identity theft, and I'm not sure whether the fraud alert prevented my identity from being stolen and any other losses or if I was just plain lucky that no important mail was in the box at the time of the theft. At that time, I immediately switched to paperless statements for my bank accounts and credit cards.

# Chapter 14

# Closing Compromised Accounts

· · · · · · · · · · · · · · · · · · · · · · · · · · · · · · · · · · · · · · · · · ·

· · · · · · · · · · · · · · · · · · · · · · · · · · · · · · · · · · · · · · · · · ·

**C**losing bank accounts (and subsequently opening new ones) isn't my idea of a fun-filled afternoon, but if your accounts have been compromised, you have to do it, which is just what this chapter helps you do. To close out your accounts, you can close and open new accounts over the phone as most banks allow this. In this chapter, I also cover what to do if you lose your ATM card: Promptly report it to your bank and ask for a new one. I also mention how check verification companies can be a great ally, especially if someone cashes bad checks in your name. Finally I discuss closing credit accounts.

## Closing Bank Accounts

When should you close your bank account? Close accounts anytime the account has been compromised, or when you notice unauthorized withdrawals on your monthly statements from your bank. Look for checks you didn't write for stuff you didn't purchase or cash you never withdrew.

Naturally, close any accounts that have been opened fraudulently in your name. Don't forget to check your credit report for fraudulently opened accounts. Notify your bank or any other financial institutions where these accounts reside; contact the financial institutions where these fraudulent accounts were opened and ask them to investigate and close as fraud because you are a victim of identity theft and tell someone there that the accounts weren't opened by you and that you've been the victim of identity theft. Send the fraud affidavit to the bank (or use their fraud form if they don't accept the fraud affidavit).

In some cases, you need to close the account even if there aren't some strange transactions because your account information has been compromised. By looking at your bank statement on a regular basis, you can catch the problem so you can do damage control by working with your bank. But close any account that has been compromised immediately no matter how small the amounts taken were. Report all missing sums of money to your bank immediately; do not wait, even if the sum is small.

Better to be safe than sorry, even though closing the account may be a pain. Closing savings accounts isn't usually as much of a pain as closing a checking account because you don't have to balance it, but both are equally important — your money is your money.

## When your ATM card goes missing

You're at the ATM ready to withdraw some cash, but you can't find your ATM card. Don't panic; let your bank know immediately — even on weekends and holidays. You can do this several ways:

- ✔ Go to your bank's online Web site and report the lost card.

- ✔ Call the bank at the number that's printed on your monthly statement and report the lost card.

- ✔ Visit a branch of your bank during business hours and report the lost card. If the bank is closed for a holiday you can contact someone at the company that backs the credit card — Visa or MasterCard perhaps — and tell them to block or cancel the card if you are unable to reach your bank.

- ✔ If your card is lost or stolen overseas, your bank may not have an international number, but the company that backs the card does.

When you report the lost card, the bank cancels the card immediately, and a new one is issued in about ten days. When you're traveling, even in foreign countries, most banks will arrange to send you a new temporary card overnight for your convenience. Remember to change your PIN as well (because you don't know if the old PIN was compromised).

If you lose your ATM card while traveling, don't use a computer from your hotel room (even in the U.S.) to go online and check your account because hotel Internet systems can be compromised (and not just wireless connections). Don't use the phone from your hotel room, either. Hotel phone systems in some foreign countries, as well in the U.S., have been compromised and even monitored by the government.

You don't need to be paranoid about using technology; you just need to be mindful that some vulnerabilities can be exploited in Internet connections and phone services from hotel rooms. This isn't true in all countries, but it helps to be cautious. The same holds true for the U.S.; most hotel phones and Internet connections are safe to use to check your bank account information, but I suggest erring on the side of caution.

If you don't have your account information, your bank may be able to get it with the last four digits of your Social Security Number (SSN) and by verifying other personal information, such as your home address and so on.

Don't check your bank information from a coffee shop, a restaurant, public computers, public Wi-Fi connections, and so on. In other words, be careful in public places.

When you get your ATM card, call to activate it. When calling from your home or another phone number that's tied to the account, you can easily activate the new card. Do so through the automated system by calling the 800 number on the sticker that's on the card when it's sent to you. Calling the 800 number from another number than the one that's on the account will require you to speak to a live person so that she can verify some personal information for security reasons.

Several years ago, I forgot to take my card from an ATM at a branch of my bank. I didn't realize that I left the card until I arrived at work. The bank was close to where I worked, so I went back to see if the card was still in the machine. The card was gone, so I immediately called someone at the bank and he cancelled the card and issued me a new one. The card arrived in about ten days and couldn't be used until I activated it. I also changed my PIN. I checked the balances in my accounts when I spoke to the bank representative on the phone, and the accounts weren't compromised, so I didn't close them. I checked my monthly statement religiously every month and encountered no problems. (Note that some cards are activated when you first make a purchase.)

To limit your liability to $50 for the lost ATM card if it's used to drain your bank accounts, you must report the loss within 48 hours; otherwise, you may be liable for $500 in losses from your accounts. At some financial institutions your ATM/debit cards have the same zero liability as a credit card. Check with your financial institution to find out if this is the case; do not assume that your bank has zero liability for its ATM cards. You need to read and understand your reporting requirements when it comes to letting your institution know that there are fraudulent or mistaken charges. Some require two business days. Please read the section of your contract under reasonable care to get all the details about your institution's policies for reporting. See the nearby sidebar, "Clarifying the zero liability issue."

## Clarifying the zero liability issue

ATM/debit cards have the same zero liability as a credit card. To clarify the zero liability issue, by law, you're held only to the $50 maximum if you weren't negligent or if you reported the issue in a timely manner. In practice, financial institutions are *not* holding to the $50, but are claiming zero liability for PR and marketing reasons. Don't take the chance that your bank will forgive any charges; report the loss immediately and check your account immediately as well to make sure that no money is missing. This means that you don't have any charges that you don't recognize as yours on your statement. With online banking, this is easy to check.

When you review your monthly account statement and notice unauthorized withdrawals on it, report it to your bank immediately. You have only 60 days from the date the account statement was mailed to you to report any unauthorized withdrawals on your monthly statement, or you can potentially lose all the money in your account.

Make sure that you add your ATM card to the list of notifications you need to make if your wallet or purse is stolen. Report the stolen ATM card to your bank within the 2-day time frame, and be sure to review your monthly statement and report any unauthorized withdrawals within the 60-day time limit.

## *Reporting to check verification companies*

If your personal checks have been lost or stolen, contact your bank and close your account. Have the bank contact someone at Chex Systems to alert him that your checks have been lost or stolen. (*Chex Systems* is the network used by banks and credit unions to report mishandled checking accounts or overdrawn accounts.) Only banks that subscribe to the service can report mishandled accounts, but as a consumer, you can report stolen or lost checks. Members report the history of account mishandling and the outstanding debt.

You can order a consumer report from Chex Systems to see what's in your file. Simply go to www.chexhelp.com and follow the link to order your consumer report.

Don't forget to contact your local police department about stolen checks. If your checks are used fraudulently, you will receive notification of that fact in writing from the merchant who had the check bounce. At that point, you can contact a check verification company (see Table 14-1) that the merchant uses and notify them of the fraud. This list isn't all inclusive; other companies are listed on the Internet. The ones on the list are simply the most widely used.

| Table 14-1 | Check Verification Companies | |
|---|---|---|
| *Company Name* | *Telephone Number* | *Web Site URL* |
| Certegy | 800-437-5120 | www.certegy.com |
| TeleCheck (owned by First Data) | 800-366-2425 | www.telecheck.com |
| Chex Systems | 800-428-9623 | www.chexhelp.com |

The SCAN report has information regarding where your checks have been cashed and have come back as non-sufficient funds (NSF) from your bank. The SCAN Web site has a forgery affidavit to use if your checks have been lost or stolen.

## Covering checks that you've written already

The checks you wrote before you closed the account need to be paid. Your bank pays the checks with funds from your new account. Table 14-2 shows the information you need to provide for *each* check you've written.

| Table 14-2 Checklist for Closing Compromised Checking Account | |
|---|---|
| *Item* | *Information* |
| Check number | |
| Payee name | |
| Amount | |
| Date written | |

Don't write new checks on the closed account. You must work with your bank to cover the outstanding checks. Shred all the old checking account's checks so that you won't use the wrong check and they won't fall into the wrong hands. Checks from a closed account in the wrong hands can cause a nightmare for you because you'll have bad checks with your name, address, and more on them. Even though the account's closed, someone can still try to use the old checks from the old account. Sometimes the fraudster will make up new checks by using your account numbers, because the necessary information — the bank's routing number and your account number — is on the checks. Both numbers appear at the bottom-right corner of your check. The first set of numbers is the routing number, and the second set is your account numbers.

Today, merchants use the point-of-sale (POS) check verification system, which works like this:

1. You write a check for a purchase and hand it to a cashier.

2. You sign your name on an electronic pad (the same one used for ATM and credit card transactions).

3. The cashier runs the check through the register and then hands you the canceled check and receipt.

   On the back of the check is bank information for the merchant and is what would be stamped on the check if the check was sent to your bank for payment. In this case, the process is completed electronically.

4. Your checking account is debited as it would be if you'd used your ATM card for the transaction.

The system helps eliminate NSF checks that pass through the company because the funds need to be available before the transaction is completed and a receipt is printed. When the funds are insufficient to cover the purchase amount, the check is rejected. The system helps everyone save money because the merchant isn't stuck with bad checks and doesn't need to raise prices to cover the bad checks and lost merchandise.

When you pay online, your bank sends the check to pay the bill with money from your account, using a different a check that doesn't have your account number on it.

## Closing Credit Accounts

Close all credit accounts you didn't open or authorize to be opened. Also, close any credit accounts that aren't used. You can close the accounts by telephone. To close an account by telephone, use the checklist in Table 14-3.

| Table 14-3 | Checklist to Close a Credit Account by Telephone |
|---|---|
| *Information Needed* | *What to Ask* |
| Card number (account number) | Balance on account and last payment. Don't forget to dispute unauthorized charges. |
| Date, time you called, and representative's name | Write down the date, time, and name of the person you talked to about closing the account. |
| Request account be closed | Notations to reflect you closed the account. |
| Confirmation letter | The date to expect the confirmation letter that the account was closed. |

You can also close credit accounts by sending a letter to the card issuer. Figure 14-1 shows a sample letter you can send to close your credit accounts. You can modify the letter to meet your needs.

Date: *mm/dd/yyyy*

To: *Name and address of credit company*

From: *Your name and address*

Account Number _____

Please close the account number listed above. The reason for closing the account is listed below. If you report to a major credit bureau, please indicate that this account was closed at my request. Also, please send me written confirmation that this account has been closed.

_____ The account has not been used in several months (the cut up card is enclosed).

_____ The account was opened without my knowledge (I am not in possession of the card). A fraud affidavit is enclosed.

I can be reached at (give a telephone where you can be reached).

Sincerely,

*Your Name*

**Figure 14-1:** Sample letter to close credit card accounts.

Closing credit accounts you didn't open is very important. To help with closing these credit accounts, use the fraud affidavit on the FTC Web site, as I indicate in the sample letter in Figure 14-1. The affidavit lets the creditor know that you're disputing the account. Along with the fraud affidavit, send a police report, especially if you're an identity theft victim. Sending these documents helps you state your case to the creditor that you aren't the one who opened the account(s). In addition, you may want to place a fraud alert on your credit report — or even better, place a credit freeze on your credit report. (The freeze is free if you've been a victim of identity theft.) The sooner you close these credit card accounts that someone else opened in your name, the sooner you'll be on the road to getting your good name back.

Whether you contact the credit issuer by phone or in writing, don't delay. Do it now so that the card issuers know that you've been a victim of identity theft and that the accounts aren't yours. When you submit the proper documents proving that you have been a victim of identity theft, such as a fraud affidavit and a police report, the credit card issuers have to address the situation with you. The police report has a case number on it, and this is information the credit issuer will request and use to verify your story. (***Note:*** Not all banks or financial institutions will require a police report, but it is a good idea if you can get one.) Credit issuers might also have their own forms for you to complete; when you write the credit issuers, ask for any forms they might have.

Some credit accounts need to be closed by writing to the creditor rather than calling them on the phone. They'll want to know that the account closing is because of fraud and as I previously state, they want more than just word of mouth.

No matter how you close the account, ask for written confirmation that the account's been closed. The credit company doesn't automatically close accounts just because you haven't used them, they're paid in full, and have a zero balance. You need to tell the company to close the accounts. Cutting up your cards (or not activating your cards) from the account doesn't close the account. Of course, you do still need to cut up the cards.

Another scenario that causes you to close a credit account is if your credit card becomes missing. Whether you lose the card or believe it's been stolen, report that it's missing to your card issuer *immediately.* The card issuer's phone number (likely a toll-free number) appears on your paper statement or online. Have your account number or SSN readily available when you call. The card issuer will probably close the account and issue you a new card right away. Any outstanding balance is transferred automatically to your new account and card number. You still need to make any payment that is due on legitimate transactions by the regular due date or you will be assessed late fees.

## Credit card fraud versus identity theft

There's a big difference between credit card fraud and identity theft, which I explain in Chapter 3. *Credit card fraud* involves the unauthorized use of one or more of your credit cards to make purchases. *Identity theft,* on the other hand, is the stealing of your name and personal information to open new accounts in your name.

If you review your monthly statement and notice that you've been a victim of credit card fraud, notify your credit card issuer immediately. You can call the number on the back of your credit card. Tell someone at the company that

you want to speak to the fraud department. After you tell the card issuer's representative what charges are fraudulent, she will issue a temporary credit on your credit card statement until she completes the investigation. For ATM and debit transactions, you get your money back ASAP. You're also notified in writing about the call you made and the charges you're contesting. This process usually takes about five to ten business days to receive the letter. In 30 days, you will hear that the credit card issuer has received your complaint. You can expect to get a resolution within 90 days.

In most cases, especially for small amounts, the credit card issuer will permanently remove the charges from your statement account balance. After checking the next month's statement, if you find the same charges again with new dates of the transaction, call the card issuer again. This happened to me, and the credit card issuer cancelled my card and issued a new one because it was a subscription authorization (recurring charge).

Most credit card companies do a better job today of monitoring their card holders' accounts in an attempt to spot fraud.

# Chapter 15

# Opening New Accounts

· · · · · · · · · · · · · · · · · · · · · · · · · · · · · · · · · · · · · · · · · · · · · · · · · · ·

## In This Chapter

▶ Opening new bank accounts

▶ Keeping tabs on your new accounts

▶ Using a new PIN for a new account

▶ Opening new credit accounts

· · · · · · · · · · · · · · · · · · · · · · · · · · · · · · · · · · · · · · · · · · · · · · · · · · ·

*I*n this chapter, I outline the things you need to do when you open your new accounts. I show you how to keep tabs on the account balances, help you pick a new personal identification number (PIN) for your new account, prompt you to change your paycheck to direct deposit to your new account, and detail how to open new credit accounts.

## Opening New Bank Accounts

After you close your old bank accounts, you need to open new ones. This is usually done in one step if the account is being closed because of fraud as opposed to consumer request. For your new checking accounts, you're issued temporary checks to use until your permanent ones are printed. The temporary checks don't have your name, address, or phone number printed on them; use them only as a last resort and be prepared for the third degree. (And note that many merchants will not accept them.)

Opening new bank accounts isn't hard, but it can be a pain, especially because you might have to go to the bank to open the account. If you are closing a compromised account, you can do that by phone; if you open a new account with that same institution, you can likely also do that by phone. If you have to go to the bank to open a new account, you must provide an ID (government picture ID, passport, driver's license, and so on) because the Patriot Act requires identification of anyone opening a bank account. The bank verifies your identification while you're there. After the verification is complete, you're asked to sign the forms after you decide what type of account you want.

As you know, banks offer a variety of accounts. When choosing what type of account to open, consider these issues:

- ✔ **Does the account require a minimum daily balance or collect a service charge?** Some accounts and banks require you to keep a minimum daily balance in your account, or the bank will charge you a monthly fee for checking accounts. Some consider the savings combined with the checking account to meet the minimum daily balance; however the bank does it, you need to maintain the minimum daily balance or you may have to pay a service charge, which varies from bank to bank.

- ✔ **Arrange to pick up your new checks at the bank.** The banker will give you temporary checks to use until the design you've chosen arrives from the printer. Have the new checks sent to the bank address, not your home address. You can pick them up at the bank. I've done this for years and haven't had a problem. With debit cards and online banking, I find I don't write as many checks as I did in the past, but I still check my statements often to make sure that there aren't any problems.

After you decide what type of account you want, complete the paperwork and give the banker some money to open the account.

The bank usually prints your name, address, and telephone number on your checks as well as your account number, bank routing number, and the bank's name and address. These checks contain all the information an ID thief needs to make up a fake ID to pass off your checks as hers, so don't make it easy for her to steal them from you.

Table 15-1 is a quick checklist to use as a guide for opening new accounts. The checklist isn't all inclusive, but it gives you a good idea of what needs to be done when you open a new account. Add to the checklist as necessary to ensure that you cover the important items.

| Table 15-1 | Checklist to Open New Accounts |
| --- | --- |
| *Account Type* | *Action* |
| Savings | Transfer balance from old, closed account. |
| | Check balance. |
| Checking | Transfer balance from old, closed account. |
| | Order new checks and have them sent to your bank for pickup. |
| | Get a supply of temporary checks. |
| | Ask for a new ATM card and make up a new PIN — *don't use your old PIN.* |
| | Check account balance. |
| | Tell your employer your new account number for your paycheck deposit. |

---

## Rerouting your paycheck

If you closed your existing account that your paycheck was deposited in, did you remember to notify your employer of the change in accounts? You don't want your paycheck bouncing around in the cold, hard world and not have a warm, friendly home to be deposited in. To make the change, your employer might need a voided check from your new checking account, similar to what you provided when you initiated direct deposit on the old account, and you might have to fill out another form. After a couple paychecks, the switch takes effect. You have to deposit your paycheck into your new account on your own for a bit.

---

## *Maintaining good records*

The balance in the new account is probably the transfer of the balance from the old account. As you did with your old accounts, keep tabs on the balances in the new accounts. Review the initial account balance and check it against your first monthly statement to make sure that the account hasn't been compromised.

Keeping good records is important. The checks you write, deposit receipts you receive, your direct deposit stub from your paycheck, and more — all this can be of value to you when you balance your checkbook. Then when you receive your monthly statement, you can keep tabs on the balance in the account.

Your savings account balance is a little easier to keep tabs on. Because you don't write checks on the account, you can check the account balance simply by reviewing the monthly statement your bank sends to you. The only thing you need to track are the withdrawals you make. Keep your ATM and withdrawal receipts so that you can compare them to your monthly statements.

### *Tracking your accounts online*

Keeping tabs on your accounts became easier with the advent of online banking, which is a great convenience. You can see your balance anytime you want and from almost anywhere. I say *almost anywhere* because you need to be discreet when accessing your online account in public to make sure that nobody steals your account information, user ID, and password. Having online, 24/7 access to your accounts means that you have no reason not to keep tabs on them.

With online banking, you can immediately correct any problems you notice. This is a benefit, especially for my checking account when I noticed the bank charged me a monthly checking account fee that was debited that day. I immediately called the 800 number and spoke to a banker. I explained that the account I have for my checking account doesn't have a monthly fee. The person I spoke to agreed and immediately reversed the charge and credited my account. Without online banking, it would've been one month before my statement arrived in the mail.

Online bank records are easy to access, and you can make a printout if the need arises. In the past with paper statements, you needed to keep them for your records. Now you don't need to keep paper records. Your bank has folders set up for the statement months, and if you need a particular month's statement, you can get it by going to that month and clicking it.

### Choosing a secure user ID and password

Online banking requires you to have a user ID and password. Choose a password that is different than any other one you are currently using. Also choose a password that isn't easy for someone else to guess but that you can easily remember because you don't want to write it down. The password needs to have letters, numbers, and special characters (@, #, &). You can use a catchphrase to help you remember the password. Catchphrases can be something you made up and only you know what it is. (If you need to write down either your password or the catchphrase, store the paper in a fireproof safe or some other safe place.)

Don't panic if you forget your password. On your bank's sign-in page, you'll likely find a Forgot My Password link, which lets you to set up a new password. If you answered security questions during the setup phase, you'll see those questions, and you must answer them to verify your identity. Here are sample questions:

✔ What is the name of the elementary school you attended?

✔ What was your favorite job?

✔ Who was your childhood hero?

Do not give real answers to these questions. Use fake ones, so if someone has real information about you, they can't answer these questions and gain access to the account.

When answering the question you choose, the answer box might be case sensitive (it should say whether it is). So if you type the answer in all caps during sign-up, you need to answer it in all caps as well. You may think I'm stating the obvious, but under pressure, you may forget and you get only three attempts before you're locked out of the system for security reasons. Being locked out isn't the end of the world. If you get locked out, call your bank and tell someone there that you're locked out of your account. The banker will refer you to someone in IT (Information Technology) who will ask you some security questions to verify your identification and then he'll reset your password.

Some banks and credit card companies reject your logon if it looks like it came from a different computer than the one you signed up on. This is the case when you purchase a new computer, add a router, and so on. This is a security feature in place because the computer looks different; the MAC address (the address of the computer that is built into the system) changes from the original you used to sign up or used previously to enter your account information. The bank or credit card company sends you an authorization number via e-mail, phone, or text message — whichever method you choose. The number is then typed in an Authorization Number box. After you do this, you're granted access to your account information. *Note:* This might not be the case for all institutions; yours may not do this. You need to be aware, however, that it may happen like this.

## Using a new PIN

So you closed your old accounts and opened new ones. You now have new account numbers, but what about your PIN? You were probably given a new ATM card. Did you remember to change your PIN, as well? Better safe than sorry if you closed the accounts because they were compromised. Use a new PIN, period! With the ATM card doubling as a debit card, I caution you to err on the safe side and change your PIN.

Debit cards are easy to use and in most cases, you don't need to sign a receipt. With selfcheckouts at grocery stores, home improvement stores, and so on, a thief can easily use a debit card without having to sign a receipt. However, the thief will need your PIN to use the card. So the better the PIN — that is the harder it is for someone to guess — the harder it is for a thief to obtain it. (Unfortunately, if the thief uses your debit/ATM as a credit card, no PIN is needed for most transactions.)

When you change account numbers for any reason, change your PIN as well, regardless of whether your PIN has been compromised. In fact, change your PIN periodically even if you haven't lost your ATM card. I know you have a great deal of passwords, PINS, user IDs, and so on to remember, but it's important to change your PIN.

When you choose a new PIN, choose one that's easy for you to memorize (so that you don't need to write it down) and hard for others to guess. PINs are usually made up only of numbers, but you can remember the numbers by replacing the numbers with letters. You can make up a catchphrase that's easy to remember and then replace the letters with numbers. For example, you could choose 47861 and remember it as the catchphrase "thank goodness it's Friday again" — TGIFA. The T is 4, the G is 7, the I is 8, the F is 6, and A is 1. This is just an example; do *not* use this for your PIN.

Don't use the last four digits of your Social Security Number (SSN) or your birthday. If you must use a phone number or birthday, use a friend's phone number or birthday, or some other number that you can remember easily but that a thief can't guess easily.

# Opening New Credit Accounts

To maintain a good credit score (see Chapter 5 for more information on credit scores), don't open two new credit accounts at one time. You're better off to stagger the new accounts because the new accounts haven't aged, so they don't have a credit history.

If you've been the victim of identity theft and filed all the proper notifications and closed all compromised and fraudulent accounts (see Chapter 14 for more details), however, you can open new credit accounts without compromising your credit rating. But don't overdo it.

So really be selective of what accounts you need and don't open accounts just for the sake of opening accounts. Check the interest rates on any new account's credit card and other accounts (new car loans, and so on) before you open them. If at all possible, stay away from the lure of a low introductory rate that will adjust in a year or so and then become a variable rate. These are similar to the teaser mortgage rates that got people into the financial mess they're in at the present time.

How many credit accounts you need or have is up to you, but you probably don't want too much debt. (To help track your credit accounts, subscribe to one of the online services from one of the major credit reporting agencies — TransUnion, Experian, and Equifax — that I outline in Chapter 5.) Today you can use your Visa, MasterCard, Discover Card, and American Express in most major department and even grocery stores, as well as at gas stations. This limits the number of cards you need. The days of "the more credit cards you have, the better" are gone. This helps limit your exposure to credit card fraud because you don't need to carry so many cards with you. One card will usually do the trick, and then you have only one to worry about losing if your wallet or purse is stolen.

## Opening credit accounts online

Like everything else today, you can apply for new credit cards online. To do this, go to the credit card company's Web site and locate the link for new applications (or whatever the card company calls it). Signing up for a credit card online is easy and convenient, but you still need to be careful about where you sign up. If you're at home and have the proper safeguards in place, use your computer to sign up. Don't use a public computer, such as one at the local library or school. Public computers are not secure and someone can log on after you and see where you went; if you didn't log out for some reason, that person can then access your account. The application is submitted to the card company electronically through its Web site.

Before you fill out any online application with personal information, make sure the site you're on is secure. To determine whether the site is secure, look for these signs:

- ✔ **A lock at the bottom-right corner of the page:** If the lock icon is in a locked position, the site is secure.
- ✔ **The VeriSign logo:** The appearance of this logo tells you the site is secure.
- ✔ **The https:// in the URL field:** If https:// appears in the address field of the online application page, you're on a secure page.

Do *not* open e-mails that solicit you to sign up for a credit card even it looks legitimate; this can be dangerous because most e-mails that solicit your personal information are bogus. If you open the e-mail and click the link to the Web page, you're taken to the site the thief set up to steal your personal information.

Go directly to the credit card company's Web site to complete the application process because it's safer. To find the Web site, call the company and ask for its URL or go to the BBB and find it. Do not just do a search and start completing the application because you may not be on a legitimate site.

## Proving your identity when opening new credit accounts

When you open new credit accounts, you'll probably need to show proof that you are who you say you are. You need to have a picture ID if you're opening the account at a financial institution different from your current one. If you've placed a fraud alert on your credit report, the alert requires creditors to verify your identity and you'll be notified by the credit bureau that an inquiry has been made about your credit. (For more details on credit reports, see Chapter 5; for information on placing a fraud alert on your credit report, see Chapter 13.)

# Part VII
# The Part of Tens

The 5th Wave                    By Rich Tennant

"We take securing personal information very seriously here."

# In this part...

An important signature of the *For Dummies* series is "The Part of Tens," and no book would be complete without it. This part contains some useful information to help guide you through the process of reclaiming your identity if you've been a victim. I also detail handy resources and security tools that you can use. Finally, I discuss how to avoid some common scams that identity thieves use.

# Chapter 16

# Ten (Or So) Tips to Make Reclaiming Your Identity Go More Smoothly

*T*he following sections tell you how to reclaim your identity in the easiest way possible. Use the following suggestions as guidelines to help you navigate your way through the process more smoothly. Today online companies will help guide you through the arduous process of reclaiming your identity. Don't get discouraged; now is not the time to quit. Hang in there, be persistent, and get it done.

## Follow a Checklist

Time to get organized. If you're the victim of identity theft, you can use the checklist in Chapter 2 to get organized and plan your counterattack, or you can create your own. Whether you use the checklist in this book or make up your own doesn't matter; you just need to follow a checklist. The checklist is your road map to help you navigate your way through the issues you face and the tasks you need to do in order to reclaim your identity. The checklist helps keep you focused on the task of reclaiming your identity after you've been a victim. By using a checklist, you'll know what's been done and what's left to do. A checklist helps you keep your sanity in this tough situation by taking a systematic approach to reclaiming your identity.

# Keep a Journal

If you take nothing else away from this book, know that the more you document about your case, the better off you are in the end. Document everything in detail, keep copies of everything you send out, and keep summaries of phone conversations. You can't over document, but you can shortchange yourself if you do it too sparingly. Your journal needs to list all the people and organizations you've contacted, their titles, dates, and a brief summary of the conversation if it was by telephone. This will be a valuable reference for your follow-up work. Documenting everything during the fight to restore your credit and good name seems like a distraction, but it isn't. Your journal can be a valuable tool in the fight.

Your journal is a record of what you did and when, and anything you can put in your arsenal to help you reclaim your good name and good credit.

Online companies that help you with identity theft have all the forms and the process online, so keeping a hard copy journal may not be necessary. However, keep a backup of all the documents you complete on a portable drive just in case the Web site for the company crashes. This way you can still continue the fight to reclaim your good name and credit.

# Complete a Fraud Affidavit

As soon as you realize that you've been the victim of identity theft, you need to complete a fraud affidavit and send it to the creditors of your fraudulent accounts. The affidavit is the first step on the road to reclaiming your identity. The fraud affidavit can be found on the Federal Trade Commission Web site as the theft affidavit (see Chapter 13 for more details). Keep copies of each affidavit you send out in your journal, along with the certified return receipt.

Completing the fraud affidavit isn't difficult, but it can be time consuming. You need to complete one for each creditor, but you can streamline the process by completing the Victim Information section and then making copies to use for all the rest of the creditors and banks to whom you're sending the form. Be sure to sign each one before you send it. Don't forget to make and keep copies for your journal.

Send the affidavits via the United States Postal Service Certified Mail return receipt. The Certified Mail receipt serves as proof that the addressee received the document. Keep the receipts for your journal.

# Record All Correspondence with Creditors

Keep a record of all verbal and written correspondence with creditors. If you choose verbal correspondence, you can use a tape recorder to make a record of the conversation, but you need to get permission from the other party before you can record the conversation. If you don't get permission, you're breaking the wiretapping law. You can ask for permission and then have that person repeat for the tape recorder that she has granted you permission. When you use a tape recorder, make sure that you preface the conversation with the repeat of the approval to record and the date, time, and the name of the person and organization's name for your records. Follow up the conversation with a written summary of what was discussed.

For written correspondence, keep a journal of who (person and organization you addressed the correspondence to), what (fraudulent account, dispute charge, and so on), when (date), where (location, store), and a brief summary of the context of the document. Also keep a copy of the complete document that was sent and any documents you receive.

# Follow Up

An important part of the process is follow-up. Just because you called and sent correspondence to close fraudulent accounts or to dispute charges does not mean that your issues will be addressed. You need to follow up, or nothing will happen.

Follow up all your telephone conversations with written correspondence and all your written correspondence with telephone calls. Your journal will come in handy to help you track when follow-up needs to be done.

Set up a *tickler file,* which lists the name of the person you contacted, and when and how you contacted him. The tickler file is used to track whom you've contacted along with the next time you should contact him for further follow-up.

Follow up within one week from your initial contact. After the first follow-up, ask when you can expect to hear from him. Mark your calendar. If you don't hear back, contact him again.

Be persistent, but be tactful. You catch more flies with honey than with vinegar; being caustic won't help your cause. If you seem to be getting nowhere with a particular person, by all means, ask to talk to someone higher up the ladder. Remember that your problem isn't her problem; she isn't the one who had her identity stolen. How you approach her will help you ensure that you're her problem, as well.

# Place a Fraud Alert on Your Credit Report

Contact one of the three credit bureaus (Experian, Equifax, and TransUnion) and place a fraud alert on your credit report. This action is helpful in keeping the identity thief from continuing to use your good name and credit. The fraud alert is supposed to guarantee that a phone call is made to you any time an application for credit is completed for verification. However, companies can (and do) choose to ignore the fraud alert and process the application anyway.

You can place a fraud alert on your credit report by contacting the fraud department of one of the credit bureaus. Even though a fraud alert on your credit report isn't a cure-all, it's a good first step to reclaiming your good name and credit.

Sometimes creditors ignore the fraud alert and credit bureaus do not have to notify you when credit is approved, so it's advisable for you to review your credit report regularly — at least monthly.

Document when you contacted the credit bureau to place the fraud alert on your credit report. You should receive written notification that the fraud alert was placed on your credit report. Each credit bureau will send you a letter.

I used the fraud alert when my mail was stolen; it was good for 90 days. The fraud alert is a good tool to help keep you safe if your mail is stolen; however, the credit freeze may be a better option. To minimize your exposure, don't receive paper statements from the following.

- ✔ Credit card statements
- ✔ Bank statements: checking and savings
- ✔ 401K
- ✔ Stocks

I didn't renew the fraud alert because no personal information was in the mailbox at the time. I changed to paperless statements after the mail was stolen.

# File a Credit Freeze

Filing a credit freeze helps you prevent further damage to your good name and credit. As I discuss in Chapter 2, a *credit freeze* is a good tool to help you reclaim your identity because it prevents the identity thief from using your credit to open accounts in your name. If you've been a victim, the freezes are free; otherwise, you have to pay to implement the freeze. (Chapter 2 has the details about costs for those who aren't victims.)

# File a Police Report

Another important task for you to do is to file a police report. The police report needs to be filed in the city, town, or county where you reside. If your mail was taken from your mailbox, you must contact your local law enforcement agency. On the other hand, if your wallet or purse was stolen, you need to file a police report where the wallet or purse was stolen.

A police report helps you convince creditors that you have in fact been the victim of identity theft. The police report should be sent with the fraud affidavit you send to creditors.

When you call or go in person to file the police report, be persistent and ask for the financial or fraud crimes division. The report will most likely be taken over the telephone, but in some cases, you can make the report online. You may receive a follow-up visit or be contacted by the detective assigned to the case, or the report number may be all the contact you have about your report. This doesn't mean that the police aren't working the case; it means that they don't need any further information from you at the present time. It may be helpful to add contacting the police to get a status report on your case to your follow-up effort.

Document in your journal the date and time you asked for a copy of the report to be sent to you, the agency from which you made the request, and the report number. When you receive the copy of the report, place it in your journal.

Filing a police report helps you when you file a fraud alert or credit freeze. The police report number is essential to filing extended seven-year fraud alerts and to file a free credit freeze. The police report adds credibility in making your case that you're a victim of identity theft and the debts that have been accumulated in your name are not yours.

# Dispute Charges You Didn't Make

Don't be pressured into paying charges you didn't make or authorize. Even if the amount is small, don't pay. The creditors will try and recoup some of their losses from you by telling you that if you pay this small amount, you'll be helping yourself because the charge won't go to collections. Well, after you dispute a charge and send your creditor a dispute letter, it can't go to collections by law until it's resolved one way or the other. Making a payment, in some cases, is considered accepting responsibility for the debt. This is an argument that can be used by creditors when you dispute the debt at a later date.

Credit card companies are usually quick to fix any charges that are truly fraudulent. I can attest to this because I've had fraudulent charges placed on my credit cards in the past.

If the credit account was opened fraudulently, request that it be closed and follow up with written documentation. Summarize the conversations in writing and place copies of any documents sent in your journal.

A fraud affidavit helps you when you challenge charges that aren't yours on accounts you didn't open. The affidavit along with a police report informs the creditor that you've been a victim of identity theft and you didn't open the accounts in question. The creditor may still push back even with the affidavit, but you must be persistent to reclaim your good name and credit. Don't get discouraged; you need to stick with the program and dispute all the charges that aren't yours and the accounts you didn't open.

If the creditor has his own paperwork for filing disputes, use it so he knows that you're serious about your dispute.

# Report Your Stolen Checks to One of the Check Verification Companies

Just reporting and closing your compromised checks at your bank may not be enough. The bank may not report the theft or counterfeiting of your checks to one of the check verification companies that I outline in Chapter 14.

Also report the loss or counterfeiting of your checks to one of the check verification companies, even if you close the account and open a new one. You want to make sure that the incident is reported and that your name isn't added to the list of people who pass bad checks. Even if you open a new checking account, the problem will still plague you.

The check verification companies have contact phone numbers for you to call and report stolen or lost checks. I list the phone numbers and several check verification companies in Chapter 14. (You can also find check verification companies by doing a Web search for them.)

Make sure that you document that you've opened a new account and that you notified your bank, the name of your contact at the bank, the date of your conversation, and the reason for closing your old account and opening the new one.

# Close Compromised Accounts

Close all compromised accounts, including accounts that were opened fraudulently or accounts to which a thief has gained access. Keep any paperwork that shows the date the accounts were closed. Also include the name of the person you contacted to close the accounts. Place all this documentation in your journal.

When you close compromised credit card accounts, don't just cut up the card and send the pieces to them. Be sure to include a letter similar to the one in Chapter 14, stating that you're closing the account and the reason. Then keep a record of all the correspondence in your journal. Record the name of your contact, the date you spoke, and a summary of any telephone conversations.

Keep your journal in a safe place. Today, online companies help you reclaim your identity if you've been a victim. I discuss these companies in Chapter 9. Most of these companies have online journals you can use instead of a hard copy journal to track your progress in reclaiming your identity. Make sure that you back up your files in case something happens to your online data.

# Chapter 17

# Ten Handy Resources

*1* n this chapter, I outline some important resources for you to use to prevent identity theft and help you recover your good name and credit if you're a victim.

# Web Sites

Here's a list of some helpful Web sites to discover more about identity theft and what to do if you're a victim. Table 17-1 provides the Web site name and URL followed by information about each site.

| Table 17-1 | | Web Sites |
|---|---|---|
| *Web Site* | *URL* | *Type* |
| Federal Trade Commission (FTC) | www.ftc.gov | Provides prevention information and what to do if you're a victim. |
| Identity Theft Resource Center | www.idtheft center.org | Non-profit that provides prevention information and what to do if you're victim. |
| Privacy Rights Clearinghouse | www.privacy rights.org | Non-profit that explains what to do if you're a victim. |

*(continued)*

### Table 17-1 (continued)

| Web Site | URL | Type |
|---|---|---|
| United States Department of Justice | www.usdoj.gov | Explains what identity theft is, how to prevent it, what to do if you're a victim. |
| Social Security Administration | www.ssa.gov | Provides links to other government agencies. |
| Equifax Midwest Equifax affiliate Experian TransUnion | www.equifax.com www.csc.com/ credit_services/ offerings/11204- consumer_credit_ products www.experian.com www.tuc.com | Credit bureaus that allow you to use credit report products for a fee, to order free credit reports, and to dispute mistakes on credit reports. |
| United States Postal Service | www.usps.com | Follow links to Postal Inspectors identity theft prevention, find out what to do if you're a victim, and use links to other government agencies. |
| Identity Theft Protection | www.identity-theft-help.us | Consumer Web site that explains how to prevent identity theft and what to do if you're a victim. |
| Truston | www.mytruston.com | Company that provides identity theft resources to help you reclaim your identity. |
| LifeLock | www.lifelock.com | Company that assists you in protecting your identity. It also provides help to its clients if they become victims. |

The Web sites I list in Table 17-1 are just some of the sites you can find that address identity theft. These sites are some of the ones that come up most frequently in identity theft searches on the Web. I find the information on these sites very useful. You may find other sites, but at least with this list, you have a good starting point.

# Major Credit Card Issuers

Table 17-2 lists the major credit cards. Visa and MasterCard are also issued by most of the major banks around the United States. The Web sites provide good general information as well as what to do if you've lost or had a card stolen.

| Table 17-2 | Major Credit Issuers |
|---|---|
| *Issuing Company* | *Web Site URL* |
| MasterCard | www.mastercard.com |
| Visa | www.visa.com |
| Discover | www.discovercard.com |
| Citibank | www.citibank.com |
| American Express | www.americanexpress.com |

Citi Cards come with a free service to card members to help you get your identity back if you're an identity theft victim. The Citi Identity Theft Solutions provide identity theft specialists to help you if you're a victim. As a card member, you will have an 800 number you can call if you're a victim and an identity theft specialist is assigned to help guide you on how to file a police report and close accounts with creditors. The Web site says that the Citi Identity Theft Specialist will stay on the phone with you as you place a fraud alert on your credit report. Also, Citi sends you an Identity Theft Tool Kit, which has fraud affidavit forms — a Security Affidavit and an Identity Theft Worksheet — and an information booklet provided by the FTC and Citigroup.

# Credit Report Services

Credit report services give you unlimited credit reports and e-mail alerts of any inquiries into your credit. All three credit bureaus (Experian, Equifax, and TransUnion) provide these services (see Chapter 5 for more details). Companies also exist that provide services that aren't affiliated with these credit bureaus. The services are worth the annual fee because you have unlimited access to your credit report. The only drawback is that you only have access to the credit report of the credit bureau's service that you subscribe to. I recommend purchasing a three-in-one report at least once per year. The three-in-one report gives the status of your credit across all three bureaus and shows side-by-side comparisons.

Seriously think about subscribing to one of these services. I find it helpful; it helps to know I can go online and look at my credit report any time I want.

# Registration Services

These are the opt-out requests that are sent to you by your financial institutions, credit card companies, and so on. The opt-out form is important because it helps you minimize the amount of credit card offers you receive in the mail or through telephone solicitations.

To opt out of other credit offers, you can call 888-567-8688 (see Chapter 2 for more details). The call takes about 30 seconds, and you'll notice a dramatic decrease in the number of credit card offers sent to you in the mail.

Here is another contact where you can opt out:

> Telephone Preference Service
> Direct Marketing Association
> P.O. Box 9014
> Farmingdale, NY 11735

The preceding address is for you to opt out of telephone solicitations. Another way to remove yourself from the telephone solicitations lists is to go to the FTC site and add your name and telephone number to the National Do Not Call Registry (www.donotcall.gov). You can add your name to the list for free.

Here are several other mailing lists you can also send correspondence to in order to opt out. The lists are as follows:

> Database America
> Compilation Department
> 470 Chestnut Ridge Road
> Woodcliff, NJ 07677

Dunn & Bradstreet
Customer Service
899 Eaton Ave.
Bethlehem, PA 18025

Metromail Corporation
List Maintenance
901 West Bond
Lincoln, NE 68521

R.L. Polk & Co. - Name Deletion File
List Compilation Development
26955 Northwestern Hwy
Southfield, MI 48034-4716

To opt out of the preceding mailing lists, you need to write a letter to each one requesting that you be removed from the list.

# Major Banking Institutions

Table 17-3 lists just a few of the major banking institutions in the United States. The intent here is to give you a list of some of the major banks. I'm sure that you can probably think of others.

| Table 17-3 | Major Banking Institutions |
|---|---|
| *Name* | *Web Site URL* |
| Bank of America | www.bankofamerica.com |
| Citibank | www.citibank.com |
| Chase | www.chase.com |

# Chapter 18

# Ten Security Tools You Shouldn't Be Without

*1*n this chapter, I briefly describe ten tips you can use to secure your computing. I discuss some of the ten in more detail in Chapters 11 and 12, but here I summarize these tips as a quick reference guide.

## Use a Firewall

A *firewall* is important to have because it protects you from unwanted malware. (See Chapter 11 for more details.) Don't rely solely on the firewall your Internet service provider (ISP) provides. The ISP firewall offers only limited protection, so it's better to have your own software firewall or hardware firewall:

   ✔ **Software firewall:** This is software you can either purchase or download for free from the Internet. You can change the settings (dubbed *rule sets*) from the default settings. If you aren't sure or really don't know what you're doing, don't change the default settings; otherwise, you may not be able to get on the Internet.

✔ **Hardware firewall:** This type of firewall is a router or computer and is usually a small box or another computer that can be configured to be a firewall. This type of firewall also includes software.

Routers can also be configured to be run as a firewall. The firewall software program, which is where you set the rules you want the firewall to perform, runs the hardware firewall.

Make sure that your firewall is updated with the latest versions of the software. Most firewall programs let you know when updates are available. When you get an update notice, update your firewall immediately.

# Use a Spyware Blocking Program

*Spyware* tracks where you go on the Internet. Issues with spyware you need to be aware of include

✔ **Adware:** Adware takes you to places on the Internet to sell you products that you may be interested in, based on what Web sites you've visited in the past. I don't know about you, but I don't want my Internet habits tracked by anyone.

✔ **Malware:** Malware is malicious software, and spyware might contain malware that can create problems for your computer.

✔ **Trojans containing a keylogger program:** The *keylogger program* captures all your keystrokes including all the usernames and passwords you type. The person(s) that puts the keylogger in the spyware then uses that information to log on to your bank account and capture other personal information.

To find and eliminate spyware from your computer, you can get an adware or spyware blocking program (such as Spybot or Ad Ware Personal) that scans and finds spyware. (Most virus protection programs also block adware.) I discuss this further in Chapter 11. To quarantine and remove spyware from your system, simply click the box next to the spyware when it's found, click Quarantine, and then click Delete.

You can get available adware programs for a fee, and you can get free programs to block spyware. Get a copy of a spyware blocker program and then set it to perform scans automatically. Also, with Windows Defender, you can set it to automatically scan for spyware. (See Chapter 12 for more information.)

No matter what spyware program you choose, make sure that you set the program to perform scans automatically.

# Get Virus Protection

Viruses are real problems for your computer. Most viruses contain some type of malware that causes your computer to not work properly, to crash, or to destroy all your data. Numerous types of viruses are on the Internet with many ways to infect your computer. Viruses are spread mainly through e-mail attachments, so don't open e-mails from people you don't know. You can read more about this in the section "Don't Open or Reply to Unknown E-Mails" later in this chapter.

To prevent viruses from infecting your computer, install antivirus software on your system. Some antivirus programs are available for a fee, but you can find free antivirus software as well. Whichever you choose, set the program to update automatically to stay current; otherwise, you risk being infected because virus writers are constantly changing and evolving them.

Installing your antivirus software once and then forgetting about it isn't a good idea. If you don't install updates for your antivirus program, you leave your computer vulnerable to being infected. Set the program to perform updates automatically so you don't have to remember. You might be surprised to see how often the software updates, because the antivirus software makers are keeping up with the virus writers. The updates include the new Windows Defender program.

Some antivirus software also scans for and quarantines adware and spyware as part of its service. I use WebRoot, but I also have adware and spyware scanners that scan automatically.

# Update Your Operating System

Operating system (OS) updates (also known as *patches* or *hot fixes*) play a critical role in keeping your computer protected. They also usually address a specific security hole in the software that can be exploited by those with malicious intent.

Windows Defender for XP, Windows Vista, and Windows 7 lets you set up automatic updates. (I discuss setting up the automatic update process in Chapter 11.) I recommend that you use automatic updates because other security features — such as a firewall — won't help if your OS has security holes.

The main cause of most system crashes is an out-of-date operating system. For instance, this occurred in 2001 when Code Red (a denial-of-service attack) was unleashed on the Internet. A *denial-of-service attack* floods a server with so many requests that it causes the server to shut down. All the computers that didn't have an update for Microsoft's Internet Information System (IIS) crashed when hit with the Code Red malware. So make sure that your computer is protected by having all the current updates installed for your OS.

Most updates require that you restart your computer for the update to take effect. Schedule updates to take place when you aren't using your computer — like in the wee hours of the morning.

# Manage Your User Accounts

Manage user accounts if you have more than one user on your system and make sure that you have a strong password for the administrator account. Choose a password that can't be guessed easily or figured out with a password-cracker program. Password-cracker programs work on two main types of attacks:

- **Dictionary:** Use of a program that runs through the dictionary and flags words that are used in passwords.

- **Brute force:** Continually tries all sorts of word combinations for passwords to find ones that are used on the system. This is blocked in companies by limiting the number of failed attempts to lock on to three. At home this is not the case; the brute force program will continue to run.

I also recommend that you change your administrative password at least every 90 days and more often if you choose. Make sure that you turn off the guest account. By doing this, you help minimize the possibility of someone signing on your computer as a guest.

# Create Strong Passwords

In Chapter 11, I discuss passwords in greater detail; however, this is as good a time as any to reiterate that a strong password is important. Follow these guidelines:

- Don't use dictionary words — for example, money and love — because the bad guys have tools that can find out your passwords by running dictionary scans.

- Use a password that no one can guess because it makes sense only to you.

✔ Use a longer (eight to ten characters), such as TgiF#$&480, rather than a shorter password, such as simply TgiF.

✔ Mix special characters — %,*, $, #, and so on — into your password. (See Chapter 11 for more about the types of characters to use to strengthen your passwords.) Again, TgiF#$&480 is a good example.

✔ Use a passphrase as your password. A *passphrase* is a password you make up in which the first letter of a word or a phrase is used in the password. For example, Thank goodness it's Friday would be TgiF. Add special characters and numerals — to make it TgiF%*&480, for instance — and you have a password you can easily remember but which others can't easily guess.

✔ Change your password at least every 90 days.

# Use Encryption

Encryption scrambles a message into nonreadable script and helps secure what's on your computer's hard drive. You don't need to encrypt all your files — just those that contain any personal information. You can purchase encryption programs for your home computer. If someone manages to gain access to your computer, he can't open the encrypted files without a key. The key is a password used to unscramble the encryption so it can be read.

Pretty Good Privacy (PGP) is one such program you can purchase. You can choose between a home or business version. PGP is easy to use and does a good job protecting your files, even when those files are sent in an e-mail. When I use PGP, I encrypt files that contain security information when I send them via e-mail. In doing so, no one outside the organization knows what the company's security issues are.

If you lose your key, you can't open your own files that you've encrypted. The information will be lost.

# Increase Internet Explorer Security Settings

Surfing the 'Net is dangerous, but you can make it safer by increasing your Internet Explorer Security settings. You can do this through the Control Panel, which I discuss in some detail in Chapter 12.

Be careful which setting you choose. If you choose the highest setting and run a firewall, you may be blocked from getting to all Web sites. You can adjust your settings as necessary by selecting Custom Setting and then choosing what you want to prevent from accessing your computer.

# Protect Shared Files

*Shared* files allow other users that have a password to access files on your computer that you're willing to share. Think of what files you want to share and make sure that they don't contain personal information before you make the files available for others to see. Hidden (administrative) shares or hidden files aren't needed if you aren't in a business environment, so you can disable them. This prevents someone from accessing the files remotely. Hidden shares are for sharing files between various computers.

You can disable hidden shares in Windows XP, Vista, and 7; just follow these steps:

1. **Choose Start⇨Run, and then type** regedit **and click OK.**

   This opens the Registry Editor.

2. **Navigate to**

   ```
   HKEY_LOCAL_MACHINE\System\CurrentControlSet\Services\
          lanmanserver\parameters
   ```

3. **Type the value word** autosharewks **and a value of** *0*.

4. **Restart your computer.**

A firewall program blocks most access to your shared files. To be safe, you can protect the files by securing a guest account. You can't turn off the guest account, but XP Home does actually let you disable the guest account because it is an integral part of XP. For Windows 7, you can turn off the guest account. For Vista Home you can't.

To password-protect the account on XP Home, do the following:

1. **Bring up the command prompt by choosing Start⇨Run and then typing** cmd **in the run dialog box.**

   This is the same for Vista and Windows 7 as well.

2. **Type** net user guest *password*.

   Replace *password* with a password of your choosing.

   The guest account is password protected. This just adds another layer of security to your computer.

# Don't Open or Reply to Unknown E-Mails

The simple rules are: Never open e-mail attachments from unknown users and never open attachments you weren't expecting. Most of these attachments contain viruses. Today, most attachments are scanned for viruses before you open them, but it's a good idea not to open the attachment in the first place.

If you do open an e-mail from an unknown source and it contains a virus, your antivirus program can help protect you by scanning the document for known viruses.

If you open an e-mail from an unknown person, you let that person know that your account is good and you will likely receive more e-mails from that person or others if your e-mail account information is shared. To make your computer safer, don't open e-mails from people you don't know.

 Set up an e-mail filter to filter out junk mail no matter what e-mail system you use at home. To filter e-mail is simple: If the person is not in your address book, the e-mail is sent to the junk mail folder. Setting up a junk mail folder is easy (in work environments, this is done automatically by your system administrator), and most free e-mail systems automatically do some filtering. You can fine-tune your junk e-mail by not accepting e-mails in your inbox from anyone not in your address book. Doing so filters out the junk and unwanted mail.

# Chapter 19

# Ten (Plus One) Common Scams and How to Avoid Them

*I*dentity thieves use numerous scams to trick you into giving personal information. In this chapter, I discuss the most common scams and how you can protect yourself from becoming a victim of them. Most of the so-called new scams are variations on the theme of these most common ones.

# Phishing

*Phishing* is pronounced "fishing" and is exactly that — except that the fish they're attempting to reel in is you and not game fish, like salmon or striped bass.

Phishing is a way to get information by sending spam e-mail to a large number of people. The e-mails can request information by saying that your ATM/debit card number and PIN (personal identification number) need to be verified by a financial institution because it "lost your data" in an upgrade to their software program, which was done because of all the fraud that's taken place. The e-mails will ask for some type of personal information.

A link for a Web site is provided for you to type your information. You're told in the e-mail that if you don't provide the information, your account will be suspended.

These e-mails often have errors in grammar and spelling, and look like someone lacking a good command of the English language wrote them.

When you click the link in the e-mail, you're taken to a Web site that isn't really the Web site of the institution mentioned in the e-mail. The site is set up for the thieves to capture your ATM/debit card number and PIN so that they help themselves to your money.

Another recent scam is circulating in which victims are sent an e-mail stating that they're under investigation by the IRS. In the e-mail, the victims are informed that they can assist in the investigation by providing "real" information and are directed to a Web site that looks official. When on the site, victims are asked to provide personal information such as their Social Security Number (SSN), drivers' license numbers, bank account numbers, and credit card numbers. The information is requested under the guise that if you cooperate, the "IRS" can quickly clear up the matter.

The IRS never sends e-mail to contact taxpayers about issues concerning their accounts. The IRS sends letters on IRS stationery in an IRS envelope sent via the United States Postal Service. Don't be duped: Ignore the e-mail and contact the criminal investigation division of the IRS to let them know that you received an e-mail requesting personal information. This is a common scam today. There are some e-mails that are supposedly from the FBI as well.

To avoid becoming a victim of phishing, just don't reply to the e-mails soliciting personal information no matter how convincing they may seem. Discard the e-mail and contact someone at your financial institution to let him know about the scam.

Internet ScamBusters, `www.scambusters.org`, lists all the known e-mail scams that are currently being distributed. You can also subscribe to a free e-mail newsletter that outlines the latest scams and is a monthly publication.

## The Bank Examiner Scam

In a nutshell, the thief approaches you stating that he's investigating a dishonest teller and says that a bank official will be contacting you about how you can help. The bank official will want you to withdraw your own money to help with the investigation. To avoid falling victim to this old scam, remember that law enforcement doesn't ask you for money to conduct an investigation. Most of the time, law enforcement conducts the investigation without soliciting any help. This helps keep the investigation covert so that those under investigation aren't alerted that they're being targeted.

Don't fall for this old scam. If someone approaches you about an investigation and says that a bank official will be contacting you about how you can help, tell her to hit the road. Then call the police to report it and give a description of the person who approached you.

# The Doctored ATM

To perpetrate this scam, the thieves install wireless equipment on legitimate ATMs to steal your ATM card number and PIN. The attachment fits over the existing card slot and looks like the original slot. This is used to read the card and capture the ATM card number. A camera is placed in the bottom deposit envelope holder and used to capture the keystrokes of your PIN. The thieves usually install several of these "doctored ATMs" in one area.

To capture the information, the thieves sit in a car nearby and receive the wireless transmissions for the doctored ATMs. The best time to capture ATM card numbers and PINs is on weekends and holidays. Armed with the information, the thieves proceed to withdraw thousands of dollars from the accounts.

To protect you from this type of scam, be wary of using ATM machines that seem out of the ordinary. For example, the card slot has cracks around the edges where the holder is affixed to the machine. If you see unusual instructions on the ATM screen, such as asking you to enter your PIN three times, be on guard. If the holder for the deposit envelopes on either side of the machine is located where a camera would have a clear shot at the keypad, cover the keypad when you type in your PIN by placing either your right or left hand over the keypad while you type in your PIN with the other hand. You should be able to shield the screen and still see what you're typing.

# Phone Fraud

Here's how this one works: You receive a call from someone, and he tells you that he's with the fraud division of your credit card company and is investigating fraudulent charges on your card. He tells you that the charges that are fraudulent come from a company that sells computer hardware that's been involved in a lot of fraudulent charges. He mentions the name of the company and you tell him you've never heard of them and have never ordered anything from them. In order to help them, he needs to verify your card number, your full name as it appears on the card, and the expiration date of the card.

Don't give your credit card number to someone who's called you. Tell him you'll call the credit card company. After you tell him that, hang up the phone and then call the number on your credit card statement and inquire about the investigation. Don't ask the caller for a callback number.

Another phone fraud is the call forwarding scam. The scam works like this: Someone calls claiming to be a bank employee and states that she's investigating why correspondence from the bank has supposedly been returned to the bank. The caller then asks a series of leading questions to get you to give her the name of your bank, is this the correct credit card name or number, and are these the correct account numbers? Next, the thief impersonates you and contacts your phone service provider to verify that your phone line has call forwarding. Now the thief poses as a telephone company employee and instructs you to leave the phone off the hook or not to answer it for an hour so system maintenance can be performed.

Armed with all this information and the fact that you aren't answering your phone or have it off the hook, the thief dials codes that forward your calls to a number controlled by her.

Next the thief uses the account information you provided earlier to use Western Union to transfer money out of your account. She also makes fraudulent charges on your credit card.

Because your calls are forwarded to the thief, she receives all the verification calls, and you're unaware of what's happening. Using this scam, a thief can steal thousands of dollars from you in less than an hour.

Don't give out personal information to strangers on the phone, and you won't fall victim to this scam.

# Card Verification

Card verification scams are usually done by phone or via e-mail. The person calling or writing says that he needs to verify your credit card information for your account at some online merchant or pay service. He tells you that the server containing the credit card numbers has been hacked into and all the data on the credit card accounts has been lost, or he tells you that he's verifying your information to make sure that it's current. The caveat is that if you don't provide the information, he'll cancel your account.

If the scam is done by e-mail, the URL provided links you to a site set up by the thieves and when you enter the information to "verify" your credit card number, name, and expiration date, they capture the information on their server. Then you know what happens: Your card is used to make fraudulent charges. When the scam is done by phone, the thief writes down all the information needed to use your credit card for fraudulent purposes.

To avoid this scam, don't give the thieves the information either on the phone or online.

# *You Won the Lottery!*

Here's how this scam works: You receive a letter, fax, or e-mail claiming that you've won a large sum in an overseas lottery game. You probably didn't know you even entered the lottery. The letter says that the lottery commission for whatever country's lotto has tried unsuccessfully to contact you about your windfall. In order to collect your winnings, you need to provide the lotto commission with your bank account information so that it can wire transfer the money to your account. Some of these scams have a form sent with the letter that asks for personal information, such as your full name (including your middle name), birth date, address, your occupation, marital status, and telephone number. Some of the forms also ask for next of kin information, including first and last name, address, telephone number, and occupation. What a great way to solicit more victims. The form also features a bank transfer section that asks for your bank's name, address, account numbers, routing number, and telephone number.

After you provide the information to the lotto commission, the only one who wins is the person who sent the letter. Imagine that! To avoid becoming a victim, don't give out this information. Just discard the letter, e-mail, or fax.

These letter scams have been successful because they play to the greed aspect of human nature. There's no such thing as free money.

# *Bogus Charities*

You're watching TV, and the phone rings. You answer, and the person on the other end says that she's from a charitable group soliciting donations. Be careful. This has been used as a ploy to get your credit card number and expiration date, or a personal check.

Legitimate charities exist that use telephone solicitation for donations. You can give to your favorite charity and still protect yourself. There are other ways to find out how to make a donation other than doing so over the phone. For instance, go online and look up the charity. The Web site will have all the contact information to make a donation. Or you can open the Yellow Pages in your area and look up the address and phone number of your favorite charity.

Another variation on this theme is the disaster relief donation scam. An example of this scam occurred right after the 9/11/01 tragedy. The thieves set up a bogus Web site and then sent a spam e-mail soliciting $25 credit card donations to help the victims of 9/11 families. The e-mail had a link to the thief's Web site, and the mail recipient clicked the link to enter the site to make a donation. The site asked, of course, for your credit card number and expiration date as well as your full name. Also, the site asked for your SSN under the guise that you can then claim the donation on your income tax as a deduction.

People who made the donation found themselves victims of identity theft. The perpetrators established new addresses and opened new accounts, using the names of the people who went to the site.

Other people were pressured into making on-the-spot donations over the phone, using the same tactics that the Web site thieves used to get personal information.

Don't stop donating to charities — just don't give out your personal information to strangers on the telephone. In most states, the charitable organizations must be registered with the state Attorney General, so check whether the charity is legitimate before you donate.

# Bogus Invoices

This scam involves phony invoices made to look like the real thing. I've been getting a number of these bogus invoices in my e-mail account recently. This may be the new trend to garner personal information from you. I've also received some bogus invoices via U.S. mail. One of the telltale signs of a bogus invoice is the lack of a phone number for an alternative contact method.

In order to comply with U.S. Postal regulations, these solicitations are supposed to have the following wording on them. The following disclaimer is easy to spot in the e-mails, but I haven't always seen the disclaimer.

**"THIS IS NOT A BILL. THIS IS A SOLICITATION. YOU ARE UNDER NO OBLIGATION TO PAY THE AMOUNT STATED ABOVE UNLESS YOU ACCEPT THIS OFFER."**

The wording is supposed to be near the top of the invoice in capital letters in bold type that is at least as large as the letters on the solicitation. Oftentimes the disclaimer is overlooked or misunderstood. The idea is to get you to pay for something you didn't order. Sometimes the scam is used to solicit credit card information.

Don't respond to invoices that don't have phone numbers on them. If you didn't order what's stated in the invoice, simply ignore it.

# Phony Brokerage Firms

In the phony brokerage firm scam, the thieves set up a Web site using the name of an actual brokerage firm, but they use a different address. Then they craft and send a spam e-mail. The e-mail usually trumpets upcoming "hot" stock to entice you into visiting its Web site. On the site, you provide the usual personal information, credit card number, and other personal information to purchase the "stock." At the time of this writing, it isn't clear whether the scam is being perpetrated to garner personal information to be used in further frauds in identity theft or whether it's collecting money for phony stocks.

In any event, don't purchase stocks from unsolicited e-mails; it's probably just a ruse to get your personal information, or it is not a good tip anyway. If you're interested in buying stock, contact one of the brokerage firms near you and set up a face-to-face meeting in their office.

# Temporary Suspension of Your Account

The temporary suspension of your account scam is set up either in an e-mail or a telephone call. The thieves use the scare tactic that your bank account (or online payment or online auction account) has been suspended. The e-mail sender or phone caller claims that the bank is undertaking a review of all its accounts to eliminate waste and fraud. You're then requested to visit the "company's" Web site to provide the information necessary to do a review of your account and to make sure that the information on file is correct. The information asked for is the usual: full name, account number, ATM/debit card number, and PIN. The e-mail sender or phone caller goes on to say that if you don't provide the information, your account will be permanently canceled.

You know what happens next! You become the victim of identity theft. So when in doubt, don't provide the information. Contact your bank instead.

# Job Scams

You probably receive several offers a week in your e-mail to work at home or as a shipping clerk or to transfer funds for various companies. These are usually scams. If you fall for them, you could lose money and put your personal information — such as your address, SSN, bank account number, and so on — into the wrong hands. Don't apply for unsolicited job offers even if the e-mail states that your information was garnered from a job Web site.

Most of these bogus job scams suck you in with the promise of thousands for working a few hours a day from your home. Some of the job scams can land you in trouble with the law because the activities you're asked to perform involve money laundering and repackaging of merchandise bought with stolen credit cards.

You can find out whether an e-mail job offer is a scam by going to www. scambusters.org. That Web site describes numerous scams. You can search by the type of scam.

# Index

## • X •

## • Y •

## • Z •